Political and Economic Liberalisation in Zambia 1991–2001

Lise Rakner

The Nordic Africa Institute, 2003

Indexing terms

Economic development

Economic reform

Donors

Political development

Zambia

Cover photo: Gisela Geisler

A rally for the Movement for Multiparty Democracy (MMD) before the 1991 transitional elections.

Language checking: Elaine Almén

Index: Margaret Binns

ISBN 91-7106-506-7

Printed in Sweden by Elanders Gotab, Stockholm 2003

Contents

Acronyms

Afronet	The Inter-African Network for Human Rights and Development
AAC	Anglo-American Corporation
ACC	Anti-Corruption Commission
ACMP	Agricultural Credit Management Programme
ANC	African National Congress
ASIP	Agricultural Sector Investment Programme
AZ	Agenda for Zambia
BoP	Balance of Payment
BOZ	Bank of Zambia
CCC	Committee for a Clean Campaign
CDC	Commonwealth Development Corporation
CFB	Commercial Farmers Bureau
CG	Consultative Group
COMESA	Common Market for Eastern and Southern Africa
CSO	Central Statistical Office
CSPR	Civil Society for Poverty Reduction
CSUZ	Civil Servants Union of Zambia
DA(s)	District Administrator(s)
DAC	Development Assistance Committee of OECD
DFID	Department of International Development
DP	Democratic Party
EAZ	Economic Association of Zambia
ECZ	Electoral Commission of Zambia
EIU	Economist Intelligence Unit
ERC	Economic Reform Credit
ERIP	Economic Recovery and Investment Project
ESAC	Economic and Social Adjustment Credit
ESAF	Enhanced Structural Adjustment Facility
EU	European Union
EUEU	European Union Electoral Unit
FAO	Food and Agricultural Organisation
FDD	Forum for Development and Democracy
FFTU	Federation of Free Trade Unions
FINDECO	Financial and Development Corporation
FODEP	Foundation for a Democratic Process
FRA	Food Reserve Agency
GDP	Gross Domestic Product
GNP	Gross National Product
GRZ	Government of the Republic of Zambia
HIPC	Heavily Indebted Poor Countries
HP	Heritage Party
IBRD	International Bank for Reconstruction and Development
IDA	International Development Association
IDEA	International Institute for Democracy and Electoral Assistance
IFIs	International Finance Institutions
ILO	International Labour Organisation's
IMF	International Monetary Fund
INDECO	Industrial Development Corporation
INESOR	Institute for Social and Economic Research, University of Zambia
IR	Industrial Relations Act
JCTR	Jesuit Centre for Theological Reflection
KCM	Konkola Copper Mines
KDMP	Konkola Deep Mining Project
LPF	Liberal Progressive Front
LUSE	Lusaka Stock Exchange
MAFF	Ministry of Agriculture, Food and Fisheries
MDP	Movement for Democratic Process

MINDECO	Mining Development Corporation
MMD	Movement for Multiparty Democracy
MOF	Ministry of Finance and Economic Development
MUZ	Mine Workers Union of Zambia
NADA	National Democratic Alliance
NAMBOARD	National Marketing Board
NASSPFU	National Association of Small-Scale and Peasant Farmers Union of Zambia
NCC	National Christian Coalition
NDP	National Democratic Party
NGO(s)	Non-Governmental Orgnaisation(s)
NERP	New Economic Recovery Programme
NLD	National Leadership for Development
NLP	National Lima Party
NORAD	Norwegian Agency for Development Cooperation
NP	National Party
NPC	National Patriotic Coalition
NUBEGW	National Union of Building and Engineering Workers
NUCIW	National Union of Commercial and Industrial Workers
ODA	Overseas Development Assistance
OECD	Organisation of Economic Cooperation and Development
OPEC	Organisation of Petroleum Exporting Countries
PAM	Programme Against Malnutrition
PF	Patriotic Front
PFUZ	Peasant Farmers Union of Zambia
PIRC	Privatisation and Industrial Reform Credit
PRGF	Poverty Reduction and Growth Facility
PRS	Poverty Reduction Strategy
PRSP	Poverty Reduction Strategy Paper
PSREC	Public Sector Reform and Export Promotion Credit
PSRP	Public Sector Reform Programme
RAP	Rights Accumulation Programme
SAP(s)	Structural Adjustment Programme(s)
SDP	Social Democratic Party
SDR	Standard Drawing Right
SIDA	Swedish International Development Cooperation Agency
TCZ	Tourism Council of Zambia
UBZ	United Bus Company
UNDP	United Nations Development Programme
UNIP	United National Independence Party
UNZA	University of Zambia
UP	United Party
UPND	United Party for National Development
UPP	United Progressive Party
USAID	United States Agency for International Development
ZACCI	Zambia Association of Chambers of Commerce and Industry
ZAM	Zambia Association of Manufacturers
ZAP	Zambia Alliance for Progress
ZCCM	Zambia Consolidated Copper Mines
ZCF	Zambia Co-operative Federation
ZCTU	Zambia Congress of Trade Unions
ZDC	Zambia Democratic Congress
ZFE	Zambia Federation of Employers
ZIMA	Zambia Independent Media Association
ZIMCO	Zambia Industrial and Mining Corporation
ZNCCI	Zambia National Council of Commerce and Industry
ZNFU	Zambia National Farmers Union
ZNUT	Zambia National Union of Teachers
ZPA	Zambia Privatisation Agency
ZRA	Zambia Revenue Authority
ZRP	Zambia Republican Party
ZUFIAW	Zambia Union of Financial and Allied Workers

Acknowledgements

My first visit to Zambia was in 1987 as a tourist. Travelling overland from Kenya to Zimbabwe, Zambia became a rather negative experience. The queue for bus-tickets to Livingstone transformed into a queue for bread as bread just happened to arrive from somewhere! I soon realized that queuing for basic commodities was an aspect of everyday life for most Zambians, together with constant road-blocks and endless harassment of citizens who failed to produce a UNIP party membership card.

Returning to Zambia during the political transitions in 1991, many things were about to change. Women in the markets, workers, trade union activists, taxi drivers, civil servants and journalists all expressed a great sense of optimism about what democracy would bring in terms of both political freedom and economic prosperity. Later visits in 1995, 1996–97, 2000, 2001 and 2002 have suggested that the 1991 euphoria 'cooled' a few years into the first MMD election period. The main reason is that politicians and well connected individuals have increasingly succeeded in reducing access to both the economic and political market-places so that at this stage they benefit only a few.

At a point in time when the political and economic reform processes in Latin America, Eastern Europe, Asia and Africa are being questioned by aid-workers, non-governmental organisations and academics in the north and south, it is important to note that people in Zambia harbour few nostalgic sentiments about the one-party era or the state-controlled economy. The question is, why did the reform processes stall in a 'grey zone' of partial reform? Moreover, what will it take to further the political and economic reform processes to the benefit of the majority? This analysis of Zambia's first decade of political and economic liberalisation addresses these questions.

I have carried out research on political and economic reform processes in Zambia for more than a decade. In the course of these years a number of personal and institutional debts of gratitude have been accumulated. A large number of politicians, researchers, donor and interest group representatives have shared their knowledge and time with me during my fieldwork. I would like to express my gratitude to all of you. This book is my modest attempt to give something in return for the generosity with which I have been met in all public and private institutions visited in Zambia.

I would also like to thank the Norwegian Research Council, the Norwegian Agency for Development Cooperation (NORAD), the Royal Norwegian Embassy in Zambia, and the Chr. Michelsen Memorial Fund for facilitating the research through funding various parts of it.

A number of people have made invaluable contributions though their comments on various parts and drafts at different stages. In particular I would like to thank Deborah Bräutigam, Theo Bull (who, regrettably, died early 2003), Peter Burnell, Siri Gloppen, Richard Joseph, Hendrick van der Heijden, Chileshe Mulenga, Joan Nelson, Nicolas van de Walle, Elin Skaar, Joe Stepanek,

Lars Svåsand, Arne Tostensen and Scott Taylor for generous and stimulating comments and inspiration.

My family has with a great sense of adventure and generosity accompanied me on many of my fieldtrips. Jon Ketil, without your encouragement, love and support—coupled with your brilliant sense of humour and sense of the absurd—it sure would have been less fun to be a researcher! I thank you, Johanne and Lars for making life so rich—and such fun!

The person who initially encouraged me to pursue the possible interconnections between political and economic liberalisation was Tor Skålnes. Sadly, you are no longer here to share your knowledge, to provide your sharp and pointed comments, or to celebrate the end result of the work. I dedicate this book to your memory.

Bergen, August 2003

Lise Rakner

1

Reform for Political Survival

Political and Economic Liberalisation in Zambia 1991–2001

This book is about political and economic liberalisation in Zambia in the period 1991–2001. The following questions of research guide the empirical analysis: How do processes of political and economic reform interrelate? And, do economic and political transition processes reinforce or hinder one another? I analyse negotiations between the Zambian government and key domestic interest groups on the implementation of structural adjustment reforms through two election periods; 1991–1996 and 1996–2001. Furthermore, I assess the dialogue on political and economic reform between the MMD government and the international donor community represented by the International Monetary Fund (IMF), the World Bank and Zambia's main bilateral donors.

The Case of Zambia

In 1991 the Movement for Multiparty Democracy (MMD), an opposition drawn from a broad coalition of trade unions, business interests, intellectuals and students, won an overwhelming electoral victory over the single party for the previous 17 years, the United National Independence Party (UNIP). As one of the first countries in sub-Saharan Africa to do so, Zambia experienced a peaceful transition to multiparty rule. One of the most significant aspects of the transition was the fact that MMD in its election manifesto (MMD 1991) committed itself to implement a liberal economic reform programme. This had been attempted since the early 1980s by the UNIP one-party government without success. Zambia thereby joined the ranks of a number of countries in Latin America, Asia, Eastern Europe, and Africa that replaced authoritarian governments with elected ones, while simultaneously attempting to implement far-reaching economic reforms.

The international donor community in turn generously rewarded the new government's commitment to both political and economic change. In the late 1980s, a new aid policy had evolved arguing that processes of political and economic reform were mutually reinforcing and should, therefore, be implemented simultaneously (World Bank 1992; Landell-Mills 1992; Moore 1993; Nelson and Eglington 1992). The peaceful transition to multiparty democracy in 1991, as well as the economic policies promoted by the new government, made Zambia a 'model for Africa' both in the eyes of the international donor community and much of the academic community (Bratton 1992; Joseph 1992; Bonnick 1997). With donors eager to promote an African 'success story' of dual reforms, as one of the few countries in sub-Saharan Africa to do so, Zambia experienced substantial growth in official development assistance (ODA) in the immediate period after 1991.

The 1991 transition and the policies adopted by the MMD government were influenced by Zambia's recent history and its predecessor's uneasy relationship with the international donor community. Among the nations of sub-Saharan Africa, Zambia suffered one of the greatest and most rapid economic declines starting in the early 1970s. According to one estimate, GDP declined by 30 per cent between 1975 and 1990 (*Southern African Economist*, June 1990). Zambia's relationship with the multilateral financial institutions started in 1973. The stability measures, and later structural adjustment programmes, introduced between 1973 and 1990 all failed to address the underlying structural problems of the Zambian economy; a large and wasteful state sector, inefficient agricultural production and an unsustainable policy of food subsidies. The World Bank and IMF's reform proposals focused, among other things, on the reduction of food subsidies to the urban population and on an increase in agricultural production by promoting small-scale farming and better price incentives for farmers. The political costs of the proposed reform measures were, however, high in a society where approximately 50 per cent of the population lived in urban areas and where the interests of workers were protected by strong and vocal labour unions. Faced with 'food riots' in the urban areas each time comprehensive reforms were attempted, President Kaunda abandoned the economic reform programmes. Due to an escalating debt burden and increasing donor co-ordination, in the late 1980s Zambia was unable to draw on financial assistance from the multilateral finance institutions and, hence, from commercial sources. The unabating decline of the Zambian economy had now become the main issue of concern for the growing domestic opposition. Former opponents of economic reform campaigned against President Kaunda and UNIP on a ticket of economic liberalisation. The forces opposing one-party rule had their organisational base in the Zambian trade union movement (Zambia Congress of Trade Unions), but also included the business community, UNIP dissidents, the churches and students.

Assuming power in 1991, the new MMD government was faced with a number of challenges. On the one hand, the government had to negotiate an agreement with the international donor community for substantial debt-relief and a new economic recovery programme. Yet, at the same time, it was necessary to accommodate to their broad-based constituency, in which large segments, most notably labour, throughout the 1980s had consistently fought against the economic restructuring measures demanded by the international donors. Both the external donors and the domestic opposition, however, demanded that the reform processes should be implemented through democratic decision-making procedures. These challenges form the focal point of this study analysing the role of three main sets of actors; the MMD government, the main domestic interest groups and the international donor community.

What, then, actually happened to the political and economic reform processes in the period 1991–2001?

Political Liberalisation 1991–2001

On November 18, 1996, Zambia conducted the second parliamentary and presidential elections under a multiparty constitution. These second elections were regarded as a crucial test of the sustainability of both the economic reform programme and the strength of the regime's commitment to consolidating the process of political liberalisation begun in 1991. The 1996 general elections suggested to local and international observers that the Chiluba government was willing to compromise the rule of law, was intolerant of criticism and willing to exploit its majority position and control of government resources to undermine its opponents. MMD used its parliamentary majority to push through constitutional amendments that denied the strongest opposition candidate, former president Kenneth Kaunda (UNIP) the possibility to contest the 1996 presidential elections. The use of a contentious voter register and an uneven electoral playing-field led both the domestic opposition and the international donors to challenge the legitimacy of the 1996 elections (Baylies and Szeftel 1997; van Donge 1998; Bratton and Posner 1999; FODEP 1996). Nevertheless, these elections indicated that after five years of continuous economic reforms—and a growing opposition to these reforms—no opposition party had emerged to challenge the ruling party or their economic policies.

The third presidential, parliamentary and local government elections were conducted on December 27, 2001. As the third consecutive elections within the multiparty constitution framework, these elections suggested that the electoral process in Zambia had become regularised. In the 2001 presidential elections there was also a succession. In the final hour President Chiluba decided to abide by the 1996 constitution limiting the president to two terms in office. Levy Mwanawasa of MMD was sworn in as Zambia's new president after the most closely contested elections witnessed in the country. With 29 per cent of the total vote, Mwanawasa was left with a weaker electoral mandate than any previous Zambian president. As in the 1996 elections, local and international election observers expressed serious reservations as to whether the electoral process had been free and fair (Meadowcroft 2002; Burnell 2002; FODEP, 2002). Again the observers accused the government of failing to create a level playing-field for the elections. Yet, similar to the 1996 elections, despite MMD's poor socio-economic record, none of the eleven opposition parties presented an alternative economic programme to that of continued economic liberalisation.

The elections in 1991, 1996 and 2001 indicate that Zambia's democracy is far from consolidated. With hindsight, a number of political incidents suggest that the democratic reform process stalled in late 1993. The new politicians who entered politics in 1991 expressing their commitment to the values of democracy and human rights, were then replaced by veteran politicians associated with the one-party rule of UNIP. In the second Chiluba administration, the government became more and more isolated and reacted in a paranoid manner to criticism from external donors, the press, interest groups and opposition parties. Contrary to expectations in the early 1990s, throughout the decade the separation between the incumbent party and the government became increasingly more blurred. Despite the stated intention to reduce the powers of the presidency in 1991, the powers of the executive office increased.

Economic Liberalisation 1991–2001

relate to public administration

Zambia's economic reform record in the 1990s is exceedingly complex and mixed. The economic reform process advanced considerably in the initial years, and significant changes in the economic policy regime were implemented between 1991 and 1994. Within the first two years, the government had completed the liberalisation of the external and domestic trade regime by eliminating tariffs, freeing the exchange rate and interest rates. Despite several exogenous shocks and uneven implementation, the MMD government maintained an open trade regime; Zambia put the COMESA Free Trade Agreement into effect in October 2000, as one of the first countries in the region to do so. Initially similar formidable steps were taken towards liberalising agricultural marketing and production. However, sporadic government involvement in the marketing of fertiliser and maize has contributed to market insecurity and an underperforming agricultural sector. The privatisation process presents a similar story. In 1996 the Zambian privatisation programme was held by the international press and the World Bank to be one of the most successful on a world scale (*Financial Times*, March 4, 1997; *World Bank Findings*, October 1996). However, the decision to postpone the privatisation of the mining industry until 1998 and to finally only sell the mining conglomerate in March 2000 had enormous adverse consequences for the economy as a whole. Overall, despite the significant and sustained changes, many important aspects of economic reform were either not implemented or implemented in a haphazard manner. The public sector reform programme, deemed essential both to balancing the budgets and to enhancing the capacity of the bureaucracy, was not implemented during MMD's first two administrations. Thus, during the 1990s the foundation was laid for a shift from a state-oriented to a market-based economy. Despite several exogenous shocks and uneven implementation, none of the reform measures implemented have been reversed. But several key reforms were never implemented. Partly as a result of uneven implementation, the Zambian economy did not experience growth in the 1990s. Most alarmingly, social indicators regressed throughout the 1990s.[1]

What can explain the Zambia development trajectory of partial political and economic reforms witnessed in the period 1991–2001? Why were some ele-

1. The *Zambia Human Development Report* 1999/2000 found that Zambia is the only country in the world for which data on the human development index is available with lower human development indicators in 1997 than in 1975 (UNDP 2001:1). Overall poverty was in 1998 measured at 72.9 per cent, with extreme poverty having risen to 57.9 per cent (Ibid. 2001).

ments of the economic reforms implemented soon after the 1991 elections while other vital reform processes were postponed? Finally, to what extent can the experience with dual reforms in Zambia during the 1990s inform the theoretical debates on the interconnections between political and economic liberalisation?

The Expectations: The Dual Reform Perspective

After a decade of poor economic results and increasing internal opposition to corruption and bad economic practices in authoritarian regimes, the early 1990s saw a new focus on political and economic liberalisation that assigned a vital role to civil society associations (Landell-Mills 1992; Healey and Robinson 1992; Robinson 1995). Acknowledging both the changing political climate and the inconclusive evidence generated from comparative research, a new consensus emerged in the 1990s arguing that economic and political reforms could be implemented simultaneously (Widner 1994; Haggard and Webb 1994; Haggard and Kaufman 1995).

Both the academic literature and the donor community's dual reform strategy expected political liberalisation to enhance pluralism in decision-making processes (Haggard and Webb 1994; Haggard and Kaufman 1995; Milner 1997; World Bank 1992). As a result, both donors and academia emphasised the implicit contradictory relationship between the two processes. Governments committed to dual transition processes were expected to face a political dilemma: economic reforms were expected to involve immediate costs yet the potential benefits were expected to be more long term and uncertain. At the same time, the process of political reform allowed potentially 'losing coalitions' access to the political arena to challenge the reform measures. As a result, transitional governments attempting to implement an economic austerity programme, while at the same time consolidating the political reform process, were advised to take advantage of the expected political period of grace (often referred to as 'the honeymoon') in order to overcome political dilemmas associated with the dual reform processes. According to this perspective, governments should, in due time before the next election, seek support from those segments of society which had benefited from the reform process. Based on a similar dual-reform logic, donors were advised to reward 'reform willing' governments with increased levels of aid in the early stages of the reform process (World Bank 1994).

The Argument: Zambia's Dual Reform Experiences

This study of Zambia's reform processes confirms the dual reform 'logic'. In the first period after the 1991 elections, a wide range of economic reforms were implemented, and domestic interest associations were only consulted to a limited extent. Key ministers in the MMD government explicitly stated their intention to take advantage of the initial 'honeymoon' period offered by the 1991 electoral majority. As a result, the MMD government did not attempt to create a broad-based consensus for its economic policies. The MMD government was, in turn, rewarded with extraordinary levels of aid. Between 1990 and 1994, aid to Zambia reached an average of US$ 951 million from an average of US$ 312 in the 1977–1989 period (Saasa and Carlsson 2002:67). However, the second phase of the first electoral term did not witness closer cooperation and consultations with domestic interest groups. In the second election period (1996–2001) the institutionalised relationship between government and interest groups established in the one-party era came to a complete stop. Disregarding lack of economic results and the fact that no sector of society had emerged as 'winners' of the economic reforms, the economic reform programme continued throughout the 1991–2001 period. The MMD government did not face an opposition that seriously challenged its economic policy in the 1996 or 2001 elections.

Thus, despite a disastrous socio-economic record, the processes of political and economic liberalisation proceeded concomitantly without seriously affecting or undermining each other. Both the political and economic liberalisation processes share a fate of partial implementation. Zambia has, thereby, joined the vast majority of African reform governments who have entered a 'transitional grey zone' (Carothers 2002) stuck in a 'partial reform syndrome' characterised by permanent economic crisis (van de Walle 2001). In the 1991–2001 period, three local, parliamentary and presidential elections have proved that despite the presence of thirty-six listed parties and around 400 non-governmental associations, there are presently almost no organisations in Zambia capable of contesting the incumbent's power. As a result, pluralism, and with it institutional proliferation, has increased MMD's autonomy from society. Stressing continuity rather than change, the Zambian case suggests that the political practices associated with one-party rule, such as centralisation of power in the presidential office and extensive use of state patronage for political gain, may prevail within the formal structures of democracy and a market economy. These rather counterintuitive conclusions are explained by the following findings.

The Decline of Interest Group Influence

Political liberalisation re-introduced multiparty elections and civil liberties in Zambia. However, the process of political reform did not result in increased political participation. Contrary to the assumptions of pluralist theory, the Zambian case study indicates that the influence of interest associations declined as a result of the economic and political liberalisation processes. The immediate effect of the economic reforms was that business, labour and agriculturual associations experienced a decline in income and membership because of increasing levels of redundancies, bankruptcies and the high cost of living. The circumstances around their reduced political influence were unique to each sector. Chiluba's trade union background ensured the MMD government initial support and extensive knowledge of the trade union movement. This enabled MMD to capitalize on the split between private and public sector unions. The fundamental division between industrialists and traders weakened the potential political influence of the main business associations. The problems of agricultural liberalisation and the dualism of agricultural sector interests rendered the agricultural lobby weak and ineffectual. Neither Zambian business, labour nor agricultural interests could be considered (or indeed, considered themselves) to be 'winners' of the reform process. While some reform measures benefited a sector as a whole, other measures hurt some sectoral interests and benefited others. As a result, no sector emerged that could be characterised as a new constituency in favour of the economic reform policies.

That economic changes could adversely impact economic interest groups is perhaps not unexpected. What is surprising, however, is that the process of political liberalisation also weakened the relative position of organised interest groups vis-à-vis the government. The creation of a large number of non-governmental associations and 36 new opposition parties between 1991 and 2001 increasingly made it difficult for traditional economic interest associations to be seen and heard in the press and in public fora and thus, to lobby government. Their weakness in terms of membership base and associational density further reduced the incentives of the government to consult with, or yield to the interests of, particular interest organisations: they did not represent a significant electoral support-base for the government. Furthermore, for economic interest associations to influence policies as envisioned in the pluralist notion of 'winners' and 'losers', it is necessary to provide channels into the competitive political processes. In the 1990s, no links were formed between Zambian economic interests and the party system. Party formation and politics centred around issues of personalities, individual ambitions and ethnic relations, and opposition parties remained exceedingly weak. No party offered an agenda that challenged MMD's economic reforms and, as a result, the interest groups representing business, labour and agriculture had few channels into political decision-making arenas. Continued executive dominance, coupled with organisational proliferation and a weakly institutionalised party system, meant the electoral channel did not function as a credible 'threat' to the incumbent government. As a result, throughout the 1990s, the MMD government was able to ignore the voices of business, labour and agriculture. Echoing findings from the comparative literature, the Zambian case study suggests that interest coalitions located within the government and bureaucracy were more influential than independent interest associations in terms of opposing and postponing reforms.

The Increased Leverage of the MMD Government vis-à-vis Its External Partners

The analysis confirms that the external actors played a central role in the Zambian dual reform processes and that reform implementation cannot be reduced to either a domestic or an international policy matter. The MMD government initially almost uncritically accepted the reform proposals set forth by the donor community. But like the Zambian government, the aid donors failed to express a coherent strategy of economic growth in their negotiations with the government. Instead, in the 1990s both the government and the donors made fiscal austerity an end in itself and a measure of reform commitment. Similar to the experiences of the 1980s, donor conditionality proved unable to stem the waning reform commitment witnessed from the mid-1990. The experiences in Zambia indicate that the specific targeting of certain reform elements and the technically formulated benchmarks offered relatively wide room for manoeuvre for the Zambian authorities. Reflecting continuity rather than a shift in donor-government relations, a partial reform syndrome was supported and maintained by the inability of donors to apply the conditionality instruments in a coherent manner. Like the domestic opposition, the donor community also proved powerless in terms of providing checks against the declining levels of governance witnessed from 1993 onwards. Despite a rhetorical commitment to a dual conditionality agenda, the Zambian case study suggests that if a recipient country (in part) follows the economic policy prescriptions, lack of adherence to principles of democracy will not be challenged by the donors.[1] Thus, the pattern of partial political and economic reforms was reinforced by continued donor support. Paradoxically, the international donor community contributed, and largely fed into, the political developments witnessed in Zambia in the 1990s of increasing executive dominance and poor financial discipline.

Introduction of the Central Actors

To take account both of Zambia's past domestic history with vocal interest groups having protested against economic reforms, and the country's conflicting relationship with the international donor community, the analysis of political and economic liberalisation in Zambia in the 1990s is envisioned as a two-level game between on the one hand, domestic interest groups and the MMD government, and, on the other hand, the international donor community and the government.

In the 1990s, an emerging literature on political and economic reform processes began to argue that it was not feasible to understand processes of reform in Africa without considering the powerful role played by the international donor community (Remmer 1995; Milner 1997; White 1998; Bräutigam 2000; van de Walle 2001). Nevertheless, Putnam's (1988) model of two-level games remains one of the few explicit theories seeking to capture the interrelationship between domestic and international policy negotiations. The main idea behind Putnam's two-level game perspective is that political leaders are constantly playing the domestic and international arenas simultaneously. Considering the starting point of Zambia's dual reform project in 1991, the need to include both domestic and international actors in the analysis presented itself.

The Domestic Policy Game between Government and Interest Groups

The previous attempts at economic restructuring in the 1980s failed, and in most accounts, the failure was attributed to the opposition from urban constituents with its organisational centre in the Zambian labour union movement. The same labour movement provided the organisational backbone of the 1991 transition process. The new President of Zambia as well as a number of minis-

1. This argument is elaborated in Rakner, van de Walle and Mulaisho, 2001.

ters in the first MMD Cabinet came from the labour movement. To many observers, it was therefore evident that the success or failure of Zambia's dual reform process depended on how the new government managed to construct a working relationship with the labour movement and more generally, urban interests (White 1996; Bratton 1992; Joseph 1992). Alternatively, the success depended on the government's ability to shift its organisational and constituent basis of support. Thus, the analysis of dual reforms in Zambia in the 1991–2001 period is structured to take account of the relationship between the state and the main societal interest associations. Focusing on the implementation of the economic restructuring programme, the analysis emphasises the relationship between the government and the main representative associations of labour (Zambia Congress of Trade Unions, ZCTU), business (Zambia Association of Chambers of Commerce and Industry, ZACCI and Zambia Association of Manufacturers, ZAM), and agriculture (Zambia National Farmers Union, ZNFU and Zambia Co-operative Federation, ZCF).

The Labour Unions

In terms of labour the analytical emphasis is placed on the Zambia Congress of Trade Unions (ZCTU). With its 19 affiliated national unions and approximately 350,000 members in 1990, or close to 70 per cent of those in formal sector employment, ZCTU was at the time regarded as one of the strongest labour movements in sub-Saharan Africa (Rakner 1992; Buhlungu and Adler 1997). Unionised labour, nevertheless, only represents a marginal part of the total labour force in Zambia. But, due to its strategic location in the urban centres, labour has constituted an important factor in Zambian political life from the days of colonialism. The unions played a key role in the struggle for independence in the 1950s. Furthermore, the unions provided the main organisation base of the movement for multiparty democracy in 1990–1991 that resulted in the transition to multiparty rule and the ascending of MMD to power. Due to its historical role as a major opposition force to the economic reforms during the previous regime, and its ties to the government through the President and three ministers from the labour union in the MMD Cabinet, the Zambian labour movement was considered to be a central societal association in the process of political and economic reforms. Again, based in pluralist, democratic theory, the assumption at the outset was that the power of labour would increase within the new political structures as democratisation is considered to favour large member organisations.

Business

Although MMD drew its organisational strength from the labour movement, the campaign financing and its international credibility, most notably with the donors, were provided by the business community. Due to the pro-business politics expressed by MMD in its election campaign, the position and influence of the business community was expected to increase in the Third Republic and to further reinvigorate a number of small business associations which had been ineffectual during the Second Republic (van de Walle and Chiwele 1994). But, in contrast to the trade unions, the business sector in Zambia is quite dispersed and private sector interests in Zambia are represented by a large number of business associations, ranging from the smaller associations, such as the Zambian Tour Operators Associations to the largest Zambia Association of Manufacturers (ZAM).[1] However, most sectoral associations are apex members of the Zambia Association of Chambers of Commerce and Industry (ZACCI). Together with ZAM, ZACCI has been the main association representing private business in negotiations and consultations with the government in the 1990s. ZACCI was created in 1938 by the local chambers of commerce as the co-ordination body for business. By 1993, ZACCI had a permanent staffed secretariat, an executive director, an economist and 8 support personnel. Including six chambers of commerce, 35 corporate members and seven trade associations (including ZAM), the membership was approximately 500 (*Profit*, December 1996).

Agricultural Interests

Together with private business interests, agricultural producers were perceived to be the main potential 'winners' of the economic restructuring measures. It was assumed that Zambian economic policies in the one-party era had favoured urban constituents (Bates 1981). But, common in Southern Africa, Zambian agriculture exhibits a multi-faceted character comprising approximately:

- 550,000 small-scale farmers, cultivating approximately 1–2 hectares of land using low inputs, little technology, relying on family labour and retaining a large proportion of production for household subsistence.
- Approximately 750 individually or corporately owned large-scale commercial farms, each cultivating 40 hectares or more of land for commercial sale, with extensive mechanisation and relying upon permanent and casually hired staff.
- An intermediate group of approximately 50,000 'emergent' farmers each cultivating 5–20 hectares with draught power and greater use of purchased inputs than smallholders (World Bank 1996a:33).

In the 1990s, the Zambian National Farmers Union (ZNFU), until 1991 the Commercial Farmers Bureau (CFB), was the main agricultural interest association in Zambia in terms of advocating and lobbying the government on behalf of its membership. Traditionally, ZNFU articulated the interests of the large-scale commercial farmers. In the early 1990s, ZNFU attempted to enlist farmers of the two other categories as well in order to increase its lobbying potential.

1. Moore and Hamalai list a number of reasons why business associations in most countries are relatively numerous, compared especially with farming and labour associations, pertaining to the higher incomes of firms, lack of resistance from workers, the small number involved in organising and lack of external reality checks on the legitimacy of their organisational existence. The central explanation, however, is that organisers are active in creating and sustaining business associations because they have an individual interest in the existence and prosperity of the organisation (1993:1895–1912).

During the Second Republic, small-scale producers were primarily represented through the Zambia Co-operative Federation (ZCF). Under UNIP's reign, ZCF became part of the party structure and functioned as a wing of the party with the sole responsibility of administering the distribution of inputs and marketing of outputs from rural grain producers. After the liberalisation of the agricultural sector in 1993, the MMD government no longer provided funding to inputs for and marketing of agricultural produce through the co-operative movement. As a result, the co-operative movement had to generate its own funding. A great number of the former co-operatives ceased to function, and some new member-organised co-operatives emerged. In addition, three new organisations seeking to represent the small-scale and emergent farmers were formed during the 1990s, including the Peasant Farmers Union of Zambia (PFUZ 1995), the National Association of Small-Scale and Peasant Farmers Union of Zambia (NASSPFU 1989) and Women in Agriculture (1995). Apart from ZNFU, the associations representing agriculture are poorly organised, financially weak and given to organisational infighting.

The External Policy Game between Government and Donors

Zambia's transition to multiparty rule had a strong domestic component with a base in the trade unions, sectors of the business community, the churches and the intellectuals. Yet, the process only gathered momentum when the domestic opposition was supported by the international donor community. In the 1980s the international donor community became increasingly more cohesive and co-ordinated on the principles of economic policy reform, based on the promotion of exports through market-friendly economic policies.[1] A second shift occurred in the early 1990s. Connecting the lack of success of the first decade of structural adjustment programmes to domestic policy issues, the World Bank first introduced the concept of 'good governance' as a solution to the political and economic failures of African states (World Bank 1989, 1992). The international financial institutions emphasised 'non-political' governance issues, such as accountability, transparency and the rule of law. This way, the World Bank and the IMF attempted not to tie their assistance to the issues of democracy and human rights advocated by the bilateral donors. Yet, while emphasising different aspects of political liberalisation, a dual conditionality agenda emerged in the 1990s supported and promoted by the multilateral and bilateral donors. Thus, international development aid in the 1990s became conditioned both on a set of macro-economic performance criteria and issues of governance and democracy.

The international donor community's increased influence over recipient countries' economic and political affairs must also be related to the inability of developing governments to attract alternative sources of private finance capital (Killick 1997). Zambia had for decades sought to avoid donor cohesion and the reforms advocated by the external donor community. In the late 1980s the sit-

1. The concept of cohesion is used to denote the range of agreements among representatives of the states and multilateral organisations within the international donor community (Sandberg 1990).

uation was fundamentally altered. In 1987 multilateral aid programmes were suspended. Due to the substantial international arrears accumulated, Zambia was no longer eligible for commercial or IMF credit (West 1989). When the World Bank withheld disbursements due to non-compliance with the country's international debt obligations in 1991, Zambia was virtually cut off from international credits. Thus, the survival of any political regime in Zambia depended upon improving the country's international financial relations. As a result, the role of the international donor community was at the outset assumed to be of vital importance for the consolidation of the new government as well as the political system introduced in 1991. Due to the former regime's lack of commitment to economic reform, Zambia's international credibility was at a low-point in 1991. In order to lay the foundations for the resumption of growth in the Zambian economy, the arrears with the IMF had to be cleared and fresh balance-of-payments support and investments had to come from donor funds. For their part, the donor community found in Zambia a potential success case for the new 'dual conditionality agenda'.

For indebted, donor dependent nations like Zambia, the international donors function both as a strong interest lobby in favour of a set of policies and the external sanctioning party in terms of further finance. The increasing application of cross-conditionality in the 1980s and 1990s, in which donors and creditors insisted on an a priori stabilisation programme with the IMF programme before lending could resume from bilateral donors, increasingly made the international donor community an external supervisor of national budgets and economic policies (Havnevik and van Arkadie 1996; Mkandawire 1996, 1999). Illustrating the central role of the external donor community, the Consultative Group meeting process was referred to as 'our external parliament' by Zambian policy makers.[1] Interviews with economic policy makers in Zambia indicated that the international donor community was regarded as the final sanctioning body of economic policies, above the National Assembly. In addition to the two main multilateral donors, the World Bank and IMF, the analysis also includes Zambia's main bilateral donors. In terms of aid disbursements, according to the statistics provided by the Development Assistance Committee (DAC) of OECD, these included disbursements from Canada, Germany, Japan, Norway, Sweden, the Netherlands, the United Kingdom, and the United States in the 1990s.

As argued above, the introduction of good governance as a condition for aid disbursements tied the operations of the World Bank, and implicitly the IMF, to the bilateral donors, the main owners of the two international finance institutions. According to Killick:

> [S]ince the end of the cold war, bilateral donors have taken the lead in extending conditionality to the sphere of political systems ... The BWIs [Bretton Woods Institutions] have sought to distance themselves from such overtly political stipulations but the enthusiastic espousal of political objectives by their major shareholders has meant that they are invariably drawn into this extension of attempted influence. (1997:484)

1. Personal interview, Ben Mwene, Secretary to the Treasury, Ministry of Finance. Lusaka, January 13, 1997.

The Multilateral Donors

While the operations of the World Bank and the IMF in the 1980s became increasingly tied, the IMF had a narrower mandate, to restore macro-economic stabilisation and growth through the introduction of a set of macro-economic policies. The IMF loans, while on concessional terms, were conditioned on closely monitored macro-economic and structural performance benchmarks (Killick 1997; Collier 1997). The World Bank, adhering to similar performance criteria, presented a wider 'conditionality agenda' including issues of governance as well as policy goals linked to poverty reduction and sectoral performance. However, in terms of their roles in promoting economic policy reform in Zambia the functions of the two multilateral institutions are grouped in the analysis. Due to the increasingly active role of the international finance institutions in Zambia from the mid-1970s onwards, close to half of Zambia's long-term external debt is owed to the multinational institutions. As a result of the multilateral institutions' position in the international financial market, a major aim of the operations of the IMF and the World Bank is to enable the indebted nations to repay their debt (Gordon 1993; Collier 1997). This, and the more limited mandate for their aid, distinguish the operations of the international financial institutions from the bilateral donor community (Collier 1997).

The Bilateral Donors

The group of bilateral actors, while not a homogenous group in terms of the size of their aid portfolios or policy goals, have a number of similarities. Bilateral donors answer to their national assemblies and, ultimately to the tax payers in their home countries. They are sensitive to criticism about donating aid to 'bad causes', in the post-cold war era increasingly seen as dictatorial regimes without development inclinations (Stokke 1996). Most of the large western bilateral donors have since the early 1990s explicitly tied their aid policies to promotion of good governance, democratic development and adherence to human rights. Observers relate the bilateral donor governments' call for democratic reforms and respect for human rights in the early 1990s to growing aid fatigue—again linked to decades of limited measurable success of aid (Killick 1996; Havnevik and van Arkadie 1996). Studies of the motives behind bilateral donor aid have emphasised commercial objectives and foreign policy objectives (Mosley et al. 1991; van de Walle and Johnston 1996). However, bilateral donors are also guided by altruistic motives (Selbervik 1997; Stokke 1995, 1996). The 'mixture' of altruism and self-interest varies within the group of bilateral donors, with the larger donors displaying the most mixed motives. However, by the late 1980s Zambia had become a relatively marginal country both in terms of security issues and international business interests. This, and the increasing coherence developed within the international donor community in the post-cold war era, meant that Zambia's bilateral donors largely succeeded in co-ordinating their aid policies. In this analysis, bilateral donors are, therefore, treated as a homogenous group.

The Sources of Analysis

The paucity of quantitative data for sub-Saharan Africa in areas such as fiscal policy and trade, and the lack of adequate data on institutional reforms is a problem shared by researchers as well as African policy makers. This analysis has attempted to utilise a variety of sources and sought to combine (and check) quantitative data with qualitative interviews and observations and vice versa. In addition to the secondary sources found in the comparative empirical and theoretical literature, the research is based on approximately 150 qualitative interviews with representatives of the international donor community, the Zambian government, Members of Parliament, representatives of interest groups, non-governmental organisations, and the Zambian academic community. Moreover, primary written material was collected in archives of various interest groups, donor organisations and the Government Archives. Parliamentary debates and newspaper articles (*Times of Zambia*, *Zambia Daily Mail*, *The Post* and *Financial Mail*) for the period 1991–2001 were collected from the National Archives and the documentary centre of the Institute for Social and Economic Research (INESOR), University of Zambia.

Outline of the Analysis

In 1991, the cards were dealt again in Zambia. A new government intent on developing the Zambian economy in cooperation with its international partners, promised to do so while abiding by the principles of democracy. The political decisions met a donor community eager to support what they hoped would become an 'African success story', showing that it is possible to achieve growth while upholding democratic practices and respect for human rights. It is to this relationship between the Zambian government, the main economic interest associations and the international donor community the analysis now turns.

Following this introduction, Chapter 2 presents the theoretical and comparative literature of dual reform processes which forms the basis for the empirical analysis.

Chapter 3 provides an analysis of the economic and political developments in the period leading up to the 1991 elections.

Chapter 4 covers the economic liberalisation process with a basis in the domestic negotiations between the MMD government and the key interest groups representing labour, business and agriculture. The first section assesses economic reform implementation in the two election periods (1991–1996, 1996–2001). The second section analyses negotiations on economic policies between the government and business, agriculture and labour in the period 1991–2001.

Chapter 5 analyses the political liberalisation process 1991–2001 emphasising domestic negotiations between government, interest groups and opposition parties. First, the chapter assesses political developments in the two election periods (1991–1996, 1996–2001). Second, the decline of interest group influence is explained with reference to three aspects of Zambian political developments 1991–2001: organisational proliferation, the weakly institutionalised party system and continued executive dominance.

Chapter 6 discusses the external policy negotiations between the MMD government and the World Bank, IMF and Zambia's main bilateral donors. The first section assesses negotiations between donors and government at the Consultative Group meetings 1991–2001 (political and economic conditionality). Section two focuses on the leverage of government vis-à-vis its donors. The final section discusses ownership in the context of conditionality based aid.

Chapter 7 summarises the main findings from the external and domestic policy negotiations over political and economic liberalisation 1991–2001. The final chapter then moves to discuss the endurance of neo-patrimonial aspects of rule in the context of political and economic liberalisation.

2

Political and Economic Liberalisation in Theory and in Africa

Do processes of political and economic reform interrelate? Is there a negative or positive correlation between political and economic liberalisation? Are democratic or authoritarian systems better equipped to carry out economic reforms intended to secure growth? These broad questions of research have long occupied political scientists. An escalating Third World debt crisis, coupled to major shifts in the economic policies of the US and UK in the early 1980s, brought issues of economic liberalisation to the centre of academic attention. In the 1990s, the wave of democratisation following the fall of the Soviet Union initiated a major and influential scholarly debate on dual reform processes. In this chapter I review the theoretical debates on the interconnections between political and economic reforms. As the discussion will reveal, the role of interest groups has been given great consideration in the academic debates on processes of economic and political reform. Very recently the literature analysing Africa's political and economic reform processes has recognised the influential role played by international aid and donors. The chapter concludes by arguing for analytical designs that integrate the role of aid and international donors to analyses of political and economic reform processes.

Interconnections between Political and Economic Liberalisation

Within pluralist democratic theory political liberalisation should entail increased freedoms for associations which will lead to a rise in the number of societal groups, and new freedoms of speech will ensure that they have a voice. Within this perspective it is anticipated that, over time, this will create problems for governments wishing to implement economic reforms, since such governments need to maintain political support in order to be re-elected, and since the electorate normally does not like to endure difficult economic restructuring, such as cuts in government spending. This is considered to be the dilemma facing new democracies attempting to implement political and economic reform simultaneously. Assuming that democratisation, at least temporarily, may undermine economic reform by encouraging political participation and empowering interest groups that are unlikely to benefit from reform, the academic and aid-related literature has over the past three decades presented various theoretical formulas to overcome this dilemma.

Among the early modernisation theorists, Lipset argued that political and economic development complemented each other in a universal process of modernisation (Lipset 1959).[1] But the idea that economic development and democratic governance complemented each other as part of an evolutionary modernisation process became discredited following the disappointing economic performance of many newly independent countries that had adopted democratic systems of government. The high growth rates of the East Asian newly industrialising countries achieved under stable, authoritarian regimes further served to discredit the early postulates of modernisation theory. These experiences supported the view that pragmatic authoritarian rule rather than democracy was necessary to bring about economic transformation. Within this perspective, the high levels of popular participation and expectation associated with processes of democratisation and modernisation were perceived to have destabilising effects on economic systems and development. In order to achieve economic growth, according to this perspective, interest group pressure and popular demands should be contained in the early and intermediary stages of a country's development process.[2]

The Argument for Authoritarianism

Two interrelated events in the late 1970s brought the issue of economic liberalisation to the centre of academic attention. An escalating debt crisis in developing countries, most notably in Latin America, coincided with a distinct shift in economic policies in the US and UK (under Reagan and Thatcher) strongly emphasising market reforms and the need to expand global markets for Western corporations. As a remedy to the economic crisis in Latin America and Africa in the late 1970s, the International Finance Institutions introduced Structural Adjustment Programmes (SAPs). The economic reform measures prescribed centred around a set of core principles involving liberal trade, competent administration, secure property rights, privatisation of state enterprises, and market-based prices, interest rates, and capital flows (Williamson 1993; Diamond and Plattner 1995; Nelson 1996). The early literature on the politics of reform regarded democratic regimes as less able to undertake the necessary economic reforms than authoritarian ones (Lal 1983; Nelson 1990). Drawing on public choice theories, most argued that interest groups were dominated by short term rent-seeking concerns and that collective action problems made it difficult for growth oriented businesses to act in concert. The rationale for this was based on the logic of collective action reasoning: the gains of reform were considered to be spread across a wide proportion of the population while the costs of the reforms were expected to fall on powerful constituents that had benefited from state intervention.[3] Thus, losers would organise to resist reforms while winners

1. The study of the relationship between democracy and economic development has a long and distinguished academic tradition. Good reviews are provided in Przeworski and Limongi (1993, 1997) and Diamond (1992).
2. S. Huntington's *Political Order in Changing Societies* (1968) became one of the most influential critiques of the early modernisation paradigm. See also Skidmore (1977) and Sørensen (1991) for a good review of the arguments.
3. On the dilemmas of collective action, see Mancur Olson (1965, 1982).

would not recognise their good fortune for some time. As a result, it would be difficult to organise 'reform winners' into a pro-reform coalition. Since authoritarian regimes appeared more able to insulate themselves from interest group pressure, many observers considered this form of state autonomy necessary for successful economic reform implementation (Skidmore 1977; Kaufman and Stallings 1989; Lal 1983; Bates and Krueger 1993; Kaufman 1985). Linking the collective action reasoning to electoral policies, most observers at the time claimed that in pluralist political systems the objective of re-election would be given priority over the pursuit of economic reform policy. Thus, it was assumed that 'political rationality' would create incentives for redistributive policies and budget deficits in order to win the next election (Haggard and Kaufman 1989; Callaghy and Ravenhill 1993).

As the decade progressed, however, comparative research increasingly began to call into question the negative correlation between economic reform and democratisation. A number of new studies suggested not only that many authoritarian regimes were incapable of dealing with economic crisis, but that many democratic regimes did have the capacity to do so (Bresser Pereia et al., 1993; Remmer, 1995). It also became evident in reports presented that the success of economic reform was determined by a host of other political, historical, institutional and international factors that were largely unrelated to the crude distinction between democratic and authoritarian regimes (Nelson 1990; Haggard and Webb 1994; Geddes 1994b). The new empirical realities of the late 1980s, including the break-up of the former Soviet empire and the emergence of new democratic regimes in Eastern Europe, Africa, Latin America, and Asia embarking on a dual process of political and economic liberalisation, introduced the dual reform perspective to the academic literature.

The Dual Reform Perspective

After close to a decade of poor economic results and increasing internal opposition to the corruption and bad economic practices of many authoritarian regimes, a new focus on political and economic liberalisation emerged that assigned a vital role to civil society associations (Landell-Mills, 1992; Healey and Robinson 1992; Robinson 1995). Acknowledging both the changing political climate and the inconclusive evidence generated from comparative research, a new consensus emerged in the 1990s arguing that economic and political reforms could be implemented simultaneously (Widner 1994; Haggard and Webb 1994; Haggard and Kaufman 1995).

One of the main differences between the authoritarian argument that dominated the debate in the 1970s and 1980s and the dual reform perspective related to the role of interest groups in decision-making. Whereas the authoritarian perspective held interest group participation to be a hindrance for growth-oriented reform policies, the theories emerging in the mid-1990s assigned a vital role to interest associations in order to achieve both economic growth and democratic sustainability. Rather than obstacles, interest groups were increasingly considered vital channels of communication between the state and society. Proponents of this view argued that greater participation and involvement in policy-making by affected social groups would ensure ownership, credibility and sustainability of the reform processes (Johnson and Wasty 1993; Robinson, 1995). Research on business associations in developing countries argued that good growth enhancing relationships between business and government were in fact possible (Maxfield and Schneider 1997; Lucas 1997). Arguably, however, the potential dilemmas associated with interest group activity were still present. According to Haggard and Webb:

> Interest groups are important not only because of their lobbying activity and role in mobilizing electoral support but also because of their capability for spearheading collective action outside routine political channels: labor and investment strikes, capital flight, demonstrations, riots and even insurrection. (1994:16)

According to the dual reform perspective, the main challenge for transitional governments attempting to implement political and economic reform simultaneously was to achieve a balance between popular demands and market-based reforms, which spelt hardship and sacrifice (Bates and Krueger 1993; Haggard and Webb 1994; Nelson 1994). To most academic observers, the collective action problems remained: mobilising support for stabilisation and liberalisation would be difficult as costs were certain but benefits unclear; sacrifices were immediate while rewards might be long postponed; losers could be easily identified: "The central political dilemma for reform is that though significant benefits may accrue for society as a whole, policy adjustment involves significant start-up costs and reduction of rents to particular groups" (Haggard and Kaufman 1992:18). Assuming that certain groups would emerge as reform 'winners' and others as 'losers', scholars stressed the need to create constituencies of support for the economic reform measures. Joan Nelson characterised interest groups as 'janus faced'—from one perspective they were part of the fundamental core of democratic practice exercising voice and forming alliances, but they could also produce disastrous policies and threaten the ability of governments to make decisions (Nelson 1994:150). Thus, the central question became how to initiate a process of reform in the face of reform-resistant interest groups. If reforms could be implemented and sustained it was hypothesised that supportive coalitions would emerge. These groups could in turn provide the new democratic regimes with electoral support. To overcome the dilemmas associated with dual reforms the most influential theoretical literature—which also became exceedingly influential among international donors and for reform implementation in sub-Saharan Africa—sought solutions in public choice models developed and tested in the context of Western democracies.

Theories of political business cycles assume that governments adjust their policymaking when faced with re-election.[1] With a basis in this literature a number of analysts have pointed to the great advantage enjoyed by new leaders as newcomers may be less beholden to the established intricate networks of

1. Political business cycle theory is mostly based on data appearing from Western democracies (Nordhaus et al. 1995; Hibbs 1977). However, a small number of studies have discussed election-oriented policies in developing countries. Bates (1988) and Grindle and Thomas (1991) are excellent examples.

patron-client relations often assumed to underpin power structures in developing societies (Bienen and Herbst 1996; Bienen and van de Walle 1991; Haggard and Kaufman 1995; Nelson 1994). The public choice literature suggests that new governments voted into power on promises of undertaking economic reforms might enjoy a period of grace, or honeymoon.[1] During this period, interest groups associated with the old regime may be discredited and/or in organisational disarray as major aspects of new institutions and procedures remain undefined and vague. In this period of early post-transition excitement, flux and uncertainties, reform-resistant groups and interests may not be able to challenge the economic reform processes. By the time the losers from reform are again able to mobilise, governments may have been able to capitalise on the reform gains by shifting to, and consolidating, a support-base among groups and associations regarded as having gained from the reform processes. Thus with a basis in political business cycle theory, many observers of dual reform processes in new democracies argued that shortly after an election newly elected governments could be expected to implement far-reaching economic reforms if the new leaders displayed an adequate understanding of the economic crisis and an ability to act quickly (Williamson and Haggard 1993; Haggard and Webb 1994; Haggard and Kaufman 1995; Nelson 1993). In the initial stages, economic considerations were expected to take the centre stage. In order to consolidate the economic reform gains after the first autocratic implementation phase, governments were in due time before the next election expected to seek to renew and institutionalise contact with groups and associations deemed to have benefited from the new policy.

Critique of the Dual Reform Perspective

Both the authoritarian perspective and the dual reform perspective share a common conviction that interest group influence is potentially harmful for economic reform processes and, further, that the position of formal interest associations will be enhanced by the introduction of liberal political reforms. However, research based in different empirical settings has called into question the assumption that every country undergoing structural adjustment has to cope with a politically aroused, anti-reform civil society.

Based on comparative studies of reform implementation in eight developing countries, Bates and Krueger (1993:455) find that organisations representing business and labour, while perceiving reforms as potentially harmful to their interests, were rarely able to block reform: "One of the most surprising findings from our case studies is the degree to which the intervention of interest groups fails to account for the initiation, or lack of policy reform."

Research by Barbara Geddes in Latin America paints a similar picture of passive or ineffectual civil society organisations. She finds that groups that have borne the cost of reforms, especially organised labour, have shown less capacity

1. The so-called honeymoon-hypothesis argues that a new party winning an election may be able to implement an economic/ideological programme perceived 'politically impossible' under the former government due to the initial legitimacy provided by the elections. See Alesina (1989).

to exert political influence than observers expected. Her research suggests that the groups with the best ability to postpone or stall processes of reform are located within the government and the bureaucracy: "... the kind of autonomy that actually contributes to better economic performance is not autonomy from interest groups but instead autonomy from politically motivated pressures to distribute the resources needed for effective policy-making and implementation" (Geddes 1994b:81–82).

Turning to sub-Saharan Africa's experiences with political and economic reforms, it will become clear that these critical perspectives are particularly relevant on a continent marked by weak interest groups, low levels of political participation and high levels of aid-dependency.

Economic and Political Liberalisation in sub-Saharan Africa

While analyses of the development potential of some authoritarian states in Asia and (until the 1980s) in Latin America reported positive results, most studies of sub-Saharan Africa concluded that authoritarianism had adverse consequences for economic development (Ake 1991; Bates 1981; Sandbrook 1985). Bates' (1981) influential analysis of marketing boards across sub-Saharan Africa suggested that authoritarianism had created a particularly negative form of interest group activity in Africa, in which urban interests were protected by the state due to political considerations, whereas rural producer interests were marginalised (1981). By examining how governments interfered in markets by lowering the producer prices for agricultural output while increasing the prices farmers had to pay for consumer goods, Bates' analysis suggested that economically irrational decisions by African leaders were perfectly rational *political* actions.

Entering the 1980s, the African state model, characterised by patron-client relations, experienced its deepest crisis since independence in the early 1960s.[1] A severe economic crisis now affected most of the continent, threatening the economic basis of the post-colonial state. Even in the most positive interpretation, by the 1980s, it was clear to most observers that African states had taken on too many tasks in trying to achieve modernity and growth, installing new institutions, infrastructure and industries in too short a time. The evidence of economic failure was seen in the failure of public enterprises, which incurred losses large enough to contribute to substantial national budget deficits. The attempts to make up for the deficits through monetary expansion again led to inflation, overvalued exchange rates and negative real interest rates. Rather than promoting growth, the state-led modernisation processes across Africa were by this time considered to have caused economic rent-seeking activities and encouraged large-scale smuggling (Jackson and Rosberg 1982; Herbst 1990; Callaghy 1990; Bayart 1993). The economic crisis, coupled with an intellectual shift in the

1. Bratton and van de Walle (1997) characterise neo-patrimonialism as the institutional hallmark of post-colonial regimes in Africa. The term is derived from Max Weber's concept of patrimonial authority; systems of rule by individuals through personal prestige and power. In sub-Saharan Africa, these patrimonial patterns co-exist with rational-legal institutions. For an excellent discussion of the 'African state model', see Jackson and Rosberg (1982).

Western world, endorsed the opinion amongst observers that the African form of government was part of the economic problem. A number of political scientists started to argue that the autocratic exercise of political authority was causally linked to the economic crisis. Authoritarian leaders, it was held, lacked legitimacy and remained in power only on account of patronage and repression (Sandbrook 1985; Herbst 1990; van de Walle 1994). Regardless of their institutional designs, authoritarian states on the African continent were deemed to be far from autonomous and strong, they were regarded as weak and penetrated by rent-seeking coalitions. Authoritarianism itself was often said to have encouraged the very formation and multiplication of such coalitions (Bates 1989; Skålnes 1995). As the economies throughout sub-Saharan Africa continued to decline, both researchers and donors began to argue that in order to achieve sustainable economic reform, it would be necessary to bring producers, and particularly agricultural export interests, to centrality (World Bank 1981). Supporting this notion, researchers began to relate the emergence of political protests to the economic crisis (Bates 1994; Herbst 1993). According to van de Walle (1994: 485), the failure of Africa's authoritarian governments to bring about economic reform and generate sustainable economic growth constituted a major explanatory factor for the widespread demands for political change occurring from the late 1980s onwards. In a similar vein, Diamond (et al. 1990) argued that the structural adjustment reforms promised an enabling environment for democracy due to economic competitiveness and decentralisation.

Concurrent with revolutions in Eastern Europe, a wave of political opposition and democratic reform swept the African continent in the early 1990s. At this time a large number of African countries joined countries in Latin America, Eastern Europe and parts of Asia in attempting to implement economic reform programmes while at the same time re-instituting competitive political systems. But, despite the critique of the post-colonial state model, and the optimism that the democratic reforms generated, most observers were pessimistic about the ability of African governments to carry out political and economic reforms simultaneously (Huntington 1991; Callaghy 1994; Bienen and Herbst 1996; Widner 1994; Jeffries 1993). Echoing the public choice argument in assuming that democratisation would increase societal pressures on government decision-making, Callaghy among others emphasised the political dilemma of economic reforms as reforms tended to create loser groups who were likely to mobilise in opposition to reforms (Callaghy 1994). Lacking the socio-economic prerequisites, such as high levels of education and literacy, and a sizeable middle-class, most observers expected political liberalisation to undermine the economic reform processes. From this perspective, the fundamental flaw of the dual reform thesis was that Africa's private sector was too limited to afford political leaders an opportunity for horizontal mobility outside the state, thereby reinforcing their interest in maintaining political control (Bienen and Herbst 1996). In a similar vein, but from another angle, others argued that democracy would transfer power from the executive to the more participatory legislative branch of government. As a result, democratisation would weaken the power and capacity of the executive to design and implement policy and thus undermine the prospects for economic liberalisation (Jeffries 1993).[1]

These pessimistic accounts referred to above placed emphasis on the ability of African governments to implement economic reforms. Another line of criticism against the dual reform perspective, emerging not least from African researchers, questioned whether it would be possible to sustain democratic reforms in the context of economic liberalisation. Holding democracy and popular participation to be the primary goal, Mkandawire (1999) claimed that the democratic transitions in Africa in the 1990s had resulted in 'choiceless democracies'. Similarly, Ake (1996) found that the current evolution of economic liberalisation and global markets so undermined the sovereignty of African governments over economic policies that the democratic constitutions were largely irrelevant. The common thread in this criticism has been that the dual reform perspective is not about democracy but about economic liberalisation and that the reform processes have been controlled from the North, most notably the United States. Cammack (1997) argued that the emphasis on procedural democracy has created a development doctrine towards the Third World that excludes social and economic goals, contrary to the democratic developments in the West. Emphasising the degree of external control over Africa's reform processes, Allen, among others, has claimed that African states are now even further removed from popular control and accountability than before the transition processes began (Allen 1998). Thus, according to this perspective, democratic consolidation cannot be expected to take place in a context of externally imposed liberal economic reforms.

The Partial Reform Syndrome in Africa

Now into the second decade of dual reform policies in Africa, tentative answers to the question of how political and economic reforms have correlated are beginning to emerge. Has, in fact, political democratisation undermined the economic reform efforts? Or have the economic reforms stalled democratic developments? For the region as a whole, arguably, the political changes witnessed since the early 1990s have been remarkable and enduring. Between 1990 and 1998 more than 70 legislative multiparty elections were convened in 42 of sub-Saharan Africa's 48 countries. Moreover, a process of institutionalising regular elections appears to have begun as 26 nations have convened second and third elections within the framework of a multiparty constitution. As argued by van de Walle, this routinisation of elections contrasts sharply with previous periods (2001:243). But from an early optimism with regard to what multiparty democracy could accomplish for sub-Saharan Africa in terms of political accountability, economic development and peace, the current perception within the academic community and international development aid circles is more mixed. The changing attitudes relate to the role of the electoral institutions and to what extent multiparty elections have actually had any *real* effect on decision-making

1. For an excellent discussion of the dual reform debate, see van de Walle 2001.

in sub-Saharan Africa since multiparty democracy was introduced. According to Carothers, most of Africa's new democracies have not yet consolidated as democracies, but have entered a 'grey zone'—one of the characteristics being the blurring of the line between the state and the ruling party (2002). Despite 'democratic maturity' in terms of the actual number of consecutive multiparty elections, the quality of the electoral process has not necessarily improved. Many observers argue that Africa's democratisation processes have stagnated and that the multiparty systems have not progressed toward democratic consolidation to the extent that democratic norms and values are institutionalised. Recent academic works find that institutional reforms have failed to produce influential 'watchdogs' and counter-forces against state malpractice and corruption—contrary to what was assumed in democratic theory (Decalo 1997; Joseph 1998). While electoral democracy exists, pluralist constitutional democracy has not challenged the hegemony of authoritarian leaders. Contrary to the expected 'participatory explosion', and subsequent reduction in executive control of reform processes, research suggests that there is an overwhelming, and growing, concentration of power in the executive office across the new democracies of sub-Saharan Africa (Joseph 1999; Walle 2001; Chazan et al. 1988). While most regimes on the continent have adopted a form of electoral democracy, with regular competitive elections, they fail to meet more substantive tests of democracy (Diamond 2002).

In his insightful analysis *African Economies and the Politics of Permanent Crisis* (2001), van de Walle finds little significant difference between Africa's democracies and non-democracies in terms of economic reform performance. Analysing two decades of continuous economic restructuring in sub-Saharan Africa, Walle distinguishes a particular reform pattern for the region as a whole; that of partial reform. According to Walle, while there has been some undeniable progress in terms of changing economic policies, this is uneven across the region's economies, given to partial implementation and vulnerable to reversals (2001:89). Echoing the critique of the dual reform perspective presented above, Walle argues that in terms of political and economic reforms on the African continent the literature on economic policy making has been too focused on societal actors. His research suggests a need to focus on state elites and the interest, economic ideas, and capacity to be found within the state apparatus as well as the state's ability to maintain key interests through periods of reform:

> In sum, the economic policy status quo is not protected by well-organized societal interests that effectively prevent governments from carrying out reform ... [t]he key obstacle to growth oriented economic policies is much more likely to have been the small number of senior state decision makers who have found it difficult to reconcile reform with their understanding of their own material interests. (2001:274)

Ten country case studies on aid and reform in sub-Saharan Africa largely support the partial reform perspective and the importance of individuals and interests within the state apparatus (Devajaran et al. 2001).[1]

1. The ten case studies are: Ghana, Uganda, Ethiopia, Mali, Tanzania, Côte d'Ivoire, Kenya, Zambia, Democratic Republic of Congo and Nigeria.

Clearly, the democratic and economic reform processes carried out in a large number of African countries in the last two decades represent significant and enduring changes. However, the literature does not report on economic and political reform processes *anywhere* on the continent having resulted in a dramatic increase in societal influence over decision-making. Contrary to theoretic assumptions, executive dominance over key political and economic decision-making appears to have increased. The continuity within political leadership and the slow progress of economic reform may relate to the way the liberalisation processes actually emerged on the continent. Robert Bates argues that Africa's liberalisation processes in the 1990s were distinguished by a number of paradoxes (Bates 1994:13). First of all, while demanded domestically, the political openings were usually supplied only in conjunction with international pressure as foreign governments and international organisations used the threat of reduced economic assistance to force the incumbent leaders to embark on the political changes. Further, while reformers sought new political beginnings, these men and women were often older politicians, once members of the government and now outsiders. Finally, in many instances the reforms were initiated by the very governments that were the object of change (Bates 1994:13). The characteristics pointed to here illustrate the dire economic situation and institutional weakness of both societal and state institutions in many nations in sub-Saharan Africa. They also underline the strong presence of a set of actors often ignored in comparative analyses of reform implementation, the international donor community. More than in any other area of the world, political and economic developments in Africa have been heavily influenced and shaped by the changing trends of the international development aid debates and policies.

The Role of the International Donor Community in sub-Saharan African Reforms

Aid until the early 1980s set few conditions and involved little co-ordination. It consisted mainly of project support. In an attempt to meet the growing balance-of-payments problems facing many sub-Saharan African nations, the World Bank in the early 1980s shifted a large proportion of its lending portfolio from project aid to programme aid. When aid in the 1980s became explicitly tied to reforms of national economic policies, systems of governance and legal processes, the international donor community acquired an increasingly stronger position in terms of influencing the policy debates on the African continent. In 1981 the World Bank entered into policy-based lending through the creation of the Structural Adjustment Lending facilities and through this, a much closer relationship between the IMF and the World Bank (Mosley et al. 1991; Gibbon 1993). The analytical basis of the Structural Adjustment Programmes (SAPs) of the World Bank which came to dominate the political and economic discourse in Africa in the next two decades, was the World Bank's 1981 report *Accelerated Development in sub-Saharan Africa* (World Bank 1981).[1] This report stated that the causes of Africa's economic crisis were to be found in the internal policies of

1. The report is commonly referred to as the Berg report named after its main author, Elliot Berg.

the African states. The report pointed to domestic misallocation, political obstacles to growth, and the over-extended public sector. Calling for a reduction in the role of the state and a strengthening of the market, the 1981 World Bank report, and the policy prescriptions generated from this report, was strongly influenced by the neo-liberal agenda dominating the political and economic discourse in the Western world at this time (Gwin and Nelson 1997; van de Walle and Johnston 1996). Whereas the development economists of the 1950s and 1960s had located sources of underdevelopment in the failures of the market and called for the involvement of an active state, development economics in the 1980s turned instead to seeing the state as the major obstacle to economic development (Mosley et al. 1991). As a result, the 1980s became a period when the trends towards increased and co-ordinated conditionality lending deepened, involving a redefinition of roles and relations within the donor community (Gibbon 1993:38). The main trend was growth in aid co-ordination and cross-conditionality. This involved bringing the bilateral donor governments to tie parts of their development assistance to the agreements already reached by the recipient nations with the IMF and World Bank.

Chaired by the World Bank, Consultative Group meetings appeared in the mid-1980s as a mechanism to improve co-ordination among donors and cooperation with the recipient governments in the field of macro-economic and structural policy reforms (Engberg-Pedersen 1995; van de Walle and Johnston 1996). These meetings became regular and the World Bank became the disseminating institution in terms of presenting and analysing economic information (Gibbon 1993; van de Walle and Johnston 1996; Lancaster 1997). According to Gibbon (1993:39): "The new regime thus involved a decisive (if willing) subordination of the bilaterals, especially evident in the case of the so-called 'like-minded' countries—the Scandinavians, Canada and Holland." By tying the disbursement of programme aid to an a priori stabilisation agreement with the IMF, the operations of the World Bank became more closely linked to those of the IMF. Increasingly, international aid to sub-Saharan Africa became linked to the principles of economic policy reform, based on the promotion of exports through market-friendly economic policies. According to critical observers, more and more, the donors resumed full responsibility for planning, preparing and implementing their own programmes (Bonnick 1997:116). In the 1980s, the Consultative Group meetings increasingly became the main channel for indebted recipient governments to raise external support required to meet their balance-of-payments needs and debt servicing obligations. As a result, recipient governments had great incentives to participate in these meetings (van de Walle and Johnston 1996:50).

The focal point of the donor community through its policy-based lending was initially to restructure the economic policies of debtor nations by reducing the role of the state in economic matters and strengthening market forces. In terms of the actual results achieved, however measured, the experience with aid to Africa's reform processes cannot be depicted as a success. By the mid-1990s, after a decade of structural reforms in Africa, it was becoming evident that the effectiveness of the various structural adjustment programmes had been limited.

The two-volume study of the effectiveness of structural adjustment programmes conducted by Mosley, Harrigan and Toye (Mosley et al. 1991) provided a most devastating critique of the reform programmes' first decade. The authors concluded that the programmes had largely been unsuccessful in terms of reaching their own objectives as over half of the programme agreements were discontinued before the end of their intended life. Evidence from the first decade of adjustment lending to Africa indicated that while African states had powerful incentives to enter into conditionality based agreements, they had much weaker incentives to implement such agreements, and often the technical and political capacity to do so was very limited. The limited results, documented in academic research as well as in the World Bank's own evaluations, prompted the World Bank to conclude that reform implementation had a *political* as well as an economic element (World Bank 1989, 1992, 1994). By the late 1980s, a shift in the perspective of the international donor community was discernible towards an emphasis on the political basis of reform implementation and sustainability. These ideas were given official sanction by the 1989 World Bank publication *From Crisis to Sustainable Growth*, which emphasised the importance of the rule of law, property rights, increased accountability of public officials, and greater transparency in decision-making. Thus, from the early 1990s onwards, the World Bank began to argue that a country's ownership of the reform programme was necessary for sustainable success (World Bank 1989). Arguably, the willingness of donors to attach political strings to their aid portfolios was motivated by both political and economic factors. The mixed experiences of a decade of structural adjustment programmes were attributed by the World Bank and IMF to problems of governance (Healey and Robinson 1992). In addition, the end of the cold war and the collapse of communism in Eastern Europe all contributed towards the evolution of a more active political stand by the donors. As argued by Kapur:

> The demise of the cold war, tightening donor budgets, and mounting frustrations at the limited results that donor assistance had produced contributed to putting 'governance' issues at the centre of the development agenda in sub-Saharan Africa. (1997:762)

Dual Conditionalities as a Response to Reform Failure

From the late 1980s onwards, a number of donor institutions began to issue statements on the need for political reforms. One of the earliest manifestations of this expansion of the conditionality agenda was the 1989 aid package to Eastern Europe, which emphasised political democracy as its precondition (Ibid.). For the international finance institutions, the growing tendency of bilateral donors to include issues of policy reform as a condition for support was initially met with scepticism. Both the constitutions of the IMF and the World Bank specifically stated that their operations should not be based on political considerations.[1] Moreover, according to observers, the inclusion of explicit political conditionality was problematic for the World Bank because it was considered to

1. World Bank: Article 4, section 10. See Lancaster for a discussion of the dilemmas of the World Bank in terms of introducing policy aid (1997:185–89).

potentially overload governments in developing countries and thereby potentially threaten or at least slow down, the economic reform efforts (Nelson and Eglington 1992; Gibbon 1993; Lancaster 1997).

However, the multilateral financial institutions also started to give higher priority to aspects of political reform. Despite the fact that the World Bank's charter restricted its activities to promoting economic development, the World Bank, in fact, was in the forefront of arguing the need for good governance as a crucial ingredient for economic development (Nelson and Eglington 1992). Good governance, in the 'non-political' jargon of the World Bank, entailed four major components: sound economic policies, competent public administrations, open and accountable governments and respect for the rule of law (Robinson 1993:90).

The means applied by donors in pursuit of good governance included either punitive measures, such as withdrawal of aid or diplomatic pressure, or positive measures, in which additional aid was provided to reward genuine reform efforts and to encourage the reform process further. Within the promotion category, aid as assistance to non-governmental associations, training of legislators and judges, electoral monitoring and support of the media became common elements (Nelson and Eglington 1992). Thus, by 1992 the multinational finance institutions, led by the World Bank through its co-ordinating functions, again came to occupy a leading role within an increasingly homogenous aid regime (Nelson and Eglington 1992; Sandberg 1990; Gibbon 1993). More and more, the international donor community held that processes of economic and political liberalisation were not only compatible, but also interdependent and should be promoted simultaneously (Moore 1993; Robinson 1995). But, whereas the World Bank and the IMF tended to see governance as a question of management of a country's resources and thus emphasised issues of accountability, transparency and predictability in public administration, other aid agencies emphasised democratisation as a goal in itself. Influenced by the European Union's Council of Ministers, the bilateral donors extended their focus and placed more explicit emphasis on human rights and democracy. Political liberalisation and democratisation were added and imposed as conditions in their own right at the beginning of the 1990s (Robinson 1993; Stokke 1995). Adding to the complex nature of implementing political conditionality, bilateral donors attached different meanings to the concepts of human rights and democracy (Gwin and Nelson 1997).

The early 1990s therefore witnessed a tendency within the international donor community to endorse the view that 'all good things go together', in other words, democracy and economic liberalisation were seen as mutually interdependent processes (Bienen and Herbst 1996).The design of aid programmes and the conduct of Consultative Group meetings in the period after 1990 indicated that the donor community as a whole had to a large extent endorsed the principles of public choice reasoning. Through increasing aid disbursements to governments undertaking both political and economic reforms, the strategy was to programme reforms in the initial stages through promotive mechanisms (Ndegwa 1997; Lancaster 1997; van Arkadie and Mule 1996). The continued economic crises on the African continent, and the donor community's new ability to appear as a unified group vis-à-vis Third World governments, suggested that the international donor community had acquired influence and leverage in the domestic policies of the indebted sub-Saharan nations on an unprecedented scale in the post-colonial era (Lancaster 1997).

The Failure of Conditionality

What has been the effect of donor conditionality on Africa's dual reform processes? According to Killick (1998), the new adjustment regime in the 1990s witnessed an increase in conditionality and an explosive growth in the explicitness and detail of the conditions donors attached to aid. Yet at the same time, evidence does not suggest that actual donor influence over policy outcomes has increased. Towards the late 1990s an emerging literature on conditionality based aid began to suggest that more co-ordinated conditions had produced less and less effective conditionality.[1] New evidence on aid effectiveness found that aid transfers to date had been ineffective both in promoting growth and in inducing policy reform except in good policy environments (Burnside and Dollar 1997; Killick 1998). White (1998) suggested that macro-economic policy reform was delayed by the massive inflow of aid to sub-Saharan Africa. Killick questioned whether the main effect of financial aid for structural adjustment purposes had been to postpone real adjustment processes by allowing governments to avoid politically sensitive decisions (Killick 1998). Stating the argument more explicitly, van de Walle (2001) has argued that donor support for policy adjustment has served an essentially conservative role by reducing the incentives to undertake policy reform. But whereas conditionality has been weak at best, external aid has resulted in a growing role for donors in day-to-day decision-making. Concluding his analysis of two decades of policy reform in sub-Saharan Africa, Walle (2001:62) argues that: "Standing between their own societies and their donors, top state elites have sought to use the policy reform process to gain maximum autonomy from both". Through their focus on technocrats, Walle maintains that the international donor community largely ignored the fact that reforms would fail without the support of the political class.

Increasingly confronted by studies suggesting that not only has aid failed to reverse bad policies, but that there may even be a positive correlation between corruption levels and aid, the international donor community have in recent years sought to develop other mechanisms for enhancing democratic accountability and the effectiveness of aid (World Bank 1998a). A growing international critique, fronted by large civic transnational movements, claims that the structural adjustment processes has been donor-imposed and led to increased levels of poverty.[2] This criticism tended to treat policies prescribed by the interna-

1. Similar conclusions are found in analyses conducted by Killick 1995, 1996; Collier 1997; Mosley et al. 1991. For an excellent review of the structural adjustment lending process in Africa, see Kapur' s article "The weakness of strength: The challenge of sub-Saharan Africa" in Kapur et al. 1997, Vol. I, pp. 683–805.

2. The works of international NGOs and social networks like Attac and Jubilee 2000 were influential for the shift in the international aid regime witnessed from 2000 onwards. The Structural Participatory Review International Network (SAPRIN) report, "The policy roots of economic crisis and poverty. A multi-country participatory assessment of structural adjustment", produced in April 2002 has further become an important document for a growing international movement to reduce Third World debt.

tional finance institutions as actually implemented.[1] As a result, structural adjustment policies have come to be seen as the root cause of most negative development witnessed in Third World countries. Nevertheless, public opinion—coupled with the negative reports on what conditionality-based aid had accomplished in terms of sustainable development—has led to a marked development in the donors' mode of thinking and a renewed focus on poverty reduction towards the end of the millennium (World Bank 2000a; Dijkstra 2002). The Poverty Reduction Strategy Processes (PRSP) adopted by the World Bank and IMF for forging poverty reduction in the context of debt relief programmes are maybe the most direct attempts by the international donor community to seek to enhance commitment to the poor and accountability to poverty reduction from the outside. All countries requesting debt-relief under the highly indebted poor countries (HIPC) initiative are required to adopt a Poverty Reduction Strategy developed through a broad participatory process (PRSP). This process aims to have a wide range of stakeholder views on issues of priority setting, resource allocations and access to public goods and services. Tied to a set of governance conditionalities, the PRSPs have placed issues of poverty reduction at the centre stage of the official agenda in a number of debtor countries. The inclusion of empowerment as a key element in poverty-reduction strategies may indicate a shift in the international aid regime and a pendulum-swing from the focus on market liberalism in the 1980s and 90s towards state intervention in selected fields. As part of these changes, a transition from *substantive conditionality*—that stressed efficiency, goalposts and results—to a form of *processual conditionality*, which lays more emphasis on inclusive participation and ownership can be witnessed.

Thus, largely reflecting the failure of the former aid regime, the new millennium introduced shifts in the international aid regime emphasising poverty alleviation, debt relief and participation. Whether participation—facilitated by externally imposed conditionalities—will lead to increased responsiveness of the national political institutions (the executive, legislators, parties, courts etc.) to the poor and their concerns will depend on the extent to which the PRSP processes are 'owned' by the national governments. It is too early to assess whether this perception is only an appearance or a factual description and if the process perspective has just been added to the erstwhile substantive approach in order to enhance the efficiency of implementation. To a certain extent, the new aid regime represents a break with the past as a result of the increasing emphasis on poverty reducing budgets, and civic participation, which attempts to break the pattern of economic policy being a process involving a few government ministers and the international finance institutions. On the other hand, the current aid policies are still imposed from the international donor community. The participatory processes are made an explicit condition for debt-relief and PRSP-grants and the participation by civil society is sponsored and financed by the external donors. The economic prescriptions are still that poverty reduction requires growth and that growth is founded on a set of macro-economic principles laid

1. This is most clearly witnessed in the SAPRIN report when it concludes that privatisation, whether implemented or not, has resulted in massive lay-offs and increased poverty.

out in the economic adjustment programmes from the early 1980s onwards. Structural reforms like the reduction of the public sector, privatisation of industries and liberalisation of trade and monetary institutions are still part of the economic conditions laid down by the external donors. It is likely, therefore, that the influence of international public actors and institutions will remain large in poor, indebted nations.

Analysing Political and Economic Reforms in Zambia

This chapter has reviewed the main theoretical debates on the interconnections between political and economic liberalisation that started to emerge in the early 1980s following the debt-crises and a major ideological swing towards market liberalism in the western world. The collapse of the Soviet Empire marked an end to the cold war era, and increasingly countries in Eastern Europe, Latin America, sub-Saharan Africa, and Asia introduced multiparty democracy while simultaneously liberalising their economies. The review has indicated that the literature has primarily been concerned with the relationship between executive governments and interest groups outside the state structures. Both the dominant literature and the main international donors considered reform implementation in electoral democracies to be a question of creating 'reform winners' before 'reform losers' could mobilise against reform. However, an emerging literature on dual reform processes began to question the capacity of societal interest groups to block economic policy proposals regarded as hurting their interests. This literature has called attention to the capacity of the state elites and forces within the state apparatus to protect their own economic interest.

But, as the review of the reform processes in sub-Saharan Africa has indicated, it is not feasible to understand processes of reform in Africa without taking into consideration the powerful role of the international donor community. Today the IMF and the World Bank lend exclusively to developing and emerging economies. The loans and policy prescriptions of multi- and bilateral donors are linked to conditions that increasingly impinge on the domestic policies of the state. Largely based on the failure of the previous aid regime, the dual reform perspective added further conditions to the already substantial list. It is therefore essential to acknowledge that in poor countries external actors (public donors as well as transnational NGOs) are active stakeholders in the domestic policy arena, through defining agendas and orchestrating alliances between interested players (Callaghy 2001).

Criticising the lack of analysis of the role played by international forces in processes of democratisation and reform implementation, Remmer (1995) has found that the theoretical assumptions made in the comparative literature to a large extent fail to capture the empirical reality found in Latin America, Africa as well as Eastern Europe. From her perspective, this reality reflects that democratisation and reform implementation represent international phenomena and that processes of democratisation have taken place under conditions of severe economic decline, involving a wide variety of transitional paths, state-society relationships and historical traditions. Similarly, a number of recent and influential analyses of dual reform implementation in sub-Saharan Africa have emphasised the need to include both domestic and international actors in the analyses (White 1998; van de Walle 2001; Devajaran et al. 2001). However, so far few explicit theories on this interaction have been developed (Milner 1997). In his seminal article *"Diplomacy and domestic policies: The logic of two-level games"*, Robert Putnam (1988) argues that the current practice of debating whether domestic politics determine international relations or the reverse is fruitless. The question should rather be put: *How* do the international and domestic processes affect one another and thus shape the actual outcome of policy reform? The main idea behind Putnam's notion of two-level games is the understanding that political leaders are constantly playing the domestic and international arenas simultaneously (Milner 1997). They are trying to achieve their various goals using these two arenas, and they face different—and sometimes contradictory—pressures and constraints from each. At the national level, domestic interest groups pursue their interests by pressuring the government to adopt favourable policies. Politicians seek power by constructing coalitions among these groups. At the international level, national governments seek to maximise their own ability to satisfy domestic pressures while minimising the adverse consequences of foreign developments. As long as the country remains interdependent, neither one of the two games can be ignored by central decision-makers (Putnam 1988; Milner 1997).

The two-level game perspective offers an analytical framework for analysing the way international and domestic processes interact and represents an important theoretical development for the understanding of political and economic reform processes. Yet, the assumptions underlying in the two-level game perspective embody the same pluralist notions guiding the comparative literature on interconnections between political and economic reform processes, namely that domestic interest groups are expected to increase their influence in multiparty political systems. To the extent that this will benefit the economic aspects of the reform depends on what role interest groups are perceived to play. If the most powerful interest groups see their interests as best protected in the present (status quo) economic situation, these interest associations may seek to block or interrupt reforms. However, to the extent that these groups can either be compensated or new coalitional ties can be created with other societal groups, processes of political and economic reform can supplement one another. In terms of the domestic policy 'game' therefore, the perspective advanced by two-level game theories closely resembles the assumptions found in the comparative literature on the politics of economic reform:

> The key to understanding policy making is to realize how the game between the *domestic* actors is played. This game depends on three variables, the differences among the players' policy preferences, the distribution of information domestically and the nature of domestic political institutions. ... Policy choices—whether for domestic or foreign policy—are the result of a strategic game among the *internal actors*. (Milner 1997:14, italics added.)

In the following, the analysis of political and economic liberalisation in Zambia in the 1990s will adopt a 'two-level game' perspective by carefully analysing both the relationship between the Zambian government and domestic interest groups and the government's negotiations with the international donor community. Tracing linkages between the domestic policy negotiations taking place between the government and key societal interest groups and the negotiations between government and the international donors, the analysis will assess the leverage of the various actors in different stages of the reform process. As the next chapter will indicate, the focus in the early 1990s by key Zambian policymakers and their main international donors on interest group resistance to reform appeared valid. Throughout the 1980s, the Zambian trade unions had resisted reforms. There were few groups in Zambia that explicitly questioned the state-developmentalist model created by the United National Independence Party (UNIP) during the period of the one-party state before the transition to multiparty democracy in 1991.

3

Political and Economic Developments in Zambia 1964–1991

From the outset, copper played an immensely important role in the economy of Zambia. With the growth of copper-mining in the 1930s, foreign capital and multinational corporations developed one of the largest mining complexes in the world on what was later to become Zambian territory. By the end of the Second World War, Northern Rhodesia was among the foremost producers of copper in the world. The growth of the mining industry led to the creation of urban centres and by the time of independence, Zambia was one of the most industrialised and urbanised of Africa's new nation-states. With a Gross National Product (GNP) of close to 2 US$ billion at independence in 1964, Zambia had one of the highest per capita incomes in independent Africa and at the time GNP was two times higher than South Korea's (World Bank 1991; McPherson 1995). Two decades later Zambia was reduced to one of the poorest countries on the African continent. From 1975 to 1991, Zambia's average per capita income declined by 2.5 per cent per annum. At the same time, the country's external debt rose from US$ 627 million in 1970 to a staggering US$ 7.2 billion in 1990. According to the UNDP's *Zambia Human Development Report* (1999/2000), Zambia is the only country in the world with data on the human development index available with lower human development indicators in 1997 than in 1975 (UNDP 2001:1).[1]

The defining event in Zambia's economic history was the collapse in copper export earnings *and* the government's response to this collapse. This chapter argues that the UNIP government's failure to adequately address the economic decline is closely related to the government's political project and the creation of a developmental state where the main economic element was the nationalisation of the main industries. The economic decline was the defining factor that triggered the political opposition leading to the 1991 political transition.

The chapter is divided into three sections. The first section describes the creation of the developmentalist state-model in the post-independence period. Secondly, the chapter assesses the effects of the economic decline on the developmentalist state model. The final part discusses the links between the economic crisis and the political opposition to one-party rule emerging in the late 1980s.

1. The Human Development Index is a measure of average achievements in a long and healthy life, knowledge and decent standards of living, developed by the UNDP.

The Creation of a Developmentalist State Model

The first independent constitution of Zambia provided for a unitary state with a strong chief executive and a cabinet selected from, but not responsible to, the National Assembly. The constitution further specifically named Kenneth Kaunda as the first president of Zambia. The struggle for national unity became from an early date the main political ambition of the new leadership, reflected in the rallying slogan adopted at the time of independence 'One Zambia One Nation' (Gertzel et al. 1984).

Between 1968 and 1971, major parts of the Zambian economy were nationalised as part of the so-called Mulungushi reforms.[1] Starting in April 1968, the UNIP government implemented the first of what proved to be a series of economic reforms by buying controlling shares in twenty-six major companies. In 1969 the state acquired a 51 per cent controlling share in the major copper-mining companies, Anglo-American Corporation and Roan Selection Trust, the two main pillars of the Zambian economy (Turok 1989:42). From 1969 onwards the government was the primary direct recipient of the revenues from the copper industry with the control of government investments vested in Zambia Industrial Mining Corporation (ZIMCO). Nationalisation effectively ended investments from abroad in Zambian industries (Burdette 1988:89). The significance of the government's decision is reflected upon by Beveridge and Oberschall:

> Each reform wave represented a challenge to expatriates, foreign investors, and foreign economic interests. Each also represented a gamble, in that outside technology and managerial personnel were making valuable practical contributions to development efforts. Each was also a gamble inasmuch as the success of the reforms depended on African readiness and ability to take the place of expatriates. (Beveridge and Oberschall 1979:46)

In theory, nationalisation was intended to shift power from foreign ownership to private *and* public Zambian interests. But the reforms of 1968 and 1969 marked a greater determination by the government to tilt the balance against the foreign private sector in favour of the public sector (Turok 1989; Beveridge and Oberschall 1979). Through state intervention in the economy the parastatal system was established on a significant scale of organisation and power, dominating all industries. The enhancement of the power of the state was symbolised by the President taking over the chairman's role of ZIMCO, the overarching parastatal (Gulhati 1989:43). As argued by Young:

> The reforms signified that the authorities had overcome any lingering preference inherited from the colonial era for private rather than public enterprise, and also that they were determined to ensure that where the interests of private export business and the interests of the Zambian economy diverged the latter would take precedence. (1973:206)

The nationalisation resulted in a rapid expansion of the public sector. The numbers of state employees grew from 22,500 in 1964 to 51,000 in 1969 and for each new job in the private sector, the state administration recruited four new employees (Pausewang and Hedlund 1986:18). Through the major state indus-

1. Named after the Mulungushi Rock venture of the UNIP National Congress where the reforms were presented and accepted.

trial conglomerate, Industrial Development Corporation (INDECO), the government became both a leading supplier and competitor to private sector business, thereby imposing heavy constraints on private enterprises (Bates and Collier 1993; Taylor 1997).[1] The magnitude of the state's involvement in the economy is illustrated by the fact that Zambia inherited 14 parastatals at independence, among them four agricultural marketing boards. After the major nationalisation effort was completed by the mid-1970s, 147 parastatals were in existence and 121 under a single holding company, ZIMCO (Callaghy 1990:289). By 1971, most major industries were owned and controlled by the government and government companies. The process of nationalisation beginning with the Mulungushi reforms in 1968, resulted in 80 per cent of the Zambian economy being state-controlled by the conclusion of the nationalisation programme in the mid-1970s.

The policies of nationalisation carried out in Zambia in the period from 1968 to 1971 were given political legitimacy by the President with reference to his philosophy of Humanism, by Zambian analysts referred to as a Christian, non-capitalist view of a good society seeking to maintain African traditions and cooperation while promoting economic growth (Beveridge and Oberschall 1979:46).[2] The nationalisation of major sectors of the economy and the aim to promote 'Zambianisation' in all sectors of political and economic life brought interest groups representing labour, business and agriculture into a close, albeit conflictual, relationship with the state.

Business Interests

As a result of the government acquiring majority shares in all major industries, large public investments were made in power, transport and roads by the state through the parastatal corporations. The parastatal sector created the infrastructure perceived as necessary for further growth. State intervention largely displaced foreign capital and personnel (Beveridge and Oberschall 1979:273). As a result of these measures, non-Zambian capital was displaced from the commanding heights of the economy and opportunities were given to individual Zambian businessmen by restricting certain sectors to nationals, which in the context of allocating businesses tended to be interpreted as 'African' rather than 'Zambian' citizen (Ibid.). Due to the limited opportunities for Africans to enter into enterprise under the colonial administration, the emerging private sector re-

1. The parastatal agencies, defined as quasi-autonomous governmental bodies outside the regular civil service with wide mandates in terms of their internal operations, became major vehicles in Zambia's economic transformation. INDECO was set up in 1960. After independence it became the central agency for the expansion of the state's industrial base. With the Mulungushi reforms in 1968, INDECO became a vast industrial giant dominating key sectors of production and distribution in Zambia. In 1969, the Zambian state acquired a controlling share in the mining industry and set up a similar structure, Mining Development Corporation (MINDECO). In 1970 when the insurance and banking industries were nationalised the State Financial and Development Corporation (FINDECO) was established. These parastatal bodies were again made subsidiaries of the all-embracing conglomerate Zambia Industrial and Mining Corporation, (ZIMCO), which dominated the Zambian economy until major privatisation efforts were undertaken after the 1991 political reforms (Johns 1980:104–26).

2. The doctrine of Humanism was introduced by President Kaunda in 1967, the main points published in two booklets entitled *Humanism* Part I (1967) and *Humanism* Part II (1974).

quired state support as it could not dislodge non-Zambian private business on its own (Ibid.). As a result, an entrepreneurial class was created with the support of the state (Baylies and Szeftel 1982). However, according to Beveridge and Oberschall (1979:245), the combined effects of the Mulungushi reforms and the doctrine of Humanism restricted business ownership and the lobbying activity of the private sector. The influence of the private business sector was further reduced by Zambia's dependence on and preoccupation with the mining industry. As copper accounted for 90 per cent of Zambia's export revenue, all other economic interests, public and private, were given secondary importance (Sklar 1975).

The racial distinction within the private business community remained after independence. According to Turok, objections to state intervention by capitalist minded Zambians were largely stilled as all classes wanted development and modernisation to proceed and it was evident that the state had sufficient capital to set this in motion (Turok 1989:45). Furthermore, local Zambian businessmen became beneficiaries of state intervention and investments.[1] Racial distinctions were evident at the level of organisation and lobbying. It was the policy of the party and government to recognise only one organisation as the representative for each industry in the country. For this reason, incentives, albeit limited, existed for African businessmen to join Zambia National Council of Commerce and Industry (ZNCCI) as membership could provide members with access to shortage goods (Beveridge and Oberschall 1979:257). Non-Africans were invited to join and no expatriate business groups were disbanded. The largely expatriate Zambia Association of Chambers of Commerce and Industry (ZACCI), had some of the most substantial African businessmen as its members. The influence and ability to petition government of both African and non-African business associations were, however, limited due to the economic weakness of the private sector group and the government's ambivalent attitude towards private business (Baylies 1980:72; Beveridge and Oberschall 1979:259). As a result, the relationship between the state and business interests became based on individual responses and networks. Based on their field analyses of business activity in Zambia in the 1970s, Beveridge and Oberschall reach the following conclusion:

> For African businessmen [and Asian and European as well] the best strategy for achieving particular aims was to activate personal relationships in individual cases. ... It was much easier to ask for and be granted exception than to modify policy proclaimed by President Kaunda. ... [Thus], [a]lthough businessmen were unable to influence the political system collectively, through individual and joint actions, they were able to have an influence on the implementation of policy. ... By mobilizing kinship, political, and other connections, the businessman could get his individual case heard and acted on by those in power. Explicit bribes and various favors often facilitated accommodation. (1979:270)

Various individual preferences and the weakness of organised private interests explain to a large extent why private business interests did not constitute a coherent organised force that the government could mobilise in favour of eco-

1. Citizens defined as Africans. The third phase of economic reforms specified that by January 1972 only Zambian owned or state owned companies would be permitted in the transport sector. Furthermore, all mining and public works contracts worth less than K 100,000 were granted to Zambian contractors (Baylies 1980:69).

nomic reforms in the direction of closer reliance on the private sector. Through a combined system of state protection and individual negotiations, the business community was split into various individual entities acquiring profits within the state-controlled economy. Despite this, Africans and non-Africans alike faced disruptions, credit uncertainties and a profit squeeze as well as competition from state enterprises subsidised by the state (Beveridge and Oberschall 1979; Gertzel et al. 1984; Turok 1989).

Agricultural Interests

Most accounts of Zambia's contemporary history relate the lack of progress of agricultural sector development to the emergence of a strong urban interest lobby, consisting of local business groups, civil servants and formal sector workers (Gulhati 1989; Bates 1981; Gertzel et al. 1984; Tordoff 1980; Burdette 1988). The new urban middle-class was neither politically well-organised nor expressing coherent economic interests, but together they prevented a forceful policy of rural development. At a time when incomes from copper-mining were high, Zambia could afford to finance a great expansion of services in the fields of education and health. But whereas access to education and health facilities grew in the urban areas, the rural areas did not experience the same levels of growth (Gulhati 1989; Burdette 1988; Bates 1976). As the welfare schemes implemented by UNIP after 1964 did not halt the poverty of the majority of the population, people moved to the cities in search of better living conditions (Tordoff 1974:155). The rural urban migration added to an already high urbanisation rate in Zambia compared to the rest of Africa. As a result of the high population concentration in urban areas, both the colonial and post-colonial governments attached great importance to the general availability of food for the urban dwellers (Bates 1981). With one of the highest urbanisation levels in Africa, the government supported urban consumers with direct and indirect subsidies that helped keep the prices for the main staple food, maize, affordable (Hawkins 1991; Bates 1981; Mwanza 1992).

The agricultural policies implemented after independence were also based on *rural* policy objectives such as reducing the dominance of large-scale, expatriate commercial farmers, and seeking to ensure fairness, national unity and economic justice (Sandberg 1990:122). At the time of independence the large-scale commercial farmers (mostly white settlers) dominated the food economy of Zambia. In 1971, as part of its policies of Zambianisation and national development, the Zambian government mandated uniform, transregional crop-pricing with the intention of equalising the market position of all ethnic groups and regions. In 1973 the National Marketing Board (NAMBOARD) was designated as the sole purchaser of maize and cotton in order to ensure fair and adequate agricultural distribution. The marketing arrangement provided some benefits to the widely dispersed peasant farming community in Zambia in terms of guaranteed prices, provision of transport and storage. But NAMBOARD proved unable to adequately perform the task it had been given as a monopoly indicated by the chronic late payments of farmers and inability to transport crops in a timely fashion. Government market control severely depressed the prices for agricultural produce as food prices were strictly controlled and kept largely below market levels. Producers were unable to find alternatives to the highly controlled domestic market since the Kwatcha was overvalued, making Zambian exports un-competitive (Hawkins 1991).

Commercial farming interests also suffered under government interference because the pan-territorial pricing system served as a considerable detriment to production for large-scale commercial farming interests (Makgetla 1994; Bates 1981). With the state establishing prices and controlling exports, there was simply not enough profit potential in a number of crops. However, as in the case of business interests, government intervention in the rural economy was also received positively by many of Zambia's emerging rural producers and entrepreneurs who saw opportunities for entering into rural trading and farming through the exclusion of Asian and white producers (Baylies and Szeftel 1984; Sandberg 1990). The dominance of expatriate farmers in the food economy at independence was challenged by the policies of UNIP and many emerging Zambian entrepreneurs as well as politicians regarded the Zambianisation as a positive development (Sandberg 1990). The main organisation representing commercial farmer interests was the Commercial Farmers Bureau (CFB), an association representing private, largely expatriate white commercial farmers. The limited influence of this association during Kenneth Kaunda's and UNIP's reign is illustrated by the fact that the Ministry of Agriculture in 1980 declared the CFB as obsolete and to be discarded in favour of the government established and controlled Zambian Co-operative Federation (ZCF). The power of the government and of the anti-commercial ideology at the time was further reflected in the response of the CFB spokesperson who reserved comment on the statement by the ministry (Sandberg 1990:198; *Times of Zambia*, January 8, 1980). As in the case of business, commercial farming interests were split along a racial line in which emerging African farmers to a large extent sought to increase their economic interests through UNIP. Organised interests were marginalised. While the rural sector as a whole was neglected in the post-independent period, both small-scale and some large-scale producers enjoyed personal benefits from the government monopolised system (Bates 1981). As a result, farming interests in Zambia did not constitute a strong lobby for economic reforms in the direction of reduced state control (Bates and Collier 1993:395).

Labour Interests

Much more than business and agricultural interests the urban work-force was considered a potential political contestant to UNIP. The unionised formal sector workers, especially the copper miners, from the onset at independence represented an organised and potentially powerful political opposition to the new national leadership of UNIP. The unions, led by the Zambia Congress of Trade Unions (ZCTU) had played a vital role in the independence movement in the late 1950s and early 1960s (Epstein 1958; Bates 1971; Gertzel 1979; Meebelo 1986). In the period after independence the UNIP government sought to control the urban work-force through economic redistribution and political co-optation. Ironically, UNIP's attempts at incorporating interest organisations into the party structure had the unintended effect of creating a financially and organisationally viable opposition movement from a trade union movement which entered the era of independence weakened by internal splits and financial difficulties.

In the first independence period, UNIP attempted to bring the trade union movement in line with its own developmental objectives through voluntary measures (Bates 1971). The power of the organised urban working class was demonstrated in March 1966 when a strike by the mineworkers threatened to paralyse the economy. The workers returned to work in exchange for a commission of inquiry into their demands (Hawkins 1991). The Brown Commission report recommended a 22 per cent wage increase for all Zambian miners and similar awards to the civil service followed (Young 1973:134). However, the wage increases did not defuse the demands from unions that the government live up to expectations created by independence. The number of man-hours lost in industrial disputes rose from 124,738 in 1964 to 579,409 in 1966 (Burdette 1988:83).

The 1971 Industrial Relations Act

By 1970 the level of strike activity and worker militarism indicated that this strategy had not been successful. The 1971 Industrial Relations Act represented a clear break with the pattern of voluntarism that had guided Zambian industrial relations to this date. While the 1965 act provided strong incentives for affiliation to ZCTU, the 1971 act made such affiliation mandatory for union registration (Gertzel 1979). The 1971 act strengthened the powers of the party and government in industrial relations through the clauses regulating strike activity and the industrial relations court. As ZCTU at the time was led by a politically oriented leadership closely affiliated to UNIP, the leadership did not react strongly to the new industrial relations policies because the act also greatly increased the organisational powers and capacity of the trade union movement as a whole (Rakner 1992). The mandatory affiliation to one central congress enshrined in the 1971 act and the enforcement of the policy of 'one industry one union' granted the unions an organisational monopoly, unifying the union movement. The automatic check-off facilities provided for in the act strengthened the national unions financially and organisationally, as their finances were secured without the unions having to spend time collecting union dues. The 1971 Industrial Relations Act (IR) therefore did away with one of the greatest problems of the Zambian trade union movement since before independence, the financial situation (Simutanyi 1995, 1996).

Ironically, however, rather than gaining control over unions through state corporatist measures, the UNIP government instead created one of the best organised and financially protected union movements on the continent. UNIP officials interviewed in 1991 emphasised the unintended consequences of IR 1971 and saw the legislation to have been one of the greatest mistakes of UNIP. In the eyes of one official:

> The party succeeded in creating a constitution which provided for unionship at all levels, and the number of unions were reduced to 19 which made it possible to group people into districts, which again became the nucleus of the ZCTU structure. This was the aim of UNIP, to create a strong and unified union movement and now, this is the base for the MMD.[1]

ZCTU was the most powerful non-state association in Zambia throughout the First and Second Republics embracing in 1991 all 19 national unions in the country (Rakner 1992:76). Its membership of around 350,000 comprised approximately 70 per cent of the total work-force in formal sector employment. The UNIP regime succeeded relatively well in utilising the ZCTU as a channel for communicating its policies to the unions as long as the economy allowed for wage increases and growing job opportunities in the parastatal sector. However, the economic decline eroded the legitimacy of the state corporatist model. From the mid-1970s onwards the trade union movement became the unofficial opposition force in Zambia. This process culminated in 1990 when ZCTU lent its organisational structure to the Movement for Multiparty Democracy and became the central force in the 1991 political transition.

Political Consolidation: The One-Party State 1973–1991

The introduction of one-party states in Africa occurred both under conditions where opposition to the political leadership was weak or non-existent and under conditions where opposition was persistent and entrenched. In Zambia, the one-party state was introduced despite considerable opposition and in a situation where opposition parties were well entrenched and when the support for the ruling party UNIP was probably lower than ever since independence (Gertzel et al. 1984; Scott 1980). At the time of independence, UNIP was the dominant party both in terms of parliamentary control and density of party support throughout the country. However, despite slogans and a quest for unity, regionalism remained a powerful force in Zambian politics. The Copperbelt was the economic centre through the incomes generated from the mining industry and this had a great effect on political mobilisation. The initial two-party system was based on UNIP drawing support from the urban settlement and mineworkers on the Copperbelt and in the Northern regions while the African National Congress (ANC) drew its support in the South. This coalition was challenged in 1966 when Lozi members of parliament (from the western region) formed an opposition party, the United Party (UP). UP quickly gained support in the Western Province and was basically a product of the growing disenchantment and relative deprivation felt by many political leaders of Lozi origin at what they regarded as Bemba domination of UNIP (Gertzel et al. 1984; Burdette 1988). The blatant sectionalist appeals made during the 1967 UNIP general conference introduced an era of frequent reshuffling in the Cabinet as Kaunda sought to stem rivalries and balance ethnic representation. Nevertheless, UP managed to mobilise support on the Copperbelt in the 1968 election campaign that led to violent clashes

1. Personal communications, Dr. K.J. Ngwisha, Director of the UNIP Research Bureau, cited in Rakner 1992:97.

between UNIP and UP supporters. As a consequence of the unrest, UP was banned in 1968 (Turok 1979).

Between 1969 and 1971 Kaunda introduced measures to minimise the impact of sectional rivalries within UNIP by instituting reforms in the party organisation. Each province was given equal votes and members on the Central Committee. This move proved controversial as it reduced the influence of the Bembas within the party. Largely as a result of this move, a fraction of UNIP with a local base in the northern provinces withdrew and formed their own party, United Progressive Party (UPP) led by the former UNIP vice-President Simon Kapwepwe. UPP attracted dissatisfied groups, non-Bemba as well as Bemba speakers, who felt themselves disadvantaged in the competition for national resources. The formation of UPP posed a major threat to UNIP as the party's majority position now was threatened both by UPP in the north and by ANC in the south. As a result, pressure to introduce a one-party state grew within the party. On December 13, 1972, Kenneth Kaunda announced the introduction of a one-party state, outlawing not only existing opposition parties but banning all future initiatives to form opposition parties. According to Bates and Collier (1993:122): "On the verge of becoming a minority party, UNIP secured its power through control of the government".

The new constitution established the President as the head of both the government and the party, thus strengthening the links between the two institutions. It further established the supremacy of the single party over the government, the hierarchical relationship being reflected in the phrase 'the Party and its Government' which regularly appeared in party documents, newspapers, TV and radio (Kaplan 1979:129).

The main task of UNIP both in the First and Second Republics was to solidify the control of UNIP and to rework the relationship between the party and the bureaucracy in favour of the party. Under the new constitution, criticism could be aired within UNIP's party organs such as the Central Committee, the National Council and the General Conference, but not outside. Government structures were matched by party structures at all levels. However, opposition to UNIP and President Kaunda's rule did not cease and forbidding multiparty competitive politics did not translate into co-ordinated and unified policies at the national level.

Under circumstances like those in Zambia, where opposition parties are banned and the one-party regime is introduced in spite of political opposition, a regime is faced with the problem of establishing a new consensus for the continuation of its rule. In the case of Zambia, a wide support-base involving pressure groups, the civil service, the army as well as the party was created through economic redistribution in the form of spoils and benefits to major groups (Scott 1980:139). As a result, a form of patron-client system crept into most transactions. Most businessmen remained within UNIP, finding that it was easier to use party ties to circumvent rules than to change the system. Furthermore, the large party bureaucracy which developed in the Second Republic had little to gain from a process of economic reform that could threaten to undermine its position. As argued by Graham (1994:152): "Access to the party system and the state resources that it controlled became the primary route to social advancement in post-independence Zambia".

The Developmentalist Model in a Declining Economy

During the first ten years after independence, the Zambian economy expanded fairly rapidly with GDP increasing at an average of 2.3 per cent annually in real terms (World Bank 1984). However, Zambia's modest luck ran out in 1974, and according to estimates, in the period between 1975 and 1990, Zambia experienced a 30 per cent decline in real per capita growth (World Bank 1990). After 1974, copper prices fell sharply on the world market. The fall in copper prices also coincided with an enormous increase in oil prices. The OPEC formation and the ensuing oil crisis, world-wide recession and the large-scale cut backs in production that accompanied it, led to a general economic uncertainty, spelling the end of high copper prices for an undetermined period. Zambia's revenues fell sharply with the decline in the price of its major export. Diversification of the Zambian economy away from copper had been an expressed political goal since independence. Nevertheless, Zambia remained dependent upon copper for 90 per cent of its exports and 40 per cent of its GDP throughout the 1970s and 1980s. As argued by Burdette (1988:95). "In essence, the [Zambian] economy was always a house of cards balanced narrowly on the prosperity of the coppermines".

In Zambia's case, the effects of the price decline were exacerbated by declining ore grades and technical production difficulties leading to a lower export volume and reduced export revenues from copper. The disorder in the copper industry caused by the government's recent assumption of management of the mines (in 1969) also added to the problems. Without revenues from copper, even productive industries were unable to produce as foreign exchange to finance imports was no longer generated. Government market controls and price limits without copper to subsidise them, spelt shortages and decreased production (Hawkins 1991; Bates 1981). In the years that followed, the Zambian economy declined rapidly. GDP growth was either negative or weak for the period 1975–1980, reserves declined and the budget balance was negative. By 1977 the government had completely exhausted its foreign reserves (Hawkins 1991:844). Thus, from 1975 onwards, Zambia was caught in a classic bind as a weakening market for the main export cut into foreign exchange earnings, in turn necessary for the purchase of increasingly more expensive industrial and consumer goods.

Zambia's situation was exacerbated by regional conflicts that cut vital export/import lines. At the time of independence in 1964 four of Zambia's eight neighbours were ruled by minority settler regimes. In the two decades to come, liberation wars took place on virtually all Zambian borders bringing military conflict to Zambia as well. But it was only when the external donors co-ordinated their aid strategies, by making financial aid conditional on economy reforms that UNIP found it necessary to reform the economy that had declined for more than a decade.

Table 3.1: Macro-economic indicators 1973-1990

Year	GDP growth [a]	Reserves [b]	Current account [c]	Budget balance [d]	Copper prices [e]
1973	- 0.9	185.5	113.3	-315.4	80.58
1974	6.7	164.4	8.4	70.0	93.23
1975	- 2.4	142.0	-726.1	-340.8	56.10
1976	4.3	92.7	-132.8	-231.3	63.64
1977	-4.8	66.3	-232.3	-190.3	59.41
1978	0.6	51.1	-321.1	-208.8	61.92
1979	-3.0	80.0	4.7	-139.9	89.49
1980	3.0	78.2	-544.6	-295.0	99.12
1981	6.2	56.2	-766.6	-210.2	79.05
1982	-2.8	58.2	-592.6	-276.5	67.21
1983	-2.0	54.5	-310.0	114.6	72.23
1984	-0.4	54.2	-162.7	-120.1	62.66
1985	1.6	200.1	-404.1	-232.7	64.29
1986	0.6	70.3	-372.1	-388.1	62.13
1987	-0.2	108.8	-256.7	-232.3	80.79
1988	6.7	134.0	-324.7	-205.2	117.93
1989	-1.1	116.2	-292.0	-71.7	129.15
1990	-0.4	193.1	-489.8	-43.8	120.72

[a] annual growth rates of GDP at constant prices.
[b] total reserves minus gold in US$ million.
[c] current account balance before official transfer in US$ million.
[d] government balance in ZK'million.
[e] London Metal Exchange copper prices US cents/pounds.
Sources: World Bank: World Tables; IMF: International Financial Statistics, 1992.

Economic Decline with No Response (1974–1983)

The economic pressures on the Zambian economy were not immediately felt by the society as the government was able to continue social spending through domestic and foreign borrowing. Until copper-prices started to fall, the Zambian government had showed no interest in the IMF or in the loan programmes from the World Bank. However, from 1973 onwards, Zambia started drawing on IMF financial resources. The World Bank was initially slow to respond to the financial requests from Zambia, due to the country's high copper earnings (West 1989:183). However, in 1978 the World Bank declared Zambia eligible, i.e. poor enough, to qualify for IDA funds, and pledged US$ 50 million per annum for the next five years at the first Consultative Group (CG) meeting it organised for Zambia (*EIU Country Report*, 3rd Quarter 1978). Neither the World Bank nor the bilateral donors took active parts in policy discussions concerning Zambia until the early 1980s. In the 1970s, the IMF was the most important external advocate of liberal economic reforms in Zambia but its application of conditionality was weak. The first two IMF stand-by agreements (1973 and 1976) contained few conditions. Zambia utilised all the financial assistance offered in both the IMF programmes, yet the balance-of-payments was not restored to equilibrium. The IMF team visiting Lusaka in 1977, described the economic situation as critical (*EIU Country Report,* 1st Quarter 1978). Due to the deteriorating economic situation, in effect, Zambia depended on the IMF and members of the Consultative Group for its foreign exchange requirement from 1978 onwards.

The Economic Crisis and Reactions from the International Donor Community

Towards the end of the decade, it was becoming increasingly clear that the Zambian economy was unlikely to recover without developing new exports and more efficient import substitution. By the late 1970s, the Zambian economy was showing signs of deterioration and destabilisation. Attempting to 're-finance' its way out of the growing external imbalances, Zambia had since the early 1970s turned to private creditors as well as the IMF. Thus, by 1978 Zambia's economic situation called for more substantial aid and in return the conditions imposed by the IMF became more severe. In exchange for the 1978 Standard Drawing Right (SDR) of the US$ 250 million stand-by agreement, at the time the largest IMF loan ever extended to an African country, the IMF imposed a strict reform package including reduced internal borrowing, a 10 per cent devaluation, reduced government food subsidies and a more realistic price and income policy (Hawkins 1991:844). The 1978 stand-by agreement was Zambia's first high-conditionality IMF programme. From 1978 onwards, the relationship between the IMF and Zambia was characterised by steady increases in borrowing, matched by even more stringent conditions. None of these agreements, however, got to grips with the fundamental problems of the Zambian economy. In 1981 the IMF extended its fund facility to be negotiated for three years. However, the programme broke down in 1982.

The Internal Reactions to the External Policy Prescriptions

In the 1970s and 1980s, Zambia became a controversial country with respect to structural adjustment reforms. The relationship with the IMF and the World Bank had an on/off character making it exceedingly hard to assess impacts of various economic policies (Loxley and Young 1990). A thread running through the Second Republic was that the pressure to continue the reform efforts came predominantly from *external forces* rather than domestic groups (West 1989, 1992; Bates and Collier 1993; Callaghy 1990). Analysing the debate and reactions to the economic crises internally throughout the 1980s, it may be held that both the government and to a large extent the internal opposition blamed the country's economic misfortunes on external forces such as the low copper prices and the heavy costs associated with support for independence struggles in neighbouring countries. According to Callaghy (1990:290), despite the continued deterioration of copper prices as well as production, the austerity measures introduced under the various stand-by agreements were perceived by the government and the public as wartime measures brought on by the turmoil in the region and by world-market forces. The economic crisis was considered temporary.

The introduction of the IMF as a major player and stakeholder in Zambia's economic policy discussions created from the onset a cleavage line between 'socialists' who found the IMF solutions ideologically distasteful and a heterogeneous group finding the IMF measures to be unpalatable but who recognised that foreign exchange from Western countries could only come through an agreement with the IMF (West 1989; Sandberg 1990). However, even the latter

Table 3.2: Zambia's external debt 1970–1991 (US$ bn)

Year	Total debt	as % of GDP	as % of exports
1970	0.63	36	63
1975	1.14	49	129
1980	2.18	61	134
1985	4.64	178	554
1986	5.71	317	769
1987	6.6	315	695
1988	6.8	200	550
1989	6.74	235	826
1990	7.22	185	719
1991	7.28	180	560

Source: Andersson and Ndulo (1994:24).

group, including the business community, offered only lukewarm support for the measures (Bates and Collier 1993:287). The limited responses to the first signs of economic crisis by the Zambian government have been attributed to the leadership's primary concern with securing its political dominance within the newly established one-party state structures (Bates and Collier 1993; Gertzel et al. 1984; Hawkins 1991; Scott 1980). As argued above, during the early part of the 1970s, UNIP sought to expand its political support-base by bringing large interests under the control of the party. As a result, the Zambian polity consisted of several political pressure groups, including the copper miners, the commercial farmers and the urban middle classes who all had acquired benefits under the existing system and, therefore, opposed any reforms perceived as a threat to the status quo (Gulhati 1989:48).

The unfortunate combination of an overwhelming dependence on one export product and the nature of the price fluctuations of this product were features which placed Zambia in a particular category when the economic problems started to make themselves felt. After implementing the single-party system, the President became the key economic player and patronage was an important mechanism employed in defence of Kaunda's and UNIP's continued rule (Gertzel et al. 1984). Tordoff argues that collective decision making was undermined by Kenneth Kaunda responding to infighting among key members of the party by taking decision-making into his own hands (Tordoff 1974:383). Similar conclusions are reached by Burdette, who argues that economic policy in the Second Republic was determined by political, historical, and ideological factors rather than systematic economic analysis (Burdette 1988:26). Describing this period as the 'bad years' in Zambia, Burdette claims that during this time, the party and the state under UNIP rule began to rot from within through serious corruption and apathy making itself felt on the national scene (Ibid.:96).

External Pressure for Reform Faces Internal Opposition (1983–1987)

In the early 1980s, the debt crisis on a world scale as well as the changing ideological climate in major Western countries began to make itself felt in Zambia too. As a result of the international recession, Zambia faced a situation where 'soft' foreign loans in the form of non-concessional financing dried up. The Zambian government thus found itself in a precarious situation where the only source of finance was foreign aid whose conditionalities were beginning to be felt. After more than a decade of short term stand-by agreements with the IMF, in 1983 the Zambian government and the IMF agreed on a more comprehensive structural adjustment package to be intensified in 1985 (Loxley and Young, 1990). The proposed changes of the structural adjustment programme agreed to went straight to the heart of Zambia's developmentalist model.

In reality, Zambia had very little choice but to follow the economic demands set forth by the IMF and the World Bank. The Extended Fund Facility negotiated for 1981 to 1984 of US$ 500 million went immediately to foreign creditors threatening to cut off deliveries to Zambia (Burdette 1988:122).[1] In addition to two IMF stand-by agreements negotiated, the year 1983 also marked the introduction of the first World Bank Structural Adjustment Programme (SAP) in conjunction with the IMF stabilisation programme. Through the joint reform programmes of the IMF and World Bank, a more substantial reform effort was put in motion. The aim was to overcome the institutional and financial weaknesses associated with the short term stand-by agreements that had previously been applied. The main thrust of the 1983 reforms was to regain financial balance, and over the next three years, three stand-by agreements were negotiated but none was successful. Implementation problems soon made themselves felt. By December 1983, Zambia failed to meet the targets for external payment of arrears and the first stand-by agreement was cancelled. By 1985, the weak exports together with an increasingly more unsustainable external payment position, led the international finance institutions (IFIs) to conclude that more comprehensive reform measures were in order (Loxley and Young: 1990:16). While the more limited reform proposals attempted from 1983 to 1985 had only succeeded in part, a whole new range of reforms were introduced in 1985. In structure, depth and institutional character, the new reform measures promised to challenge the centralised state controls and the developmentalist state model developed in the post-independence period.

In October 1985 the government began to dismantle the control regime by liberalising the exchange rates and prices in order to promote and expand the role of the private market. The 1985 reforms entailed liberalisation and decontrol of the central bank interests rates, the creation of a foreign exchange auction and a planned complete elimination of subsidies on maize and fertiliser in addition to previously announced but unimplemented policies: the reduction of government subsidies by eliminating price controls in the state sector, reduced budgetary deficits, reduced spending, improved economic management, a restructuring of the parastatal enterprises, reform of the tax system, and a reduction of civil service by 25 per cent (Callaghy 1990:292). However, widespread

1. The short-term arrears pipeline of payments to suppliers of imported goods had reached US$ 500 million and 17 months delay. As a result, the British Export Guarantee Department withdrew general cover to exporters in early 1979. Other countries followed suit and until the foreign auction began in October 1985, import prices included a premium of up to 70 per cent to cover the cost to the seller of the pipeline delay (West 1989:197).

scepticism and outright opposition to the reform measures was reflected in the press, within the party bureaucracy and the trade union movement (West 1989, 1992; Rakner 1992). More than anything, the 1985 adjustment measures hurt the government's political base, the urban population and the large public bureaucracy within UNIP and the state.

Internal Reactions to 'Externally Imposed' Demands for Reform

The fact that the first serious reform effort only took place *after* the 1983 parliamentary and presidential elections, from which the political leadership survived almost unscratched, illustrates the national leadership's insistence on setting political survival needs before economic survival. This is a trend that runs through the 27 years of Kaunda's leadership (Bates and Collier 1993; Callaghy 1990; Hawkins 1991). In accordance with the personalised leadership structures developed, the adoption of the reforms was secured by Kenneth Kaunda, in fact the sole supporter of the economic reforms in the Central Committee. In the Cabinet, the President only had the support of the governor of the Central Bank and the Minister of Finance (Bates and Collier 1993:408). While this was enough to adopt the reforms, it was no guarantee for their survival.

In Zambia, the main political problem was that the costs of almost all the reforms would be borne by urban consumers including the large party and state bureaucracy created by UNIP, the strong and centralised trade union movement, and the parastatal enterprises. All these interests were brought under party 'patronage' in the economically prosperous years after independence (Callaghy 1990). From 1985 onwards, major economic restructuring efforts were attempted. The introduction of an auction system for the allocation of foreign exchange was a central element of the new liberalised regime. The move to an auction had a powerful effect on the exchange rate almost immediately as bureaucratic allocations ceased to confer high rents (Bates and Collier 1993:129). According to a number of observers, the economic reforms produced results almost immediately (West 1992; Hawkins 1991; Bates and Collier 1993; Callaghy 1990; Loxley and Young 1990). However, the auction had severe effects on important political constituents. Broadly speaking, the auction favoured manufacturing over agriculture, private firms over parastatal companies, large businesses (and thus, often foreign) over smaller ones i.e., mostly Zambian-owned companies. For urban consumers, the effects of price liberalisation were serious. As part of the reform programme, the government increased its charges for transport and communication services, housing and schooling. In the public opinion, the auction was widely understood to be the cause of the sudden increase in costs as firms saw this as an opportunity to raise their prices to market clearing levels. A widespread public opinion appeared to be that the auction led to depreciation of the currency that again led to inflation. As a result, the auction came under severe attack by the Central Committee of UNIP as well as in the press (Bates and Collier 1993).

Due to the rising costs, the labour movement resisted the economic reform measures. From the close alignment created in the early 1970s, in the early

1980s the relationship between the government and the trade union movement changed radically.[1] The issues of conflict between ZCTU and UNIP, in the period after 1983 revolved around UNIP's management of the economy (Rakner 1992). ZCTU's own documents regarding their policy stand on economic issues confirm that throughout the 1980s the trade union movement was the most outspoken *opponent* of the IMF advocated economic reform measures (ZCTU 1986). In October 1984 a wave of strikes began in the insurance sector, spreading to the entire financial sector. By January, the strikes had spread to the health sector and patients were turned away from hospitals due to the strikes. The strike wave culminated in June the same year when 85 miners rioted and burned mine buildings. In November 1985 the ZCTU withdrew from all the boards of parastatal enterprises to which it belonged in protest against the foreign exchange auction which had raised the cost of living beyond acceptable limits and against economic reforms in general (Rakner 1992).

For a year the government stood firm against the pressures from the trade unions, surpressing and outlawing strikes in all essential areas in 1985 (Hawkins 1991). However, as the reforms continued, resistance to the reform process increased. In April Kenneth Kaunda replaced the economic advisory team that had negotiated the 1985 reform programme. This team had been anchored in the government bureaucracy and had close ties to the international donor community. A new group of advisors was formed of people with close ties to the party bureaucracy and the Central Committee (Bates and Collier 1993: 413). According to one observer, the reform process in reality collapsed when the General Secretary of UNIP complained publicly in October 1986 that the IMF reforms had created Zambia's main economic problems (Callaghy 1990:291). The final blow to the reform process came in response to the government's announcement of the decontrol of maize prices in December 1986. This move brought about one of the greatest outbreaks of unrest in Zambia since independence. Rioting shook the Copperbelt and Lusaka and left 15 people dead. These events profoundly shook the UNIP government and its immediate response was to restore the subsidies, nationalise the milling companies and blame the IMF (*EIU Country Profile,* 1991–92:5). Increasingly, political survival needs dictated economic policies. As argued by Callaghy:

> Over the next four months, President Kaunda wavered over whether to continue the reform effort or end it. External actors and small and isolated technocratic elements argued for the continuing of the adjustment programme, while everybody else wanted to terminate it. An important background was the growing concern about the public's response to elections scheduled for 1988. (1990:296)

On May 1st, 1987, reform attempts in Zambia came to an end when the President in his May Day speech announced that Zambia had suspended their participation in the IMF and World Bank sponsored structural adjustment

1. The political conflict between the trade union movement and UNIP had already become manifest in 1981 when UNIP introduced the Act of Decentralisation (the local government act) which the trade unions contested. The other main issue of conflict in the Second Republic relates to economic policies, in particular the implementation of the economic reforms proposed by IMF (Rakner 1992; Nordlund 1996). For good reviews on trade union views on economic adjustment in Zambia, see Gibbon 1992; Akwetey 1994; Simutanyi 1995, 1996.

programme. In its place, a home-grown New Economic Recovery Programme (NERP) was introduced replacing market reforms with administrative procedures and bureaucratic controls. Both the speech and the document indicated the Zambian government's desire to extract itself from the pressures of its foreign creditors. The 1985 reforms were extremely unpopular with nearly all parts of the population, including politicians, bureaucrats, labour leaders and domestic businessmen fearing for their ability to compete. Clearly, the political costs of the proposed reform measures were high in a society where 50 per cent of the population was located in urban areas and urban consumer and labour interests were protected by a strong and vocal labour association. Few, if any, of the influential political groups saw themselves as potential economic beneficiaries of the economic changes. According to Callaghy (1990:293) "All of these actors believed that the benefits of reform would go to external actors and resident foreigners, white farmers, Greeks and Asians".

A tale that runs through the period of the Zambia-IMF/WB economic reform relationship is that the politicians, the press and even the oppositional forces like the trade union movement consistently blamed the economic misfortunes on external forces, most notably the IMF (Akwetey 1994; Bates and Collier 1993; Rakner 1992; Callaghy 1990). While most analyses of Zambia's failed structural adjustment efforts in this period are ascribed to internal opposition and lack of a constituency supporting reform, studies have also emphasised the weakness of the donor community's response to the economic needs of the reform process (Gulhati 1989:48; McPherson 1995; West 1989, 1992; Sandberg 1990). Opposition to the economic recovery programme was aided by the fact that its benefits were uncertain and far down the road. The lack of confidence on the part of donors, banks and investors that Zambia was willing to implement the reforms further contributed to the reform collapse (McPherson 1995; Callaghy 1990). Analyses of the donor response both to the foreign exchange auction and to the liberalisation of maize marketing indicate that funding was far from adequate and often delayed (West 1989; Sandberg 1990). As noted by the World Bank:

> The financing and sustainability of adjustment programs are mutually reinforcing. Inadequate funding was partly the reason for the political reversal in Zambia [and] Ghana's effort was helped by the availability of finance. (1988:6).

In the case of Zambia, the Western donor institutions had insisted that market mechanisms take the place of inefficient state controls since the late 1970s. The demands and conditions were increasingly more pronounced and insistent. Zambia's ability to bypass these institutions was further limited due to her financial needs and lack of alternative financial sources for securing her foreign exchange needs. According to one observer, Zambia was effectively bankrupt before agreeing to undertake a comprehensive structural adjustment programme in 1985 (West 1992:4). In theory, the leverage of the Western financial institutions and donor governments was great. But, in reality, the external institutions lacked influence in the face of unravelling agreements. The implementation of the 1985 programme indicated that the international donors were virtually powerless and unable to interfere after the President changed his economic team in April 1986 from the group who had negotiated the programme to some of the strongest critics of a market based economy. Analysing donor-recipient relations in Zambia from the perspective of donor cohesion, Sandberg sees the abandonment of reform in 1987 as a reflection of donor cohesion beginning to fracture. Sandberg cites the effects of the Nordic donors and UNICEF beginning to publicly criticise the social effects of the IMF and the World Bank conditionality measures as an explanatory factor for the dwindling unity among the donors (Sandberg 1990).[1] As Zambia attempted to implement its go-it-alone economic recovery programme, the simple economic facts were still that Zambia was in desperate need of foreign funding for its foreign exchange requirements.

Home-Grown Reform Hampered by the Magnitude of the Crisis (1987–1991)

The New Economic Recovery Programme (NERP) was announced on May 1st, 1987. An interim national development plan was to be superseded by a 4th national development plan in 1989. With this decision, Zambia deferred its participation in the structural adjustment agreement and reduced its debt servicing to 10 per cent of net export earnings after deducting the foreign exchange requirements for oil imports and the copper industry, Zambia Airways and fertiliser imports. In practice this meant that 6.5 per cent of export earnings would be devoted to debt servicing while the nominal debt servicing burden in real terms was 150 per cent of exports, arrears taken into account (Loxley and Young 1990:51). The introduction of NERP meant that the government was abandoning the short-lived attempt at liberalising the Zambian economy and returning to state-controlled mechanisms. In this respect, it is interesting to note that ZCTU immediately announced that *despite* its conflictual relationship with UNIP, the trade unions supported the break with the IMF and the new national recovery programme (ZCTU 1987). The announcement made clear that in terms of economic policies there was a general agreement between the government and the trade union movement. However, the NERP attempt was opposed by Zambia's donors. While the planners worked on their documents, Zambia's decision to service debt by less than 10 per cent of GDP led the international finance institutions, followed by major bilateral donors like the United Kingdom, Germany and the United States, to cut financial aid to Zambia. The decision to break with the international finance institutions and limit the debt servicing thereby became a decision of great consequence. It meant that Zambia had to 'go it alone'. Arguing that the donor cohesion was still intact under the leadership of the international finance institutions, Loxley and Young (1990:63) argued that: "So poisoned are the relationships with the IMF and the World Bank, and so influential are these institutions in the donor community, that it is difficult for Zambia's policies to receive a fair and objective assessment".

With an economic decline into its second decade, a decade of declarations of economic reforms resulting in a number of cancelled agreements, a staggering

1. The UNICEF sponsored research report *Adjustment with a Human Face* (Cornia et al. 1987) sparked a critical debate within the donor community. The report criticised the heavy reliance on financial and fiscal reform in the structural adjustment programmes. The report concluded that donors had given insufficient attention to the cost of adjustment for the poor and for social development more generally.

debt and continued economic decline, few donors had much faith in the Zambian NERP. As a result, international interest in Zambia, both within private financial and public donor sectors, was low. For the international donor community, the NERP represented a return to the statist model that had been attempted in Zambia since the late 1960s. However, while NERP represented a shift to control over policy-making from the financial institutions to the bureaucrats responsive to the UNIP party, it was not a complete reversion to the old way of policy making. According to Bates and Collier, the home grown economic recovery programme promoted learning (Bates and Collier 1993:425). In essence, NERP called for structural adjustment of the Zambian economy. Unlike former Zambian official analysis, this document attributed inflation to excessive government spending rather than depreciation of the exchange rate. In the short run, NERP succeeded in reducing inflation and the benefits were targeted on the urban poor, thus decreasing the levels of labour unrest (Ibid.: 425). However, it did not take long before the problems of a virtual ending of gross foreign lending made themselves felt: "[By 1989] it was widely acknowledged that the intimidating proportions of Zambia's current debt would require the intervention of the donor group" (Loxley and Young 1990:vii).

Economic Crisis and the Birth of a Political Opposition Movement

After two years of going it alone, Zambia resumed talks with the IMF and in the spring of 1989 the government again began to dismantle the control regime with the aim of restructuring the economy in the context of escalating foreign debts and arrears. The new economic reform process culminated with the September 1989 approval by the IMF and the Zambian government of a Policy Framework Paper (GRZ 1989). Again, maize prices increased three-fold and price controls were dismantled. Subsequently, 14 donor countries and 8 international agencies in a Consultative Group meeting indicated that they would provide Zambia with US$ 450 million provided they continued an economic reform programme. To reduce the high subsidy burden of mealie meal, the government introduced a selective coupon system targeted only at poor urban households. The decision to exclude the rural poor from the coupon system suggests that the measure was intended to appease the trade unions (Saasa 1994:16). Commenting on UNIP's decision to invite the IMF back and to reopen the negotiations, the trade union movement again expressed a negative attitude to the structural adjustment measures:

> For these obvious reasons, we in ZCTU condemn the move by the authorities to invite the IMF to come back and work with us. We know what it means. We recommend that the Party and its Government should join those forces at international fora which are calling for a renewal of the path of development of indebted economies such as the Zambian economy, through debt relief on a massive scale. (ZCTU 1987:8)

UNIP's attempts to compromise yet again between externally expressed demands for economic liberalisation and an increasingly outspoken trade union movement were overtaken by political events on an international scale towards the end of 1989. Increasingly, economic dissatisfaction and discontent with

UNIP's reign was translated into demands for a return to multiparty politics and a new government. In December 1989, The General Council of the ZCTU declared its intentions to work for the reintroduction of multiparty politics in Zambia, requesting other individuals and associations in Zambia with similar objectives to join forces with them (Rakner 1992). In a press release ZCTU's President, Frederick Chiluba, declared that Africa should abandon the one-party system since the founders in Eastern Europe had done so (*Times of Zambia*, December 31, 1989). ZCTU repeated the plea to return to multiparty politics at the UNIP National Convention in March 1990. This time, the trade union movement was supported by party back-benchers as well as people from the business community. These calls were, however, unanimously rejected by the UNIP leadership. Anxious to regain the political initiative after increasing pressure from the national opposition and the international donor community in the months that followed, President Kaunda responded to the multiparty demands in May by announcing a referendum on the reintroduction of multiparty electoral competition. He stressed that UNIP would campaign for a 'no' vote on pluralism as previous experiences with electoral competition had led Zambia to ethnic violence. The referendum campaign was, however, overtaken by political events. When the government doubled the price of maize meal in June 1990, it led to three days of riots and looting in Lusaka and regional towns. The riots killed 27 people. Unlike the riots in late 1986, this time, the disturbances had a much broader political cause than the restoration of food subsidies. By now, the anger of the crowds had shifted from the IMF and food-prices to President Kaunda and UNIP's handling of the economic system:

> While the food riots of December 1986 had focused on the price of mealie meal, those in June 1990 focused on the political system itself. The rioters attacked the party and the single-party system. They identified the political system as the source of their economic woes. (Bates and Collier 1993:429)

The June riots became the beginning of a string of political events leading to the 1991 electoral victory of MMD. On June 30, 1990, a rebel army lieutenant announced in a broadcast from the government radio that a coup had been staged. Jubilant crowds, surging into the streets to celebrate the defeat of UNIP and Kenneth Kaunda by an unknown army lieutenant, were disappointed when hours later UNIP's Secretary General went on air to announce that the coup had failed. In this context of profound popular discontent, an alternative ruling coalition made its first appearance. A National Interim Committee for Multiparty Democracy formed in July 1990. The committee was chaired by former Minister of Finance Arthur Wina, his deputies were the President of the ZCTU, Frederick Chiluba (in charge of operations and organisations) and former Minister of Foreign Affairs, Vernon Mwaanga (responsible for publicity). The labour movement became the popular base and organisational core of the movement (Rakner 1992). Thus, from July 1990 onwards, a broad coalition of the trade unions, students, academics, the business community and parliamentary back-benchers started to organise an alternative political platform for the reintroduction of multiparty politics (Lewanika 1990). The importance attached to the trade union movement as the organisational base of these processes is illustrated by the following quote by Aka Lewanika and Derrick Chitala, two of MMD's founders:

> The ZCTU, which had been carrying out an open campaign for multiparty democracy, was a critical institution in our struggle for democracy. For one thing, Mr Chiluba and Mr Zimba [General Secretary of ZCTU] had not only vowed to spearhead the multiparty democracy at a time when many citizens were afraid of airing such sentiments, the ZCTU also possessed functional structures across the country which could be very useful in the campaign. Obviously, the ZCTU was an indispensable ingredient in the new democratic struggle (Lewanika and Chitala 1990:vi).

On December 4, 1990, the parliament removed article 4 of the 1973 Constitution which had enshrined the one-party state and guaranteed UNIP the status as the sole legal party. The Movement for Multiparty Democracy and nine other parties registered. The oppositional alliance held its first national convention in February 1991 and the ZCTU president Frederick Chiluba won the presidential candidate elections of MMD by an absolute majority. The chairman of the trade union movement thereby became the main opposition candidate against Kenneth Kaunda. In August 1991, UNIP and Kenneth Kaunda capitulated to the strong pressures from the multiparty advocates and opened up for direct multiparty elections. Constitutional amendments passed by the parliament on August 24, 1991, replaced the 1973 one-party constitution. The most important change from the 1973 constitution was article 21 legalising opposition parties and thus putting an end to the implied unity between the UNIP party and the government.

The Economic Policies Adopted by the Opposition

The Zambian parliamentary and presidential elections took place on October 25, 1991 and were by international monitors and press considered free, peaceful and fair. The fact that Kenneth Kaunda immediately accepted his loss of office contributed to the historical significance of the Zambian transition process. In view of the strong interest generated by the elections, the voter turnout of 43 per cent of the registered voters was low. The MMD won 125 seats out of a total of 150 seats. Of the 25 seats secured by UNIP, 19 were in the Eastern Province where UNIP won all the contested seats. Unlike many other African nations that over the next few years would implement multiparty rule, the Zambian political transition was by most observers considered to be driven by an internal opposition rather than threats of reductions in aid from the international donor community (Bratton 1992; Andreassen et al. 1992; Ihonvbere 1996; Nordlund 1996).

Considering the fact that UNIP's loss of popularity and legitimacy was so closely related to the various reform attempts, especially related to food subsidies, it was perhaps ironic that MMD in its campaign promised to implement a structural adjustment programme. However, after 27 years of Kaunda and UNIP, the latter years marked by precipitous economic decline, the Zambian people appeared willing to accept what was then perceived to be short term austerity in return for the promise of future economic stability and growth. Thus, the period

Table 3.3: Parliamentary election results 1991

Party	Candidates	No of seats
MMD	149	125
UNIP	150	25
NDP	5	0
NADA	3	0
DP	1	0
Independents	21	0
Total	**329**	**150**

Sources: Krennerich (1999).

Table 3.4: Presidential election results 1991

Candidate	Total no. of votes	Percentage vote
Frederick Chiluba (MMD)	972,753	75.8
Kenneth Kaunda (UNIP)	310,761	24.2

Sources: Krennerich (1999).

Everyone wanted structural reforms & economic liberalisation

1990–91 witnessed the rather peculiar situation of both UNIP and MMD campaigning for structural reforms and economic liberalisation. According to a number of observers, more than indicating a pro-adjustment position by major segments of the Zambian electorate, the economic policies campaigned for and supported in 1991 were an indication of anti-UNIP sentiments, including the economic project attempted for the past 27 years (Rakner 1992; Bratton 1992; van de Walle and Chiwele 1994). Yet, given labour's important position within the opposition movement and its previous negative stand on the IMF/World Bank sponsored structural adjustment programmes expressed as late as 1989, MMD's adoption of a neo-liberal economic agenda in the 1991 election campaign appears puzzling. Partly, MMD's pro-reform stand is explained by the fact that although the labour movement provided the organisational backbone of the movement, finances came from the business sector. By 1990, the long quiescent Zambian business associations became part of the coalition seeking to topple UNIP from power. Given UNIP's disastrous economic record, few in the business community favoured a continuation of UNIP and Kaunda's regime when presented with a viable alternative. Signalling a clear shift in popular attitudes from the 1980s, the authoritarian regime of Kenneth Kaunda and UNIP was largely perceived to be the cause of the Zambian economic malaise. The movement for multiparty democracy grew out of Zambia's disastrous economic situation. The rapid rise and success must therefore also be understood against the background of severe economic decline and mismanagement and the discontent this had created not only among the majority of Zambians but also the international donor community.

In Zambia, the political and economic reform processes begun in 1991 had a strong domestic support at the outset. However, the role played by the international donor community in terms of reform advocacy and pressure should not be underestimated. The end of the cold war had facilitated a new consensus around the principles of dual reform processes and thus, strengthened the unity within the international donor community. Zambia's dire economic situation made it clear that a return of large-scale financial assistance from the international community was paramount to the new government's political survival. Zambia's 1989 agreement with the World Bank and IMF was cancelled in the summer of 1991 when Kenneth Kaunda refused to cut maize subsidies right before the 1991 elections. In the pre-election period, President Kaunda abandoned spending limits set by the economic reform programme, raised salaries for civil servants and increased subsidies on maize and housing. MMD was now faced with the formidable challenge of institutionalising its rule and forming a coherent party structure from a 'rainbow coalition' of business interests, labour, students, intellectuals, church representatives and converted UNIP party officials. At the same time MMD needed to turn an economy around which had been showing signs of decline for almost 20 years. The trade union movement had played the vanguard role in undermining the Kaunda regime but the same union movement had displayed its opposition to economic restructuring throughout the 1980s. Arguably, the main cluster of the opposition forces now forming a government were either rooted in, or dependent on, the state through the developmentalist state model formed and nurtured during the First and Second Republics (White 1996:206). Thus, the new MMD government was facing a paradox as the social forces which organised the transition to democracy were running the risk of being weakened by the actions of the new regime (Woods 1992:89). It is to these potential political dilemmas associated with the implementation of economic reforms under a liberalised political system the analysis now turns.

4

Economic Reforms 1991–2001

The Relationship between the Government and Domestic Interest Groups

There is nothing more difficult to carry out, nor more doubtful of success, nor more dangerous to handle than to initiate a new order of things. For the reformer has enemies in all those who profit by the old order, and only lukewarm defenders in all those who would profit by the new—Machiavelli, The Prince.[1]

Arguably, the economic prospects for Zambia seemed good in 1991 when the first democratically elected government took over. But after almost a decade of continuous structural adjustment programmes, the record on Zambian policy reforms in the 1990s is exceedingly complex and mixed. On the one hand, during the 1990s the foundations were laid for a shift from a state oriented to a market based economy. Most importantly, despite several exogenous shocks and uneven implementation, none of the reform measures implemented have been reversed. But, over time, the MMD government's commitment to economic reform waned. Clearly, much less progress was made in terms of restructuring the economy by the second MMD government (1996–2001). This chapter assesses the implementation of economic policy reform by the two Chiluba-administrations (1991–1996, 1996–2001).[2] Furthermore, the chapter analyses the consultations between the government and the main economic interest groups in three main areas of reform; privatisation, trade liberalisation and agricultural liberalisation. The analysis of economic reform implementation in Zambia in the 1990s reveals that the MMD government took advantage of its 'honeymoon' in the early 1990s and implemented economic reforms with limited consultation with interest groups. But, rather than broadening consultation through the creation of potential growth coalitions as anticipated in the theoretical literature, over time, the government's relationships to economic interest groups were discontinued. Both business and labour became marginalised due to falls in membership and internal differences related to the economic reforms.

Economic Reforms in the First Chiluba Administration (1991–1996)

Throughout its election campaign, MMD advocated for a complete shift in economic policies, involving a change from the system of public monopolies to a

1. Quoted in Geddes 1994a:43.
2. Appendix 1 provides a chronological list of the main economic developments in the period 1991–2001.

greater reliance on markets, private networks and institutions. The party's commitment to fostering private sector growth and a limited role for government was spelt out in the 1991 election manifesto stating that: "The government restricts itself to rehabilitate and build socio-economic infrastructure with a small public sector in the midst of a basically private enterprise economy" (MMD, *Manifesto* 1991:14).

The economic situation had deteriorated dramatically in the second half of 1991 as Kaunda chose to ignore the reform programme agreed to with the donors in a bid to win the October 1991 elections. In his opening speech to the National Assembly President Chiluba made no secret of the difficult task ahead. According to the President:

> We have found an economy in ruins. This year, as before, Zambia's economy has declined. The decline of 3 per cent, linked to the 1 per cent of the year before, means ... that the standard of living of our people has actually fallen by some 10 per cent over the last two years. ... Adding insult to injury, they have contracted external indebtedness to the point where we owe something like one thousand United States dollars to the rest of the world for every Zambian. Our economy is in ruins and even the ruins are in danger.[1]

Soon after attaining power, the MMD government adopted a structural adjustment programme agreed to with the IMF and World Bank.[2] MMD's 1991 Manifesto and the Policy Framework Paper agreed to with its multilateral financial partners emphasised three main economic goals; to restore macro-economic stability through monetary and fiscal reforms; to facilitate private sector growth through liberalising price and exchange-rate regulations and remove trade restrictions, and, finally; to remove the public monopolies in the industrial and agrarian sectors.

Macro-Economic Stabilisation through Monetary and Fiscal Measures

The government identified the attainment of macro-economic stabilisation as its most immediate objective (McPherson 1995). An attack on inflation was identified as the most urgent task to restore macro-economic equilibrium. To achieve this, the government instituted thoroughgoing monetary and fiscal reforms to cut fiscal deficits and growth in money supply. The government immediately addressed the issue of subsidies as a drain on the government budget. In December 1991, the government eliminated subsidies on mealie meal (maize), the main staple food in Zambia.[3] This was a significant political action, considering the fact that all attempts to reduce maize subsidies earlier had resulted in major internal

1. Frederick Chiluba's Opening Speech to the National Assembly, November 29, 1991.
2. The previous government had already negotiated a complete reform programme with the donors, which remained viable despite its suspension in September 1991. The new structural adjustment agreement was, therefore, essentially the same as the 1989 Policy Framework Paper that the Kaunda government had agreed to with the donor community after a short spell of home-grown economic reforms. A new Policy Framework Paper was, nevertheless, produced by the MMD and the multilateral institutions in early 1992 (GRZ 1992). This programme differed little from the earlier programmes and included all the significant reform measures advocated by the MMD during its election campaign.
3. This resulted in a price increase of almost 700 per cent as a 25 kg bag of maize-meal increased from K 225 to K 1,800 from October 1991 to October 1992 (Seshamani 1996).

uprisings and termination of agreements with the international finance institutions.

However, while 1992 was a year of promise in terms of economic reforms, the economy was adversely affected by a number of external as well as internal factors, the most serious being the severe drought reducing the agricultural output by 39.3 per cent (GRZ, *Budget Address* 1993:3). By late 1992, it was becoming evident both to the Ministry of Finance and the donor community that lack of budgetary control constituted a major impediment to the attainment of macro-economic stabilisation (GRZ, *Budget Address* 1993:5–6). While the elimination of expensive programmes such as the consumer maize subsidies was critical to reducing the budget deficit, the most important measure to strengthen budgetary control was taken in the 1993 Budget when the MMD government implemented a cash budget system. This institutional innovation implied that the Bank of Zambia would refuse any government transaction unless adequate funds had been made available, in other words, if there was enough revenue to support it at the time.[1] Thus, the government could no longer resort to printing money in order to cover expenses. With the new budgetary procedures, extraordinary expenditures could only be financed from additional tax increases or expenditure cuts (GRZ, *Budget Address* 1993:10). In order to put the new rule into effect, the Ministry of Finance and the Bank of Zambia created a joint committee to monitor fiscal and monetary conditions which met three days a week to oversee virtually all cheques going out of the Ministry of Finance's accounts (Bonnick 1997).

Of equal importance in terms of reducing the growth in money supply was the auctioning of treasury bills introduced in the 1993 Budget to provide a market mechanism for determining interest rates and siphoning off large amounts of excess liquidity. The treasury bill tender implied that domestic debt was to be financed by the sale of new treasury bills to members of the public. On the domestic revenue side, the creation of the semi-autonomous Zambia Revenue Authority (ZRA) in 1994 constituted an equally important development. Through ZRA, tax-records were computerised and the former government-employed tax collectors were retrained. The implementation of Value Added Tax (VAT) in 1995, which replaced the former cumbersome system of sales tax, was another important mechanism intended to broaden the tax-base.[2] Arguably, therefore, particularly in the first years, important reforms were carried out that laid the basis for macro-economic stabilisation.

Liberalisation of Imports, Trade and Exchange Rates

The MMD government also wanted to encourage the private sector to take the lead in the productive activities. In order to encourage foreign investments and enhance the confidence of the local business community, the government started to decontrol foreign exchange. A Bureaux de Change system for foreign ex-

1. For a useful account of the initiation and early experiences with the cash budget, see Bonnick 1997.
2. However, as agricultural commodities were exempted, arguably VAT has contributed less to the goal of broadening the tax-base than expected (Rakner and Gloppen 2003).

change was introduced in October 1992, and by December that year the official exchange rate was unified with the Bureau rate (GRZ, *Budget Address* 1993). With these changes, the exchange rate became fully market-determined.[1] The 1994 Budget further eliminated the Exchange Control Act and thus allowed both citizens and non-citizens to open foreign currency accounts (GRZ, *Budget Address* 1994). As one of the very few countries on the African continent to do so, Zambia made its national currency fully convertible from early 1994 onwards. Funds now flowed freely in and out of Zambia. The final restriction in the foreign exchange field was removed in April 1996, when the Bank of Zambia allowed ZCCM to retain 100 per cent of its foreign exchange receipts to supply the market directly (BOZ 1997; Kani 1996). Since the nationalisation of the mines in the late 1960s, the mining company's lack of access to foreign exchange generated from mining had meant that only limited capital was reinvested into the mining industry.

Reforms in the domestic money market constituted another significant area of reforms implemented in the first few years after MMD attained power. In 1993, the Bank of Zambia removed all restrictions on bank lending and deposit rates. The liberalisation of the money market resulted in the entry of several commercial banks and non-bank financial institutions, ranging from insurance companies to pension funds. Extensive reforms within the external trade regime were commenced in 1992. Over the five-year period, all licensing and quantitative restrictions on imports and exports were eliminated. The tariff structure was compressed and simplified. The level and dispersion of customs duty rates which ranged from 0 to 100 per cent prior to 1991 and with 11 tariff bands, by 1996 ranged between 0 and 25 per cent with only four bands (GRZ, *Budget Address* 1996; Seshamani 1996; Taylor 1997). In terms of changing its economic policy regime and its regulatory environment, despite exogenous factors such as the severe drought, Zambia could by mid-1994 claim to have one of the most liberal foreign exchange regimes in Africa, and an impressive record in terms of inflation and fiscal probity.

Evaluations of Zambia's adjustment efforts after 1991 have emphasised the pace of the process of economic liberalisation as one of the government's most remarkable achievements (van de Walle and Chiwele 1994; Seshamani 1996; Kalyalya and Lushinga 1996; World Bank 1996a, 1996c). In terms of structural reforms, however, the record is far more varied.

Institutional Reforms

In the first years, the economic recovery programme consisted of many efforts to *undo* things, like state controls over prices, the abolition of the foreign exchange control act, the foreign exchange control department in Bank of Zambia. These were the first generation of reforms that did not require much development management capacity to put them through. Politically, however, they were

1. Thus, the government abandoned the practice of seeking to control the exchange rate through administrative means. This had been the practice throughout the Second Republic, save for a short spell of foreign exchange auctioning in 1985–86. See Chapter 3.

difficult to accomplish as they involved change in attitudes and social costs (Heijden 2000). Alongside the stabilisation and economic liberalisation measures, the MMD government initiated several institutional reforms involving both the creation of new institutional frameworks and the dissolution of existing ones in order to facilitate private sector growth. These reforms required the Zambian government to *do* things, to re-organise and create new institutions. Successful reforms included the establishment of Zambia Privatisaton Agency (ZPA), Zambia Revenue Authority (ZRA), and the Pension and Insurance Authority. But, Zambia's record in this area proved much more varied than in the areas of stabilisation and liberalisation. Three major reform processes; public sector reform, agricultural liberalisation and privatisation of the state-owned industries were pursued very differently by the first Chiluba government.

The Public Sector Reform Programme (PSRP) was launched in 1993. The programme promised to cut 25 per cent of the civil service within 3 years and to improve the conditions of service for the remaining staff in order to retain and attract the best candidates (GRZ, *Budget Address* 1993). However, while 15,000 contract daily employees with no job security were retrenched in 1992, no retrenchment of civil servants had taken place by early 1999.[1] The contentious nature of this reform, and its potential political implications became pronounced when the Minister of Finance in March 1996 announced that the PSRP was put on hold indefinitely (*Times of Zambia,* March 22, 1996). Based on interviews with senior policy-makers in Zambia, the main obstacle to the PSRP exercise appeared to be the cost of reforms. Since the legally mandated retrenchment costs amounted to 10 years salary for each employee, the most economic approach for the government was simply to retain workers rather than retrench them. According to estimates of the Central Statistical Office, rather than a leaner civil service, as promised by MMD in its election campaign, the civil service grew by 19 per cent between 1989 and 1994. Arguably, the government pursued the process of liberalising agriculture with more rigour.

Agricultural Liberalisation

Throughout the Second Republic, political factors dictated agricultural policies.[2] The MMD government set out to alter this long-standing arrangement. Announcing its withdrawal from the marketing of agricultural inputs in 1993, the government appointed a small number of principal buying agents and allowed private traders to enter the maize market. This implied that co-operative societies were no longer allocated government funds for handling marketing or for the purchase of maize from farmers (GRZ/MAFF 1995:3). However, a com-

1. According to a World Bank evaluation study of the Zambian structural adjustment programme, the Zambian government is still required by law to hire recent graduates in the teaching and medical professions (World Bank 1996b:28).
2. After independence, the UNIP government increased and broadened maize subsidies substantially, partly to keep both producers and consumers satisfied and in part in keeping with its development doctrine. Agricultural subsidies had their origin in the 1974/75 agricultural season when the government introduced uniform national producer prices (pan-territorial prices). This resulted in maize production dominating the agricultural sector, accounting for approximately 70 per cent of land cropped and 85 per cent of crop production (World Bank 1993).

bination of the stabilisation measures on credits and interest rates and, finally, the size of the 1993 crop recovering from the disastrous drought in 1992, created huge transitory problems. With hindsight, the largest transitional problem was the fact that the agricultural liberalisation was carried out before the economy was stabilised. With interest rates running as high as 300 per cent, private investors largely neglected the risk-prone and politically sensitive agricultural sector and invested instead in the lucrative, and virtually risk-free, government treasury bills. On the one hand, the bumper crop tested the capacities of the new, evolving production and marketing structures. On the other hand, farmers entered the 1992–93 season with pressing financial needs after one of the most devastating droughts ever during the previous year. The combination of extremely high interest rates and the cash budget put a strain on the government allocated finances for marketing the 1992–93 crop which in turn had dire consequences for the 1993–94 crop. The lack of private sector response forced the government back into the market as a buyer. However, due to the restrictions of the cash budget, the funding was given in the form of promissory notes, or forward sales contracts. The financial obligation this incurred on the 1994 budget in turn put a severe strain on the cash budget. Thus, as a consequence of market liberalisation taking place simultaneously with macro-economic stabilisation, the newly emerging agricultural trade sector faced a harsh financial environment. An IMF evaluation of the structural adjustment reforms during the first Chiluba administration concluded that liberalisation carried out in the early phases of the reform programme created economic distortions that, coupled with a devastating drought, hampered growth in the agricultural sector (Botchwey et al. 1998). The move to capital account convertibility and interest rate liberalisation prior to the attainment of stabilisation created inflation leading to a credit crunch in the private sector. This again delayed the emergence of rural food markets and reduced the private investments required for structural change. Arguably, the MMD government displayed much more 'political sensitivity' in the area of privatisation of state-owned companies.

Privatisation of State-Owned Industries

In its 1991 Manifesto, the MMD government committed itself to privatising the state-owned industries (MMD 1991:4).[1] The process of privatisation followed a very different implementation pattern to that of agricultural liberalisation. The MMD government moved quickly to amend the Privatisation Act in the National Assembly, but the privatisation process did not gather momentum until after 1995. The 1992 Privatisation Act consigned the specific responsibility for privatisation to the Zambia Privatisation Agency (ZPA). Despite the official commitment to leaving business to the private sector, the initial portfolio of ZPA

1. Until the 1990s, the majority of Zambia's state-owned industries were managed under an umbrella management institution, the Zambia Industrial and Mining Corporation (ZIMCO). Pressured by the international donor community, Zambia had begun to sell state-owned companies during the last stages of the Second Republic. A Technical Committee on Privatisation within the Ministry of Commerce, Trade and Industry set up in 1990 had carried out some preliminary work. But by the time of the political transition in 1991, no privatisation transactions had taken place.

indicated a rather careful approach to the privatisation process. From its inception, apart from some key ministers, the privatisation process had only lukewarm support even within the Cabinet. As a result, neither the mines nor the utility companies were included in the government's original privatisation portfolio. While some government ministers had argued for the inclusion of the mines from an early stage, the general feeling within the MMD government at the time was that this issue was too controversial to include at an early stage.[1] The lack of consensus on the issue of privatisation, even within the MMD Cabinet, became public in September 1992. At this stage, the Minister of Commerce, Trade and Industry, Ronald Penza, declared that the government had decided to remove the utility companies and ZCCM (the mining company) from the negative list and eventually privatise these industries as well (*Times of Zambia*, September 22, 1992). Two days later the MMD vice-president, Levy Mwanawasa, contradicted the statement of the Minister of Commerce by stating that the sale of ZCCM should wait until it was known how the rest of the privatisation process fared. He then added that the sale of the mines could take up to 20 years (*Times of Zambia*, September 24, 1992). According to observers, the whole privatisation programme was almost derailed when the Minister of Commerce announced the intention to privatise ZCCM and the utilities companies (*Financial Mail*, November 24–30, 1992).

Instead a careful process was opted for where the smaller companies were privatised first. Dividing the sales-process into tranches, small companies were to be the starting point before moving to the medium sized companies, leaving the large companies to be privatised last.[2] Despite the lack of support and the slow beginning of the privatisation process, and most notably, the failure to take action towards the mining sector, by 1996 the privatisation programme in Zambia was cited as one of the government's key successes. The World Bank attributed the success of the privatisation programme to the fact that the process through the Zambia Privatisation Agency was predominantly private sector driven, with little interference from the government (*World Bank Findings*, October 1996; *Times of Zambia*, October 15, 1996).[3]

Economic Reforms 1996–2001

After a contentious election on November 25, 1996, Frederick Chiluba and MMD were returned to the presidency and government. The economic policy platform of the second Chiluba administration was laid out in the 1996 MMD Manifesto and the policies elaborated in President Chiluba's Opening Address to the National Assembly.[4] However, in the period 1996–2001, reform implementation was inconsistent and lacked the vigour and determination of the first years in office (essentially 1991–1993/94). In terms of budgetary discipline, the

1. The 1991 MMD *Manifesto* only said the following of ZCCM: "... as with other state enterprises, ZCCM's monumental empire shall be reviewed and re-organised" (MMD 1991:4).
2. The Privatisation Act, 1992, section 38 divided the state owned enterprises into 4 tranches.
3. The success of the privatisation programme was at this time (1996) further highlighted by most respondents both among the external donors, government officials and independent local analysts.
4. January 17, 1997.

Table 4: 2 Privatisation in Zambia

Progress date	Companies privatized
June – December 30, 1992	Privatisation Act passed in parliament, information of programme carried out, establishment of ZPA
January – June 30, 1993	2
July – December 30, 1993	4
January – June 30, 1994	6
July- December 30, 1994	3
January – June 30, 1995	3
July – December 30, 1995	27
September 30, 1996	108
November 30, 1996	166
December 30, 1997	200
December 1998	223
August 31, 2000	244
July 2001	254
Total privatisation portfolio	**278**

Source: Zambia Privatisation Agency: *Progress Reports 1993-2001.*

government's commitment to the economic reform process was low in the second election period. The reductions in bilateral balance-of-payments support in 1996 and 1997 and freeze of all balance-of-payments support in1998 was not met by government savings or increased tax-efforts. Rather, domestic borrowing increased, which affected the economy negatively. But despite several exogenous shocks and uneven implementation, the MMD government maintained an open trade regime; Zambia put the COMESA Free Trade Agreement into effect in October 2000 as one of the first countries in the region to do so. Shortly after, a SADC Trade Protocol was signed and by now Zambia had joined free trade agreements with all its major trading partners in Africa. In contrast, in the 1996–2001 election period the government's commitment to liberalised agriculture was inconsistent. Sporadic government involvement in the marketing of fertiliser and maize throughout the election period contributed to market insecurity and an under-performing agricultural sector. Similarly, the public sector reform programme, deemed essential both to balancing the budgets and to enhancing the capacity of the bureaucracy, was not implemented. In the second Chiluba administration, the public sector reform came to a complete stop even though public sector reform constituted a major part of every single aid agreement between the Zambia government and the World Bank and IMF. As a result, two Enhanced Structural Adjustment Facilities (ESAF I and II) with IMF were discontinued. And, while the pace of privatisation was considered impressive in the first Chiluba administration, the delayed sale of the most economically significant asset, ZCCM, proved extremely costly.

Macro-Economic Stabilisation and Liberalisation 1996–2001

A number of factors suggest that the Zambian government's commitment to economic reform waned in the second half of the decade. While no major reform measure was reversed, major reform initiatives, such as liberalisation, the implementation of the cash budget and the establishment of Zambia Revenue Authority (ZRA) happened in the first years after the 1991 transition. In principle, the MMD government remained committed to expenditure control and management as the cash budget stipulated that there could be no net monetary financing of government deficits. According to Bonnick (1997:318), the cash budget should have meant that Zambians stopped pushing the costs of current spending onto future generations. However, after some years, the procedure that was meant to curve fiscal deficits, became a mere window dressing activity. Despite austerity measures being introduced and maintained, budget allocations indicate that government consumption levels remained high throughout the 1996–2001 election period. Throughout the second Chiluba administration, expenditure decisions at cabinet level were not effected by the cash budget but financed by supplementary budgets (Taylor and Aarnes 2002). A technical mission from the World Bank studied the effects of the off-budget expenditures of the Zambian public sector (World Bank 1998b, 2000b; Taylor and Aarnes 2002:36). The study showed that total budget deficit including all off-budget activities was between 14 and 18 per cent of GDP in the 1995 to 1997 period. Only about 2,5–5 percentage points of this was due to "normal" budget operations. The rest was used to cover off-budget activities and deficits in the remaining state-owned industries. In the period 1996 to 2001, supplementary budgets increased spending for defence and the office of the president in particular, leading to a very arbitrary budget process and distortions in resource allocation in the public sector. Seemingly adhering to the expenditure restrictions imposed by the cash budget, the government failed to pay its suppliers.[1] Suggesting that the costs of a compressed economy was not carried by the government through reduced spending, but rather by the private business sector, business complained that the Zambian government commissioned services from the private sector but failed to pay more than a third of the bills due to restrictions in the cash budget.[2]

Agricultural Liberalisation 1996–2001

Throughout the 1990s, agricultural liberalisation had a destabilising effect on the industry. Some product diversification took place as a result of the liberalisation efforts and marketed production of tobacco, cotton, wheat, and groundnuts, among other products, increased in the 1990s. However, agricultural policies in Zambia revolve around the question of government involvement in the marketing of fertiliser and maize. While the government in principle remained committed to liberalisation of the sector, growth was continuously hampered by poor implementation practices, limited supply response, and adverse external conditions.

As argued above, the 1992 drought meant that government imported and distributed maize and domestically produced maize was bought at a stipulated

1. International Monetary Fund 2000; This issue is carefully assessed in the study by Hendrick van der Heijden (2000), an advisor to the Ministry of Finance (1990–1998).
2. Personal interview, Theo Bull, (ZACCI) Lusaka, January 15, 1997.

price. In the 1993/94 season the government introduced agricultural credits. But the state-funded marketing system proved incapable of collecting maize and paying producers on time, and the result was a rapid accumulation of debt in the farming sector. In 1994/95 the liberalisation policies were implemented as the government refrained from announcing into-mill-prices, government warehouses were leased to private traders and most of the state-owned agribusinesses were privatised. Nevertheless, the government continued to import and distribute fertiliser through a new programme, the Agricultural Credit Management Programme (ACMP). This programme was meant as a temporary measure and the government's stated intention was to move away from the fertiliser and credit market altogether. But, the programme was continued in the 1995/96 season and the volume of fertiliser distributed by government increased. ACMP also continued in the 1996/97 season.

In 1997, government signalled a further departure from its basic position of free regional trade in agricultural produce as the government banned the importation of wheat flour in order to counter dumping from other states (*EIU Country Report*, 3rd Quarter 1977). In 1998, the MMD government instructed a new establishment, the Food Reserve Agency (FRA) to import and distribute fertiliser. Again, in principle, FRA was intended as an emergency back-up and the MMD government's stated policy was that the private sector should replace the state in maize procurement and the purchase and distribution of fertiliser. But, the deviations from the stated policies of agricultural liberalisation became more marked in 1998 under the new Minister of Finance, Edith Nawakwi. Announcing that FRA was instructed to import the fertiliser needed for the season, arguably, the government sent confusing signals about the actual role of FRA. Due to the quantities of fertiliser FRA was instructed to import for the 1998/99 season, it became a major competitor to the private sector and observers accused the government of treating FRA as an agricultural marketing board (Scott et al. 1998; *EIU Country Report,* 1st Quarter 1998:18). The confusing government signals combined with a good harvest, FRA sold imported food at a loss in 1998 and out-bidded private traders. FRA was unable to ensure repayment of large amounts of outstanding credits, and as a result, it had no money to import maize and fertiliser for the 1999 season, resulting in a food deficit. In the 1999/2000 season the government again used FRA to implement a fertiliser distribution scheme. An extensive evaluation of the scheme reached the conclusion that the target groups were not reached and that repayments by farmers were less than 50 per cent (Taylor and Aarnes 2002). The government's move to restrict farmers export licences in order to subdue domestic prices in 1999 was yet another example of a shallow commitment to agricultural liberalisation (*EIU Country Report*, 3rd Quarter 1999:16). Underlining the confusing agricultural policies by the MMD government in the second election period, in April 2000 the government banned FRA from distributing farming outputs due to lack of financial resources (*EIU Country Report*, May 2000:22).

The various government interventions in maize procurement and agricultural inputs demonstrated above indicate that despite an overall commitment to a liberalised marked, government has intervened in maize production through successive rural credit schemes. While there has been no official price control on food in Zambia since 1991, government is considered to intervene to keep retail prices down particularly during election periods. Partly because the government has doubted private traders' ability to fill the vacuum left by total state withdrawal, FRA has been employed in the distribution and marketing of maize and fertiliser. However, FRA has also presented opportunities for patronage to members of parliament. According to observers:

> Agricultural policies in Zambia have turned more and more towards policies dictated by political considerations (to win the votes of the farmers) and by the desire to create opportunities for personal gain for a small elite of politicians and business people who carry out the import trade in agricultural commodities. Over the last decade there have been a number of examples of this. (Taylor and Aarnes 2002:6)[1]

The list of who was in debt to FRA publicised in the Zambian press in January 2000, including a number of politicians and well connected people, adds credence to the statement above (*The Post,* January 28; *EIU Country Report,* May 2000:22). Arguably, the erratic policies and institutional innovations witnessed in MMD's agricultural policies in the 1996–2001 period closely resemble the government's handling of the privatisation process.

The Privatisation of the Zambian Consolidated Copper Mines

Due to Zambia's dependence on copper, the privatisation of the mining conglomerate was always the main issue in terms of a potential economic turnaround. It was only in 1996 that the government accepted the advice to begin the process of privatisation of the Zambia Consolidated Copper Mines (ZCCM) in unbundled units by open tender, with the aim of reaching agreements before June 1997. As will be discussed further in Chapter 6, this decision was made during a fierce debate with the bilateral donors in the aftermath of the 1996 presidential and parliamentary elections. The international bidding process for the main assets was closed on February 28, 1997 and 26 companies submitted their bids. However, shortly after the process of bid analysis and evaluation had been initiated, President Chiluba removed the mining conglomerate from Zambia Privatisation Agency's (ZPA) portfolio. The president picked a new negotiating team to be led by Francis Kaunda,[2] executive director of ZCCM from 1973 to 1991. In November 1997 negotiations on the sale of the main assets were completed and finalisation of the transaction agreements with the Kafue Consortium[3] was scheduled for March 1998. This bid was considered good by independent observers, considering the fact that copper-prices had fallen by 35 per cent since earlier in the year (Barraclough 1998; Bull 1998, 1999). However, in yet another surprising move, involving the dismissal of the Minister of Finance Ronald Penza in March 1998, the government turned down the bid. Several attempts were made to reach an agreement between the Kafue Consortium

1. See also Economist Intelligence Unit (*EIU Country Report,* May 2000:22) for a similar analysis and conclusion.
2. Francis Kaunda is not related to Kenneth Kaunda, the former president.
3. Comprising Angolovaal Mining, Phelps Dodge, Noranda and the Commonwealth Development Corporation.

and the Zambian government, but finally the consortium withdrew from the negotiations. The surprising turn of events in 1998 extended ZCCM's loss-making record by another two years. ZCCM losses by 1999 were estimated at some US$ 200–300 million, the equivalent of 6–9 per cent of GDP (Barraclough 1998). Only the maintenance costs of the ZCCM mines were estimated to cost the Zambian government US$ 1 million per month.

In December 1998 the directors of Anglo-American Corporation ratified a Memorandum of Understanding on the sale of ZCCM asset packages. After substantial pressure from the international finance institutions, in 1999 the government began to entertain the uncertain possibility of a much lower offer from Anglo-American Corporation. It was expected that sale would be completed mid-March 1999, but the final sale of the mines was only completed on March 31, 2000. The privatisation put a stop to ZCCM's accumulation of public debt. However, the stock of already acquired debt was still left with the Zambian government since the new owners did not take over any of the company's debt.[1] As a result of the price and the remaining debt, the sale of ZCCM's main assets was met with criticism and resentment within Zambia as the deal with Anglo-American Corporation for the sale of Konkola Deep, Nchanga and Nampunde was considerably less advantageous in every respect than the offers turned down in October 1997 and April 1998 from the Kafue Consortium. But due to ZCCM's losses, and the fact that much of Zambia's international development assistance from the mid-1990s onwards had become tied to the sales of the copper-mines, the Zambian government had little choice but to accept the offer from Anglo-American Corporation.

At the time of writing, the developments in the copper sector are highly uncertain. In late January 2002, Anglo-American Plc., the major shareholder in Konkola Copper Mines (KCM), informed government that it would not proceed with further investments in KCM, citing financial losses linked to declining world copper prices and failure to secure funding for the Konkola Deep Mining Project (KDMP), which was the main basis for its investment in Zambia in March 2000. The summary provided by the *EIU Country Report* provides a fair summary of the way the second Chiluba administration handled the privatisation process:

> A fair criticism of the previous government is that if it had completed the copper mines privatisation earlier, in 1997, selling to the Kafue Consortium, led by the Angovaal subsidiary, the higher copper prices between then and now would have helped fund the rehabilitation of both the Nchanga plant and the machinery and the development of the Konkola Deep Mining Project, potentially reducing the amount of financing needed. (*EIU Country Report*, February 2002:25)

Economic Reforms 1991–2001: Opportunities Lost

After almost a decade of uninterrupted policy reforms, the record in terms of economic growth, employment creation, investments and poverty reduction in Zambia

1. When ZCCM was privatised in March 2000, the total outstanding debt guaranteed by the government was about 590 million US dollars. See: "Zambia Finalizes Sale of State Copper Mine Group", *The Financial Times*, April 4, 2000.

Table 4: 1 Macro-economic indicators 1991-2001

	1991	1992	1993	1994	1995	1996	1997	1998	1999	2000	2001
GDP growth %	-4.0	-2.8	6.8	-8.6	-4.3	6.4	3.5	-2.0	2.2	3.1	4,0
Exchange rate ZK:US$	127	172	600	687	879	1213	1336	1862	2388	3111	3611
Inflation (av) %	92.6	165.1	187.3	54.6	34.9	46.3	24.8	24.3	26.9	26	21.4
For-ex reserves $USm	184.6	184.2	192.3	Na	222.7	222.7	239.1	69.4	45.4	244.8	195
Investment/GDP	11.0	11.9	15.0	12.7	13.1	14.8	13.6	14.4	13.8	na	na
Consumption/GDP	91.6	100.7	88.8	88.4	82.7	91.5	91.9	94.8	94.6	na	na
Current account balance(US$) (b)	-307	-117	-88,00	-185	-314	-491	-449	-574	-532	-583	-668
Current account balance (% GDP)	0.3	-4.1	-0.9	1.4	-4.2	-3.7	-6.2	-8.0	-6.3	- 7.5	-14.3
Copper output ('000 tonnes)	387	432	403	354	307	320	325	293	266	256	299
Foreign debt (US$ bn)	6.82	4.9	5.1	6.39	7.04	7.1	6.9	6.9	6.5	6.2	6.1

Sources: Ministry of Finance and Economic Development (MOF): *Economic Report 1991-2000*; Bank of Zambia (BOZ) *Annual Reports* (1991-2001); GRZ: *Budget Address* (1992-2001), Heijden (2000); Economist Intelligence Unit (EIU) *Country Profiles* (1991-2002), GRZ: *Policy Framework Paper 1995–1998* (1995c).

is weak. In terms of macro-economic growth indicators, the Zambian economy has shrunk and is now smaller than it was in 1991. With a 25 per cent increase in population over the last decade, per capital income has dropped by 4 per cent annually in the last decade, thus extending the long period of economic decline that began in the 1970s. Mineral production has declined throughout the decade, formal employment has been reduced in all sectors but public administration and social indicators reveal that poverty and infant mortality have increased since the 1980s. Zambia's most notable success in terms of macro-economic stabilisation has been to bring inflation under control. And while the pronounced 'national enemy number one' has been subdued during this period, it has not disappeared completely.[1]

A fundamental question in the case of Zambia is why a government committed to reform, with a wide mandate for change from its population and with donor finances to support it, achieved so little in terms of growth. Pointing to a variation of key policy events indicating shifts in commitment, most respondents interviewed in Lusaka shared the opinion that the government's commitment to economic reform had declined. In a number of watershed events, beginning in 1993 with the replacement of Guy Scott from the Ministry of Agriculture and Emmanuel Kasonde from the Ministry of Finance and culminating with the sacking of Finance Minister Ronald Penza in 1998, experienced, competent and reform minded ministers were removed from the Cabinet. With hindsight, it is clear that the MMD leadership that entered State House in 1991 included some exceptional people with regard to reform commitment as well as capacity. Increasingly, junior people, displaying a stronger commitment to the MMD President than an economic development strategy replaced the experi-

1. The Minister of Finance, Emmanuel Kasonde, in his 1992 Budget Address, first formulated the naming of inflation as the nation's number one enemy.

enced and reform minded ministers. Clearly, the quality of the cabinet ministers 1991–1996 was higher than in the second election period. However, commitment to reform during the two Chiluba administrations should be disaggregated. Commitment to economic reform in Zambia varied across issues and across parts of the Cabinet throughout the 1990s. The MMD government was united in its resolve to attain stabilisation in 1991. Furthermore, there was a relatively strong support for the liberalisation measures implemented and the re-invigoration of the private sector, including some privatisation. But, the public debates in the early 1990s indicate that the MMD government was never united over the privatisation of ZCCM. The reactions to the agricultural liberalisation from various Cabinet ministers from 1994 onwards further indicate that few in the MMD government had considered the implications of substantive agricultural reform. Public sector reform had very limited support in the influential political circles of Zambia.

After a decade of continuous austerity measures and growth prospects still appearing dismal, a waning reform commitment may be expected. The government's lack of commitment to key reform measures such as the privatisation of the mines and the reform of the public service has constituted a major impediment to growth in the last decade. To what extent can the uneven reform implementation witnessed and the apparent waning commitment to reform be linked to societal resistance? Can it be argued that resistance from the social forces within MMD's rainbow coalition reduced government commitment to reform? Turning now to the relationship between the government and the associations representing business, agriculture and labour, the question is addressed by analysing how the MMD government related to the main interest groups in the two election periods.

Consultations between Government and Interest Groups 1991–2001

In 1991 the Chiluba government not only accepted the structural adjustment programme already agreed to by Kaunda in 1989, albeit abandoned by him in the summer of 1991, but accelerated its pace. Partly, the economic policies of MMD must be understood on the basis of the 1991 election results. The election campaign and the actual vote indicated that a large majority of Zambians had come to associate economic decline and mismanagement with one-party rule in general and the leadership of Kenneth Kaunda and UNIP in particular. As argued by Bates and Collier (1993), the popular attitude displayed in 1991 represented a distinct shift from the situation in 1987 when the population had protested against the economic reform measures per se and *not* the political system. The 1991 elections therefore provided the government with a wide mandate for change. As argued by one informant: "Anyone who had a manifesto in 1991 that was not UNIP's could flag it. People voted for change, not for MMD, but because they wanted to get away from UNIP".[1]

1. Personal interview, Gideon Phiri, Chief Executive of Zambia Association of Chambers of Commerce and Industry (ZACCI). Lusaka, September 13, 1996.

MMD's Honeymoon (1991–1993)

The fact that the Zambian economy was close to spiralling out of control added to the generally felt consensus among the political leadership that economic reforms were essential.[1] The breaking of UNIP's 27-year-long rule further paved the way for so-called new brooms to come into the Zambian political elite who for a long time had been disregarded by the socialist-oriented ideology of UNIP for their pro-business attitudes. The entry of new people into government, disenchanted with the unwillingness of the former government to restructure the economy, meant that the reform attempts were supported by a group of committed ministers and bureaucrats in key leadership positions. Thus, the combined effect of an economic crisis, a new leadership, and legitimacy provided by the substantial electoral support gave the government considerable flexibility in terms of economic policy-making.

Personal interviews with key policy-makers and representatives of the major interest groups in Zambia indicate that consultations between government and interest groups were limited to formal representation on various government committees in the first years of MMD's rule. The clearest statement indicating the MMD government's awareness of the opportunity granted by the large electoral mandate was given by the first Minister of Finance, Emmanuel Kasonde:

> I was lucky as prior to taking office Chiluba had told me that I would be offered the Ministry of Finance if we were to form a government. I therefore had a year in which I followed economic events very closely and when we formed government we were able to hit the road running in order to implement my ideas quickly. I was also aware of MMD's popularity, if I had to make unpopular decisions it had to be done during the honeymoon period, otherwise it would be very difficult. In other words, necessary but unpopular decisions had to be quick. I was very interested in using the political status of the MMD government to make economic advancements. ... I use the singular I because the cabinet did not contain many economically trained brains and I myself had to train them.[2]

Confirming that the MMD government intended to use its 'honeymoon' to implent far-reaching reforms, the statement by Kasonde also underscores the limited political support-base behind the reform measures within the cabinet and society as a whole.[3] By moving quickly on the contentious issues such as maize subsidies, the budget deficit, the exchange rate and inflation, MMD ensured that the opposition would not yet have mobilised effectively. In their election campaign, some MMD politicians had alluded to the fact that, if elected, MMD would eradicate maize meal subsidies. Furthermore during the election campaign MMD met formally with donors and promised to undertake radical reforms, including the removal of maize subsidies.[4] However, MMD had also

1. The importance of an economic crisis situation for the initiation of economic reforms is noted in a number of comparative studies, see Grindle and Thomas 1991; Leith and Lofchie 1993 and Nelson 1994. See the discussion in Chapter 2.
2. Personal interview, Emmanuel Kasonde, MMD Minister of Finance 1991–1993 (and 2001–). Lusaka, October 7, 1996.
3. The statement of the Hon. Mr. Kasonde was also confirmed in personal interviews with Hendrick van der Heijden (Lusaka, December 9, 1996); Felix C. Kani, Director of Economics, Bank of Zambia (Lusaka, October 3, 1996); and Ben Mwene, Ministry of Finance, Secretary to the Treasury (Lusaka, December 19, 1996).
4. Personal interview, Hendrick van der Heijden, External Financing Advisor, Ministry of Finance 1991–1999 (Lusaka, October 28, 1996); Aka Lewanika, Minister of Technology and Vocational Training 1991–1993 (Lusaka, June 1, 1995).

during the campaign promised cheaper food and to put an end to starvation (Rakner 1992). When subsidies were withdrawn in December 1991, prices increased by almost 700 per cent. In marked contrast to the previous attempts by UNIP to reduce subsidies, this time there was hardly any political opposition. According to observers, the reforms were carried out smoothly because contrary to the UNIP government, the new MMD government was united in its resolve to remove the subsidies (van de Walle and Chiwele 1994). It may also be argued that the reforms did not provoke reactions because most groups, including the trade unions (ZCTU) and the employers' federation (ZFE), were informed of the increase in maize prices in advance (*Times of Zambia,* December 14, 1991). Comments from various sources in the trade union movement after the announced subsidy cut illustrate both the shifting position of the trade unions in terms of economic reform policies, and the general support given to MMD. In stark contrast to its position on food subsidy removals in the Second Republic, the President of ZCTU, Fackson Shamenda, now emphasised that ZCTU supported the subsidy removal, that the workers felt that interim measures should have been carried out to lessen the suffering of workers (*Times of Zambia,* December 17, 1991).

Breaking away from Labour

The MMD government's deliberate policy of not negotiating with key economic interest groups in the first years in office was most pronounced vis-à-vis the trade unions. Trade union leaders confirmed that the government's reluctance to consult provoked the unions. ZCTU accepted the need for economic reforms in general, but was critical of the government's handling of organised interests. As emphasised by the General Secretary of ZCTU:

> We knew the government was going to implement SAP in 1991 and we appreciated the need for it and saw it as inevitable. But we have not been happy about the failure to consult with various interest groups. We wanted to be constantly consulted at the time implementation was carried out but this has not happened. As a consequence, government has gone ahead with reform at a pace or speed which is not in line with the development of a social safety net for the vulnerable groups.[1]

Concerned about the limited communication with the MMD government, ZCTU, nevertheless, granted the MMD government a period of grace, as illustrated by the statement from ZCTU's President, Fackson Shamenda:

> We are not interested in partisan politics. We only have a soft spot for MMD in that we must work with the government. You cannot antagonise the man you will work with tomorrow. Many people of Zambia belong to no party and the MMD government is for all the people. (*Sunday Times of Zambia*, August 15, 1993)

The Weakness of Interest Groups

MMD's large electoral majority, interpreted as a mandate for change, reduced the government's incentive for wide-ranging consultations with interest groups.

1. Personal communications, Alec Chirwa, General Secretary, Zambia Congress of Trade Unions (ZCTU). Kitwe, December 2, 1996.

But interest groups also had to reorient themselves to the new political and economic realities. With regard to business interests, their own representatives acknowledged their organisational weakness as one explanation for the lack of consultations with government in the initial years of reform implementation. Having been suppressed under a control regime for so long, business associations strongly supported the new government. Furthermore, both the new government and the external donor community saw the business sector as the country's new engine of growth. Yet, as remarked by a member of the business community:

> The private sector was still recovering from the powers that had been thrown into their hands. They simply did not know how to react to the attitude that you are now suddenly perceived as the engine of growth. ... [T]he business community had for so long been used to distrust government and expect inconsistencies that the real partnership did not take place until two years ago.[1]

Despite the sensitive nature of agricultural liberalisation, and the fact that even the most moderate attempts at reform had failed under UNIP's reign, MMD set out to implement these reforms in a 'shock therapeutic' manner.[2] As argued by the executive director of the Zambian National Farmers Union (ZNFU):

> In terms of being consulted we knew what was coming as an organisation. That was not a problem. However, they did not talk to the actual 97 per cent of farmers affected by the reforms. They were not using radio; in fact their 2,000 extension workers could not discuss commercial aspects with the farmers as they were restricted to technical matters. There was no attempt to publicise the effort and no attempt at thinking through the consequences.[3]

The statement above from a representative of the predominantly commercial farmer controlled association was also supported by the representative of the Peasant Farmers Union (PFUZ):

> Regarding consultations, I can say that there was no warning at all to the peasant farmers about the liberalisation. This was the biggest mistake as there was no warning, no cushioning. Agriculture was just left alone and the policy was to let them feed themselves. It was like a flock of sheep without a leader.[4]

It is not surprising that interest group representatives criticise a government for lack of consultations in a situation of rapid reform implementation. But in Zambia the government representatives largely shared the views about consultations expressed by the representatives of the interest associations. According to a senior bureaucrat in the Ministry of Agriculture, Food and Fisheries (MAFF):

> I can guarantee you there were no MAFF extension workers going out into the rural areas to warn people about the changes ahead. People say the implementation moved too fast, and I find it hard to disagree. What is certain is that the flow of information did not move

1. Personal interview, Gideon Phiri, Chief Executive, Zambia Association of Chambers of Commerce and Industry (ZACCI). Lusaka, September 13, 1996.
2. See West (1989) and Sandberg (1990) for two insightful analyses of the agricultural liberalisation attempts during the 1980s.
3. Personal interview, George Gray, Executive Director, Zambia National Farmers Union. Lusaka, October 2, 1996.
4. Personal interview, Roger Phiri, Assistant General Secretary, Peasant Farmers Union of Zambia. Lusaka, October 10, 1996.

fast enough. Some of our extension workers are still in the Second Republic mentality. People did not know what to do with their produce, they were so used to government buying all their produce.[1]

The statements from a wide range of stakeholders within the labour unions, business, and agriculture indicate that the MMD government did not attempt to bring interest associations, nor the bureaucracy, into the process of implementing the economic reforms in the initial period. All statements indicate, firstly, that the MMD government felt more comfortable with its wide, but undefined, electoral support than it did with a corporatist structure involving consultations and mutually binding agreements with interest groups. In terms of agriculture, it may be argued that MMD also had a political motive for not working with the established interest groups. Initially there were only two associations the government could have worked with.[2] Of these, the co-operative associations (ZCF) were of limited interest to MMD as they had become associated with the UNIP party machinery in the Second Republic. MMD's willingness to carry out the contentious reforms within agriculture may at least partially be explained by its interest in reducing UNIP's political networks to the grass roots by aiming to sideline the co-operatives and strip them of finances. A number of observers noted that MMD politicians, who otherwise might not have favoured liberalisation, were easy to convince about the virtues in the instance of agricultural liberalisation because maize subsidies had long been provided through channels strongly linked to UNIP. The MMD politicians could appreciate the fact that subsidy removal weakened UNIP's position in the countryside (van de Walle and Chiwele 1994; Graham 1994).[3] The association representing agriculture that MMD could be expected to work with was the ZNFU. Since changing its name from Commercial Farmers Bureau to Zambian National Farmers Union in 1991, the largest farming association in Zambia had sought to widen its membership to include small-scale farmers in order to become politically viable.[4] Despite this expansion, ZNFU's membership was still small in terms of numbers. Furthermore, its policies were still associated with the interests of commercial farmers. With a paying membership of 350 ZNFU could not be regarded as an encompassing association. A clear statement on the manner of implementation and degree of consultations between the MMD government and interest groups in the first election period, and the lack of political weight attributed to ZNFU, was given by the Minister of Agriculture responsible for carrying out the policy of agricultural liberalisation:

The organisations, like ZNFU have a contradictory agenda. And nothing we could do would be right for them. As a result, I did not work with them. I saw my role as getting

1. Personal communications, A.K. Banda, Director, Policy Planning, Ministry of Agriculture Food and Fisheries (MAFF). Lusaka, November 27, 1996.
2. The National Association of Peasant and Small-Scale Farmers Union (NASSPFU) was officially established in 1989, but did not begin to operate as an organisation before 1994.
3. Interviews with representatives of the co-operative movement indicated similar sentiments. Personal communications, Bethel N. Sakala ZDC. Lusaka, January 7, 1997; Zandani Lungu, ZDC. Lusaka, January 7, 1997.
4. ZNFU has since 1991 sought to include farmers in the small-scale category by sponsoring their membership in order to use the larger membership as lobbying clout. As a result, small-scale producers by 1996 comprised the 87 per cent of the ZNFU's membership. Personal communications, George Gray, ZNFU.

the policy going. I did not have to work with these guys as the commercial farmers' vote does not carry very much.[1]

Political Consolidation (1994–2001)

Judging from newspaper reports and responses from the main economic interest groups and civil society groups representing the churches, human rights and civic education, in terms of economic reform implementation MMD's period of grace came to an end in late 1993. Both the local and international press linked the problems of MMD and President Chiluba to the economic reform process that so far had produced few winners. The criticism of the economic reform measures was particularly linked to three areas of reform. First, the process of agricultural liberalisation was considered to have harmed both the commercial and subsistence categories of agricultural producers, local businessmen, and urban consumers. Second, the process of privatisation, starting with the eradication of subsidies to state owned companies, had resulted in redundancies of large groups of formerly state employed workers. Third, the effects of the open trade policy adopted by Zambia in 1993 created substantial transition problems for the Zambian manufacturing industry which found it impossible to compete with imported products.

The poorly managed agricultural policies were the first issue that turned public opinion, opposition parties and MPs against the economic reforms. Increasingly, newspaper reports appeared in which various ministers questioned the economic reform programme, reflecting both divisions within cabinet on the reform measures and lack of discipline within the party and the government.[2] Hereafter, increasingly, controversies unfolded over the economic reform programme more generally as immediate results and poor management of the reform process began to make themselves felt in all sectors of society. ZCTU was the first association to officially withdraw its support. The Catholic Church followed by condemning the economic adjustment programme for its lack of compassion and care for the poor. The farmers' association, ZNFU, became increasingly more critical after the failure of the liberalised market system in the 1993/94 season. The growing criticism and emerging divisions were also evident within the business community.[3] When the business associations accused the structural adjustment programme of having butchered Zambian industry, the government was arguably left with a rather limited support-base.

The comparative literature on the implementation of dual reform processes argues that whereas some reform measures, most notably issues related to macroeconomic stabilisation should be left to a small insulated technocratic team, other areas of reform, particularly institutional reforms, might benefit greatly from wider consultations with a wide range of interest groups. Further, the dual re-

1. Personal interview, Simon Zukas. Lusaka, December 13, 1996.
2. An example is provided by the Director of Industries at the Ministry of Commerce, Trade and Industry who complained that the structural adjustment programme had led to the de-industrialisation of Zambia (*Times of Zambia*, April 20, 1994).
3. A series of articles in the business publication *Profit* debated the issue of structural adjustment reforms under headings like "SAP—ill-conceived, alien and misguided", *Profit*, January, 1994.

form literature expects reforming governments to initiate closer contacts with interest groups when approaching elections.[1] But the discussion above reveals that in the initial years, the MMD government did not apply a variety of tactics and attitudes to interest associations. A number of observers on the process of economic and political liberalisation in Zambia commented on the government's failure to communicate its policies, even when they were doing things right.[2] As the discussion below will demonstrate, rather than increasing contact with societal interest groups in an attempt to create a pro-reform coalition, in the Zambian case the contact with interest groups declined in the second part of the first election period. In the second Chiluba administration, the contact between the MMD government and the main economic interest groups was minimal. While business and agricultural interests were not met with the explicit attitude of non-negotiation as labour was, on the whole, none of the interest associations representing labour, agriculture or business was able to provide a strong and unified approach in terms of fighting for their special interests as regards the three major areas of structural reform: agricultural liberalisation, trade liberalisation, and privatisation.

Agricultural Liberalisation and Responses from Interest Groups

The liberalisation of the agricultural markets has by some observers been rated the greatest failure of the MMD government (Seshamani 1996; Saasa 1994). As discussed above, the initial pace of implementation put the non-stabilised economy under great pressure. Most of all, the process of replacing a set of, albeit poorly functioning, state monopolies, with decentralised private networks resulted in tremendous dislocations for the large majority of rural small-scale producers. For this group, state subsidies for maize production had become the only social welfare mechanism from the state. Due to the subsidised grain marketing system the maize sector was very sensitive to political interference. Generally, the problems encountered in the implementation of the agricultural liberalisation greatly undermined the confidence in the economic reform measures.[3] The criticism towards MMD's economic policies and the structural adjustment programme emerging from 1994 onwards was largely related to the troubles encountered in the liberalisation of agriculture (van de Walle and Chiwele 1994:36).

Commercial farming interests in Zambia were negatively affected by the government controlled prices and subsidised foodstuffs in the Second Republic and the farming community was expected to be among the major beneficiaries of the change in policy (Bates and Collier 1993). However, as argued above, agriculture failed to rebound in the 1991–2001 period due, in part, to poor and incon-

1. See the discussion in Chapter 2 on winners and losers and 'the grooming of growth coalitions'.
2. Personal communications, Dominic Mulaisho, Managing Director Shonga Steel, Governor, Bank of Zambia (1992–95). Lusaka, October 10, 1996.
3. An article appearing in *Profit* magazine illustrates the critical attitude of commercial farmers towards the MMD government due to its handling of the liberalisation of the grain markets: "The mad maize merry-go-round", *Profit*, August 1993:12–14.

sistent implementation. The three droughts that required the farmers to borrow substantial amounts of funds in order to finance inputs for the next season must also be considered influential. Borrowing in circumstances of severe macro-economic imbalance placed a heavy burden on the farmers as interest payments rose dramatically. Furthermore, the initial liberalisation caused similar dislocations for agricultural producers as for the manufacturing industry as Zambia liberalised its trade prior to rationalising its tariff regime.[1] Given the level of development and lack of competitive advantages, Zambian agriculture was unable to compete with its two main trading partners, South Africa and Zimbabwe, both in export and domestic trade. Imports of agricultural products from the neighbouring countries greatly undermined Zambian locally produced goods. ZNFU claimed that while structural adjustment had opened the door to an enabling environment for the farmers, it then cut their legs off. ZNFU blamed "the cabinet of traders [for making it] hard to invest in productive sectors" (*Profit*, August, 1995). Towards the end of the first election period, the ZNFU was more sceptical to agricultural liberalisation fearing that trade liberalisation would effectively kill agriculture in Zambia. Criticising the government for lack of support, in the form of subsidies, ZNFU by 1995 argued that the structural adjustment programme had in fact made things worse. Claiming that the liberalisation policies had broken the farmers, the association called for a more gradual implementation procedure (*Financial Mail*, August 8–14, 1995). Thus, while the commercial farmers had favoured the policies of liberalisation presented by MMD in 1991, when faced with the consequences of high interest rates, limited access to credit, and competition with imported agricultural products they began to doubt the policies. According to the first Minister of Agriculture, Guy Scott:

> [ZNFU] was not a large organisation, but they were basically in agreement on our policies. However, they were terrified when interest rates went up. These high interest rates killed out and destroyed the whole industry. The [farmers'] lobby was too weak when the interest rate started to escalate in 1993.[2]

Other observers argued that the inconsistency of the government's agricultural policies constituted the main reason why the commercial farmers started to doubt MMD's commitment to the liberal agricultural policies (GRZ/MAFF 1996; World Bank 1996a; van de Walle and Chiwele 1994; *Profit,* August 1996). As argued above, the government continued to send double messages to the farming community throughout the 1990s regarding price-setting, the role of government as a buyer of last resort and the issue of subsidising inputs. The continued inability of the government to invest in infrastructure and productive industries further made it difficult for the large majority of farmers to reap the benefits of the reform measures. Budgetary allocations continued to favour the urban sectors, most notably the administration (Seshamani 1996; Mwanawina et al. 1996).

The ZNFU successfully lobbied government to remove almost all agricultural products from the free trade agreement with Zimbabwe in 1996. When the

1. Personal interview with the Executive Director of ZNFU, George Grey. Lusaka, October 2, 1996. See also ZNFU *Annual Report* 1996 and GRZ/MAFF 1995, 1996.
2. Personal communications, Guy Scott, Minister of Agriculture 1991–1993. Lusaka, September 13, 1996.

MMD government in 1997 banned importation of wheat flour, ZNFU applauded the move, indicating the association's declining support of liberal policies (*EIU Country Report*, 3rd Quarter 1997). Two years later, ZNFU tried to force the government to increase export licences to farmers, but the government refused in order to subdue domestic maize prices (*EIU Country Report*, 3rd Quarter 1999:19; ZNFU *Annual Report* 1999). These examples indicate that both the government and ZNFU sent unclear signals to the market regarding their support for a liberal agricultural market for grain produce and inputs.[1] However, generally, the capacity of farmers to lobby the government on behalf of member interest was limited throughout the 1990s. ZNFU with approximately 350 paying members could not be regarded as an encompassing association. As a result, the complaints raised by ZNFU were usually not responded to by the bureaucrats in the Ministry of Agriculture. MMD politicians claimed that the criticism raised by the farming associations could not be taken as a response from farmers as their membership was too low to be seen as representative of the farmers as a group (*The Post*, August 16, 1994). In order to increase its lobbying capacity, ZNFU after 1991 sought to bring small-scale farmers into the organisation. However, including farmers outside the ranks of the large and technologically efficient commercial farmers meant that a great variety of views were brought under the umbrella of ZNFU, as evidenced by the many conflicting statements offered on the issue of agricultural liberalisation.

Conflicts of Interest between Small and Large-Scale Farmers

For the small-scale farmers agricultural liberalisation was regarded negatively. As argued by a representative of the Zambia Co-operative Federation (ZCF), the complete change from government monopoly institutions to market based decentralised systems of marketing created severe dislocations for the small-scale producers:

> For small-scale farmers in the far out rural areas where there are no roads and no infrastructure, MMD's agricultural policies created problems. There is no private sector to take over here as it is profit oriented and it is simply not profitable to market produce from these areas. As a result, the small-scale sector is left without a market for their produce. Traders then take advantage of the small-scale farmers and go out to buy at the end of season at a price lower than production cost and lower than what government used to buy for. There are as a result mixed feelings. ... It is true that there is a tendency of defaulting credits among small-scale farmers. This is a hang-over from the Second Republic when credit was dished out. The slogan was the 'government for the people of the people'. As a result, people saw a government thing as belonging to no one and there was no need to pay back. If they did not repay, the government would still pump in credit next year. Then MMD brought in the principle that credit should be a business and unless repaid there would be no cash for the next season. ... However, there are now only private traders who do not go to the small-scale farmers and they have to sell under profit. As a result, they are not able to pay back and thus the system forces them to default.[2]

1. The conflicts arising over the issue of credit repayment by the small-scale producers were a recurrent issue in the public debate and in the relationship between ZNFU and government. See *Profit*, August 1993; *The Post*, February 17, 1995; *The Farmer*, January 1995. See also World Bank 1996a; GRZ/MAFF 1995, 1996.
2. Personal interview, Bethel Sakala, Development Service Co-ordinator, Zambia Co-operative Federation. Lusaka, January 7, 1997.

The Peasant Farmers Union's representative offered a similar analysis of the effects of agricultural liberalisation on the small-scale producers:

> The liberalised agricultural production and marketing had enormous side effects on the peasants. It has been like a sudden heavy storm crushing the productive sectors of agriculture. Suddenly they stopped agricultural credit which incapacitated the peasants and made them even poorer. As agricultural credit finance was put into private hands, the cost of production rose beyond the reach of the poor. Peasant farmers could not afford to pay for inputs like seeds and fertilizer and they have gone without any crop for the past 2–3 seasons.[1]

The problems encountered in the process of agricultural liberalisation in Zambia reflect the general political dilemmas associated with dual reform processes. The statement by the Minister of Agriculture illustrated the political dilemmas facing a government committed to a liberalisation process with such a limited support-base:

> If you go to the remote areas and tell them not to grow maize you will get shouted down, neither the farmers nor the political leaders will accept it. Maize is not only food it is also the social security card. This is the cash crop which school fees and uniforms have come out of.[2]

The government's 'solution' to this political dilemma was to maintain some forms of indirect subsidies to the small-scale farmers, while still in the main implementing the agricultural liberalisation measures (World Bank 1996a; GRZ/MAFF 1996). The contradictory nature of the government's attitude to the liberalisation of maize marketing was reflected in public statements of the various cabinet ministers. Judging from the coverage in the local press, during the planting time, the various ministers appeared to address farmers. In May–July the government ministers seemed to be responding to the needs of urban constituents fearing the price of mealie meal.[3]

Due to the implications felt by the large majority of small-scale producers, apart from the donor community and a few reform minded ministers and bureaucrats, the attachment to liberalisation was not deep among most domestic actors involved in agricultural policy.[4] By 1996 four associations were officially registered as representing agricultural producers at the national level. However, neither the National Association of Small-Scale and Peasant Farmers Union (NASSPFU, established in 1989 but only effective from 1994 onwards), nor the Peasant Farmers Union of Zambia (PFUZ, registered in 1995) could claim to be strong lobbying associations on behalf of the small-scale producers. As a result, the lobbying activities of the farming associations were not met with a great deal of support and to a large extent, the calls for change were ignored by the MMD government throughout the election period. This may be interpreted as reflecting a general lack of interest by the government in entering into

1. Personal interview, Roger Phiri, Assistant General Secretary, Peasant Farmers Union of Zambia. Lusaka, October 10, 1996.
2. Personal interview, Simon Zukas, Minister of Agriculture. Lusaka, December 13, 1996.
3. The cycles of the agricultural policy process were confirmed in interviews with the two Ministers of Agriculture, Guy Scott and Simon Zukas as well as George Gray (ZNFU).
4. In what political analysts regarded as the first shots of the 1996 election campaign, President Chiluba in February 1995 reassured agricultural producers that the government would ensure that marketing reached where the private sector did not reach (*The Post*, February 17, 1995).

dialogue and consultations with interest groups. However, it also reflects the low levels of capacity of these associations. As the representatives of agricultural associations could not claim to represent the bulk of the producers, the government had few incentives for consulting with these associations. The frustrations felt within government concerning the lack of cooperation and the limited capacity and reach of agricultural associations were expressed by the Permanent Secretary in the Ministry of Agriculture:

> In terms of support from the community, I would have wished for a lot more. The ZNFU have been involved at all stages of this process. They will tell you a different story now but that is a lie. They have been very vocal, however, now a different song is being sung. There is lack of determination and they are now reacting only to the pain of the moment. But it was inevitable that liberalisation would cause disruptions. I would have wished for more help from them in terms of education of the farmers and peasants. ... There must be organisations representing farmers on the ground. My hope at this time is the emerging peasant and small-scale organisations. I hope that they will be of help and that they will be efficient.[1]

Perhaps more than any other sector in Zambia, agriculture underscores the barriers against generating political support-bases around economic policy reforms in Africa. Due to their numerical weakness, no agricultural organisations could provide an electoral support-base for MMD. ZNFU was critical to the effects of liberalisation, due both to the fact that the effects had hurt their members, and because the implementation had not been consistent. While ZNFU's policies support of the liberalisation policies varied considerably in the 1990s, they never reversed their policy. Until shortly before the 2001 elections, at the level of leadership, the two new associations representing small-scale and peasant farmers, as well as the co-operative federation, expressed commitment to a furtherance of the liberalisation process, with more cushioning measures. While the associations at the executive level endorsed liberalisation, in meetings with their local members, often reported in the press, the views were far more negative.[2] Thus, in terms of agriculture, it cannot be argued that a large sector of agricultural interests has emerged which could be characterised as a 'winning coalition' and a useful constituency for the government. Due to the weak agricultural associations, opposition to the government's agricultural policies was often voiced by populist sources like the press and MPs representing rural constituencies. Similarly, the size and composition of the two main business associations rendered a pro-reform coalition unlikely. Many businesses were negatively affected both by the rapid trade liberalisation and the way the privatisation process was carried out.

Business Responses to Trade Liberalisation and Privatisation

In the 1991 election campaign, MMD promised that they would return the economy to the market and the private sector. The business sector was expected to become more influential due to both the reversal of that sector's marginalisation under the former regime, and to the strong presence of businessmen in the

1. Personal interview, A.C. Sichinga. Lusaka, January 16, 1997.
2. Personal communications, Simon Zukas, Guy Scott and Hans Hedlund, Programme Co-ordinator of Economic Expansion in outlying Areas. Lusaka, September 19, 1996.

new parliament. However, as MMD's economic policies became more erratic after 1993, the positive relationship between business and the MMD government gradually gave way to mutual distrust.

ZACCI and ZAM initially endorsed trade liberalisation, as part of their general support of MMD's economic reform project. The more direct criticism of the government's economic policies appearing from sectors of the business community in 1994 addressed the imbalances created by the full-scale liberalisation of the Zambian external trade regime. While all the protective measures to shield the local manufacturing industry from competition were removed, for revenue purposes, the government insisted on maintaining a high duty on imports of raw materials. Without protection or subsidies in any form and facing competition from imported finished products subsidised in the country of origin, the Zambian manufacturing industry was not able to compete. Throughout 1993, the local press carried articles focusing on the plight of the Zambian manufacturing industry (*The Weekly Post,* October 22–28, 1993; *Times of Zambia,* January 15, 1994; *Profit,* January 1994). In a series of advertisements claiming that the Zambian manufacturing industry, like the rhino, was threatened with extinction, the Zambian Association of Manufacturers (ZAM) accused the government of killing the industry (*Times of Zambia*, August 10, 1994; *The Post,* August 12, 1994). The government's reactions to the criticism from the business community indicated that criticism was neither expected, nor appreciated. The government, feeling that it had already done a lot to ease the problems of Zambian industry, appeared genuinely puzzled by the campaign.[1] The Minister of Commerce, Trade and Industry (Dipak Patel) condemned ZAM for taking a confrontational stance instead of communicating directly with the government (*Profit*, September 1994; *The Post*, August 16, 1994). However, as argued by ZAM, the fact remained that most of the economic reform measures so far put in place by the government were biased in favour of commerce (*The Post*, June 17, 1994).

Reflecting the broad membership of ZACCI, the main business association was rather passive on the issue of the liberalisation policies having created a bias against the manufacturing industry. Based on the campaign carried out in 1994, arguably, ZAM, with a much more limited membership and lacking an organisational apparatus, was more successful in terms of lobbying for their member interests than the larger ZACCI (Taylor 1997). Persistent complaints from the manufacturing industry led the government to introduce the concept of countervailing duties in 1995 with the aim of countering any protective measures instituted by other countries in the region (GRZ: *1995 Budget Address).* According to one observer, the cumbersome process of processing claims had by the 1996 elections resulted in few benefits for the local industry (Seshamani 1996:11).

From 1993 onwards, the government's economic policy mix of an overspending public sector and a very tight monetary policy in combination with the political uncertainty created a very negative situation for the business sector in Zambia. The main Zambian business associations withdrew their support for

1. Personal interview, Gideon Phiri, Chief Executive, ZACCI. Lusaka, October 2, 1996.

parts of the economic reform programme as the effects of trade liberalisation and privatisation were felt by their members, many of whom had been beneficiaries of the state-controlled economy. But regardless of the protest and lack of support from business, despite several exogenous shocks and uneven implementation, the MMD government maintained an open trade regime throughout the 1991–2001 period. As one of the first countries in the region to do so, Zambia put the COMESA Free Trade Agreement into effect in October 2000. Illustrating the MMD government's autonomy from domestic business interests, the Deutsch Presse-Agentur's comments on the 2000 African Competitiveness Report noted that: "The Zambian government's determination to uphold an open trade regime in the face of opposition from segments of the private sector remains one of the country's major attractions for foreign investment".

ZACCI's limited ability to address the perceived imbalances between benefits geared for trade as a result of the market liberalisation measures and the institutional regulations and investments required to facilitate the growth of a local manufacturing industry was illustrated by the President of ZACCI:

> Some of our business members think that liberalisation has gone too far as some businesses have suffered. There are a number of businesses in this country which due to liberalisation have not been able to compete. It is, however, a question of approach. As a federation, we do not adopt a one voice approach. Some say liberalisation is good and let the bad businesses die if they cannot compete. We take the both schools approach and at that point it is up to government to decide.[1]

According to a business confidence survey from 2001–2002, a large number of businesses reported that Zambia's free trade policy was as a major impediment to their business.[2] Used to tariff protection, trade liberalisation meant that local firms lost state protection and had to compete with imported products. Based on the survey results, arguably, both the business associations and individual businesses seemed to regard their uncompetitiveness and lack of capital as a result of unfair competition from abroad rather than as an effect of government policy, such as an overspending public sector and tight monetary policy (Taylor and Aarnes 2002:17).

Divisions within the Business Community on the Issue of Privatisation

The business associations initially supported the privatisation process. But in the press debates following Minister Penza's statement on the mining industry in 1992 (see discussion above), contributions from the business community did not figure centrally. Alluding to the lack of support offered by the business sector, the Minister of Commerce challenged the business community to market the privatisation programme as a positive measure for economic development at ZACCI's 1992 annual meeting. Penza further accused ZACCI of having played the role of the spectator in the privatisation exercise so far (*Times of Zambia*, September 26, 1992). Other ministers also indicated frustrations with the limit-

1. Personal interview, I. Chamwera, President, ZACCI. Lusaka, October 14, 1996.
2. The business confidence survey was carried out by Nordic Consulting Group, Zambia, covering the period June 2001 to April 2002. 100 companies in Lusaka and on the Copperbelt were interviewed in four successive rounds of interviews (Taylor and Aarnes 2002).

ed support from the business community.[1] The limited role played by business in the initial stages of reform implementation underlines the argument about the need for business to redefine its role in a new political environment. But the lack of involvement also illustrates the diverse nature of the Zambian business community. Comprising a small group of non-black entrepreneurs and a larger black business class which to a large extent had risen to prominence through the state industrial sector, the business community was never a united pro-privatisation lobby. According to ZACCI's representative on the ZPA board:

> The big disappointment [in terms of privatisation] has been that there was no market, no one was able to buy companies as there are few Zambians coming from a business background with capital. Most of us have a background in the parastatal industries and we have no capital.[2]

ZACCI presented a rather ambiguous view on the privatisation process. In principle the business organisations supported privatisation and criticised the government for moving too slowly. The views expressed by various members of the business community, however, varied considerably. These divisions were also reflected in the reporting of the business magazine *Profit,* which at times strongly criticised the government for moving too slowly, in particular with respect to privatising ZCCM (*Profit,* May 1993; July 1993; January 1994). At other times, even the editorial voiced some very critical comments, often connected to the lack of Zambian participation in the process (*Profit*, April 1995). As the privatisation process gathered momentum from 1995 onwards, a racial division reminiscent of the First and Second Republics re-emerged within the Zambian business community. This division limited the strength of ZACCI in terms of lobbying the government. Due to the financial constraints generated by the fiscal reforms, the lack of growth in the Zambian economy, and the fact that a majority of local Zambian businessmen had their background in the public sector, few black Zambian businessmen were able to reap the benefits of the privatisation process which gathered momentum in 1995. Thus, the majority of the black business community did not regard themselves as beneficiaries of the privatisation process. The view expressed by a member of ZACCI's board is illustrative of views expressed by a number of African businessmen interviewed:

> ZACCI is supportive of the privatisation programme, however, with one caveat: More should and could have been done to enable Zambians to take part in the process. As it is now, it is terribly skewed towards international investors. The problem of the way this has been handled is that the privatisation effort has brought this government no new friends as no sectors of the economy have really benefited. This points to a worrisome aspect of the sustainability of the process. There is a situation where people are saying hey, what have I benefited from this situation? ... The problem is that the government does not worry about empowerment or ownership of reform by the population. This brings us into conflict with our neighbouring countries where empowerment is the main concern.[3]

1. Personal communications, Aka Lewanika, Lusaka, September 17, 1996; Guy Scott, Simon Zukas and Emmanuel Kasonde. Before becoming Minister of Commerce in the first MMD Cabinet, Ronald Penza was Chairman of the Lusaka Chamber of Commerce.
2. Personal interview, Abel Mkandawire, vice chairman of ZACCI and President of the ZPA Board. Lusaka, January 8, 1997.
3. Personal interview, Mebelo Mutukwa, Chairman of Zambia Chamber of Commerce and Industry, Fiscal and Monetary Committee. Lusaka, November, 1996.

Responding to this criticism of the privatisation process increasingly appearing in Zambian newspapers as the 1996 elections approached, the Zambia Privatisation Agency (ZPA) launched a number of public relations initiatives.[1] Answering the allegations that the privatisation process had so far only benefited foreign investors and non-Zambian citizens, ZPA argued that 80 per cent of the companies had been sold to Zambians. This figure, however, also included non-black Zambians with a registered company in Zambia. Further, as argued by representatives of the Zambian business community, regarding assets, the four biggest companies sold, accounting for 80 per cent of the value, all went back to their colonial-time owners.[2] Commenting upon the limited number of local beneficiaries of the reform measures, a policy advisor at the Bank of Zambia argued that:

> The downside [of privatisation] is that due to the level and state of our economy not many Zambians are able to participate in the process. In a sense we have replaced one form of ownership with another instead of creating more enterprises and businesses.[3]

According to the MMD leadership, the government of Zambia and the private sector formed a partnership of prosperity and growth in the Third Republic. A number of seminars were arranged where the government asked the business community to contribute their views, and both ZACCI and ZAM were represented on a number of government boards and committees. Nevertheless, according to ZACCI, the meetings were often poorly organised and the ministers were not well informed (*Profit*, April 1996). As a result, in interviews with respondents from a broad spectrum of the business community, few were able to cite examples of policy outcomes that had resulted directly from the committee representations. Generally, as MMD started to consolidate its political power-base, it increasingly disregarded domestic business views and interests. In the second election period, formalised, regular meetings between Zambian business associations and the government were discontinued. In part, the changing attitude towards business related to the fact that business could not provide the government with meaningful political or economic support. The precarious nature of Zambian business meant that it could provide few benefits (in the form of employment provision, tax revenues, etc.) to the state. Moreover, representing less than 20 per cent of formal sector employment, the private sector did not constitute either an electoral threat or a useful political ally for MMD. By the late 1990s, ZACCI became completely marginalised due to a dramatic fall in membership resulting principally from the effects of economic policies on its members. Partly agreeing to criticism raised by the government, ZACCI's current leadership admits that the MMD's trade policies and the privatisation process have split their members and as a result, it has not been possible for the association to speak with one voice.[4]

1. ZPA, 1996: "ZPA forum. Statement by the Executive". Hotel Intercontinental (October 17).
2. This comment was raised and supported by businessmen represented at the ZPA Forum.
3. 1994 Budget Address by the Minister of Finance, Ronald Penza (GRZ 1994).
4. Interview with Nelson Chisenga, acting Chief Executive, Zambia Association of Chambers of Commerce and Industry (ZACCI), December 28, 2002. The interview was carried out and transcribed by Dr. Edgar Bwalya, University of Zambia.

The marginalisation of interest groups as a result of the economic reform process was, however, most marked in the case of the trade unions, considering their prominent position in the Second Republic.

Privatisation and the Trade Union Movement

From late 1993 onwards the Zambia Congress of Trade Unions (ZCTU) again became an outspoken critic of the economic reform measures. From a very early date the trade union movement criticised the government for failing to consult with labour by ignoring the tripartite agreements. Expressing the frustrations felt with the lack of dialogue between the government and labour, by 1993 ZCTU's President Fackson Shamenda declared that a breakdown of communications between the government and the labour movement had occurred:

> It is shocking to see how this government is approaching industrial relations. It is tantamount to blackmail. Over this issue, I would say that even the Second Republic was much better. (*The Weekly Post,* September 3–9, 1993)

Attempting to influence the economic reform process more directly, ZCTU in December 1993 made a trip to the World Bank and the IMF to plead for more lenient benchmarks and to allow economic reforms to be implemented gradually. The reaction from the government to ZCTU's initiative illustrated that the government and labour movement had different perceptions on what was to be the role of a trade union movement in a liberalised environment. The Minister of Labour argued that the unions should stop acting as a shadow government as in a democracy, trade unions were only one of many interest associations. Subsequently, they should stick to issues pertaining to the interests of their members and lobbying of government (*Times of Zambia,* December 16, 1993). The government did not summon the representatives of employers and employees for tripartite meetings as stipulated in the industrial relations regulations. According to the tripartite agreement, these meetings were to be called every quarter. However, by 1994 only four meetings had been held. Furthermore, the outcome of the meetings left the unions with the impression that the government had no intention of following the advice of the trade unions.[1] The practice of the MMD government clearly broke with the policies of the one-party era when industrial relations between the government and the labour movement had been a significant part of the policy process.

Prior to the 1991 transitions, the trade union movement had advocated the need for some privatisation.[2] However, the debate on the potential sale of ZCCM in 1992 demonstrated that the unions were adamantly against this. The President of the Mine Workers Union (MUZ), Francis Kunda, simply stated that privatisation of ZCCM was out (*Times of Zambia,* September 23, 1992). After

1. Personal interviews, Alec Chirwa, General Secretary ZCTU, Kitwe, December 2, 1996 and Austin Muneku, Research Economist ZCTU, Lusaka, October 18, 1996. Lack of dialogue with the government was also one of the complaints voiced by most participants at a ZCTU and ZFE conference held on "The impact of the SAP", Andrew's Motel, Lusaka 17–18 October, 1996.
2. As early as 1973 Newstead Zimba, the General Secretary of ZCTU, suggested that it was easier to deal with private employers than the state as the former did not employ the security forces during labour disputes (Baylies and Szeftel 1984:85).

public outrage which involved the miners union, ZCTU, the churches, the press, and members of the MMD Cabinet, Minister Ronald Penza backtracked and declared that the government could wait 20 to 30 years before privatising the mines (*Times of Zambia*, September 26, 1992). The position of the trade union movement in the initial stages of the privatisation reform was illustrated by the statement of the General Secretary of ZCTU:

> We disagree with the pace and the definition of privatisation. We argue that it is not necessary to privatise public companies that are doing well and making profit. It was our understanding that only loss-making public companies were going to be privatised. ... We expected foreign bidders to be invited not only to take over public companies but to set up parallel private companies to compete with the existing companies.[1]

The policies of liberalising the trade and exchange markets as well as the process of privatisation provoked the sharpest reactions from the labour movement.[2] According to statistics from the Central Statistical Office, approximately 30,000 workers were made redundant in the formal sector economy between 1992 and 1996 (CSO 1995, 1997). ZCTU claimed the number to be closer to 50,000 (Banda and Muneku 1996). The level of retrenchments posed serious challenges to the trade union movement both in terms of defending the economic well-being of its membership, as well as the financial burden created by the loss in trade union membership. Yet according to statistics from the Ministry of Labour, the number of strikes were drastically reduced from 1990 to 1994.[3]

By 1994, the effects of privatisation in the context of an economy in crisis were beginning to make themselves felt by the number of companies closing down, or down-sealing their operations, and thus retrenching workers. The uncertain future of many of the union members led the trade union congress to take a more cautious approach towards privatisation. Stressing that privatisation had been carried out without consideration of the loss of jobs and the situation of the Zambian work-force, the trade unions started to criticise the process of privatisation. Citing concern over employment and security standards and anti-union sentiments in the new private companies, ZCTU called for a commercialisation of state enterprises as an alternative to privatisation (ZCTU 1994c). According to ZCTU's own documents, the pronounced negative stance towards privatisation from ZCTU was sparked by the high profile liquidations of Zambia Airways and the United Bus Company in 1994. The two major transport companies were liquidated by the government prior to the planned process of privatisation. As the companies were liquidated, the employees were by law only entitled to three months salary. Despite the high number of employees in the two companies, and the uncertainty facing the public at large due to the transport shortages, the Minister of Finance declared that the airline and bus company would not be treated differently from other parastatals being liquidated (*Times of Zambia*, November 11, 1994). Realising that the terminal benefits

1. Personal interview, Alec Chirwa, ZCTU.
2. ZCTU 1994a, 1994b, 1994d, as well as personal interviews with labour representatives.
3. According to the numbers presented by the Ministry of Labour, the number of strikes went down from 103 in 1990, to 102 in 1991, 91 in 1992, 48 in 1993 and 15 in 1994. However, the number of workers involved and man-hours lost was high for all the years apart from 1994. ZCTU, 1994d: "1994 Quadrennial Congress Report of the Secretary General". Kitwe, October.

agreed to in the collective agreement before the liquidation would not be paid out, workers in the two companies protested in the streets of Lusaka (*Financial Mail*, December 20–29, 1994; Times of Zambia, December 31, 1994). The public outcry generated from these processes shook the trade unions' confidence in the privatisation process (ZCTU 1994c). In meetings with the government, the trade unions had been reassured that the national airline would be financially rescued (ZCTU 1994e). However, as Chapter 6 will discuss further, the government was at the same time under pressure from the international donors to liquidate the airline due to the implications of continued subsidies for the macroeconomic situation. Stating publicly that Chiluba had failed the workers more than Kaunda ever did, ZCTU's General Secretary Alec Chirwa declared that the honeymoon was over and ZCTU was now set on a war-path with the government (*The Post*, December 27, 1994). By this stage, however, the difference of opinion on the economic reform programme had also set the trade union movement on an internal war-path.

Trade Unions Split

In contrast to the labour congress, moving from a general support of privatisation in 1991 to a critical stand when the effects started to be felt, the Mine Workers Union (MUZ) in 1994 changed from a negative stand on the issue of privatisation to endorsing the privatisation plans of ZCCM. Towards the end of 1993, the President of MUZ delivered a statement strongly supporting MMD's economic policies. The statement came at a time when ZCTU issued increasingly more critical views on the economic policies of MMD (*The Post,* October 29, 1993). Representing a sector which was assumed would grow after privatisation, the mineworkers began to advocate a more speedy privatisation of the mines, arguing that despite the prospect of immediate retrenchments, the long term prospects for workers would be better with the mines in private hands.[1] The statement of MUZ's secretary of information is illustrative of the mine workers' pro-business stand which became more pronounced in the period after 1994:

> Our position is alien to trade union movements in UK and Germany who say they are opposed [to privatisation] due to retrenchments. We see it the other way around; simply because when we nationalised, the proceeds from industries went to develop other sectors like agriculture. ... In the mines there has been no new technology and whatever the strength of a union you cannot retain wages and levels of employment if the company cannot sustain the wages. We see no other alternative but to arrest this trend of production. We must ensure fresh injection of capital and the only way to do this is through privatisation. We have miners who have worked under parastatal ownership and we have miners who have worked under private owners and the levels of employment and ability to pay living wages certainly point in favour of the latter.[2]

1. For documents describing the position of MUZ on privatisation and the modes of privatising the mines, see MUZ 1994, 1996a, 1996b.
2. Personal interview, Muchimba, Research and Information Officer, Mine Workers Union of Zambia (MUZ). Kitwe, December 5, 1996.

Table 4: 3 Zambia Congress of Trade Unions (ZCTU) membership 1991–1997

Total	1986	1990	1994	1995	1996	1997[a]
	348.960	357.967	312.389	295.747	230.000	270.000

[a] Increase reflecting the reaffiliation of three unions.
Source: ZCTU 1996; Banda 1997.

MUZ's President, Francis Kunda, was also the vice-President of the ZCTU and the internal differences within ZCTU thereby became public when the MUZ President announced his intention to contest the leadership position of ZCTU at the October 1994 Quadrennial Congress, something that had rarely occurred in ZCTU. Immediately, the contestations became linked both to national politics and the economic liberalisation process. The ZCTU President told the press that the contest was instigated by the MMD government to have him and the General Secretary removed in order to install 'yes men' to head the labour movement. ZCTU's President claimed that the MMD government was not happy with the position ZCTU had taken on the structural adjustment programme (*The Post,* August 19, 1994). When the opposing candidates lost the Quadrennial elections, the President of MUZ called a press conference and announced that his union was breaking away from ZCTU (*Times of Zambia,* November 4, 1994). Four other unions declared their intentions to leave ZCTU, including the teachers union (ZNUT), the building and engineering workers union (NUBEGW), the union of commercial and industrial workers (NUCIW) and the financial workers union (ZUFIAW).[1]

The 1994 split of the trade union movement indicated a division on economic reforms. The private sector unions claimed that ZCTU spent its resources primarily on the public sector unions. Commercial workers felt that they had fought their industrial struggles alone and therefore questioned the value of submitting 30 per cent of the trade union funds to the Congress.[2] According to MUZ:

> Implicitly ZCTU has a bias towards public sector unions at the expense of others. At the ZCTU general conference all unions were asked to strike to help CSUZ. Then the other unions said, why did you not all come forward for us? ... The bottom line is that there is a split along the lines of various positions towards economic reforms: There is a split between commercial and public sector unions. The perception of the public sector unions differs from the perceptions of the commercial unions which are facing the real brunt of economic reform while public sector unions are procrastinating and still debating.[3]

The labour movement left Livingstone as a divided and weakened organisation. The split was a serious blow to the trade union movement as a whole. ZCTU's influence was greatly reduced when the teachers, the miners, the financial and commercial workers, all significant unions in terms of influence and size, left the mother-body. The financial situation of ZCTU was also greatly affected as the

1. ZCTU 1995; see also *Times of Zambia*, October 27, 1994. This was also repeated in personal interviews with Robinson Sikazwe and Alec Chirwa.
2. Personal interviews, Ignatius Kasumbu, Ass. General Secretary (Business), Zambia Congress of Trade Unions (ZCTU), Kitwe, December 6, 1996; Austin Liato, Vice-President, ZCTU, Lusaka November 5, 1996.
3. Personal interview, C.B. Muchimba, MUZ.

ZCTU was one of the best organised & influential union movements

five unions were among the largest and subsequently, subscription fees were affected. The trade union movement had already lost a great number of members due to retrenchments. The 1994 split further weakened the already threatened position of ZCTU, which before 1991 was recognised by most observers as one of the best organised and influential union movements on the continent. In addition to fighting government over the pace, and effects of, the structural adjustment programme, ZCTU's strained resources and capacity were thereby locked into attempts to reconcile the disputes within the labour movement. Comparing the position of labour within the pluralist system it had fought so hard to attain, to the position it held within the one-party state, a labour representative argued that:

> It is ironic that Chiluba managed what the Kaunda regime never did; to weaken and split the trade union movement. ... ZCTU is weakened organisationally due mainly to loss of membership. It does no longer enjoy the strength it used to. ... The problem is that there now is a government that deliberately ignores the unions and deliberately clips the strength of the unions. ... I think the government will make sure reconciliation is not taking place and I can see a new federation being recognised with a national centre that will most likely declare its sympathy to MMD.[1]

Partly defeating these negative projections, in December 1997, three of the break-away unions rejoined ZCTU—the commercial and industrial workers union (NUCIW), the building and engineering workers union (NUBEGW), and the teachers union (ZNUT). However, the mine workers union (MUZ) and the financial and allied workers (ZUFIAW) remained outside ZCTU. In 1998 a second union federation was established, the Federation of Free Trade Unions (FFTU). MUZ, however, reunited with ZCTU in 1999 and ZCTU is still by far the biggest federation in Zambia. But, the combination of internal differences and the significant retrenchments occurring in the 1990s have reduced the trade unions from a powerful actor to a marginal actor. Illustrating the current weak position of the Zambian trade union movement, an editorial in *The Post* recently posed the following question: "Can they [the new leadership of ZCTU] defrost the ZCTU and bring it back to life again?" (*The Post* November 26, 2002).

Economic Reforms and the Role of Interest Groups

This chapter has indicated that the two MMD administrations (1991–1996 and 1996–2001) implemented the economic reform programme agreed to with the international finance institutions in a partial and uneven manner. In the second election period, the government's commitment to the economic reform measures waned. The uneven implementation and remaining high levels of public spending created an uncertain environment for business and brought MMD on collision course with its donors in the late 1990s.

The analysis of consultations between the MMD government and the main economic interest groups confirmed that the reform measures met with resistance from most interest associations. When the effects of the economic reform

1. Personal communications, Robinson Sikazwe LO/ZCTU.

measures started to affect ZCTU's membership, the trade unions officially withdrew their support to the MMD government. Business associations were affected by the rapid liberalisation of the trade regime. Similarly, the process of agricultural liberalisation created transitional problems for commercial farmers as well as small-scale producers. After a few years, the initial business support for the economic reforms waned. However, this chapter has argued that the opposition from interest groups cannot explain the inconsistent implementation of the economic reforms witnessed by the MMD government from 1993/94 onwards. Due to the weak numerical base of Zambia's economic interest groups, and the fact that the economic policies split the organisations and greatly affected their membership, these organisations did not represent a coherent societal opposition to MMD's economic policies. The government went ahead with trade liberalisation and agricultural liberalisation. The process of privatisation was slower and the public sector reforms have still not taken place. The slow and uneven implementation of aspects of the economic reform programme suggests that the MMD government, like its predecessor, lacked autonomy from powerful vested interests in the state bureaucracy.

The Role of Zambia Industrial and Mining Corporation (ZIMCO)

Arguably, one sectoral interest appeared to be in a better position than most in terms of curtailing the privatisation process. As illustrated above it was only after the holding company Zambia Industrial and Mining Corporation (ZIMCO) was dissolved in March 1995, after intense donor pressure, that the privatisation process gathered momentum. Evidence suggests that ZIMCO used a wide variety of tactics to stall the privatisation process, from personal attacks on the leadership of ZPA, to lobbying various ministers, leaking sensitive information to the press and providing illegal retrenchment benefits to selected managers. ZIMCO attempted, and partially succeeded, to slow the process of privatisation. As argued by a senior manager in Zambia Privatisation Agency:

> The main challenge in the whole process of privatisation and the main stumbling block has been ZIMCO. This is most definite. I joined the company [ZPA] in 1993 and I can remember hurdle upon hurdle from the ZIMCO head office. We felt we were fighting a giant. We tried meeting with the ministry of labour, the unions, but all our efforts failed. The ZIMCO head office was very powerful and they were wound up in the process as they had their own interests to protect. There were so many unnecessary quarrels. Without ZIMCO the privatisation would have been carried out much faster.[1]

Almost from its inception in 1992, a contentious relationship developed between the newly installed privatisation agency (ZPA) and the state holding company for the parastatal companies, ZIMCO. Numerous reports indicate that ZIMCO attempted to block sales of companies under its portfolio (*Weekly Post*, May 22–28, 1992).[2] Furthermore, the conflict between ZIMCO and ZPA

1. Elisabeth Jere, Managing Director, Social Impact Division, ZPA. Lusaka, December 6, 1996.
2. ZPA announced the sale of the first two companies, Autocare and Eagle Travel, on June 8, 1993. Immediately, a debate unfolded in the press charging ZPA with having sold the companies 'for a song', according to ZIMCO (*Zambia Daily Mail*, June 8, 1993). Furthermore, breaking the agreement with ZPA, ZIMCO insisted on paying out benefits and pensions to managers, despite the continued running of the two companies (*Zambia Daily Mail*, June 17, 1993).

was played out in public and from an early date ZPA became discredited in the press.[1] The analysis has indicated that the state holding company ZIMCO constituted an interest coalition with great ability to hinder the process of privatisation. It was only when ZIMCO was dissolved in 1995, after considerable pressures from the international donors, that the privatisation process in Zambia gathered momentum. Thus, the privatisation process in Zambia suggests that interests located within the government structures may have greater incentives, and ability, to stall economic reform processes than independent interest groups representing labour, agriculture and business.[2]

A Reform Process without Winners?

Contrary to expectations, in Zambia the influence of interest associations representing key sectors of the economy declined as a result of the economic reforms. In each case, the unions, farmers and business associations had to adjust to the transition of the regime from state corporatism to a form of pluralism. Yet, the circumstances around their reduced political influence were unique to each sector. Chiluba's trade union background provided the MMD government with initial support and extensive knowledge of the trade union movement that enabled MMD to capitalize on the split between private and public sector unions. The fundamental division between industrialists and traders weakened the potential political influence of the main business association, ZACCI. The problems of agricultural liberalisation and the dualism of agricultural sector interests in Zambia rendered the agricultural lobby weak and ineffectual.

The Zambian experience suggests that neither Zambian business, labour nor agricultural interests could be considered (or indeed, considered themselves) to be 'winners' in the reform process. While some reform measures benefited one sector as a whole, other measures hurt some sectoral interests and benefited others. As a result, no sector emerged that could be characterized as constituency favouring of the economic reform policies. The racial dimension further challenges the expectation that reform winners could be political constituencies for the government. Arguably, in Zambia the groups that benefited most from the reforms implemented were the politically least useful—Asian and white farmers and business owners who are few in number and historically favoured by the former colonial policies. But maybe most importantly, in order for economic interest associations to be able to influence policies as envisioned in the pluralist notion of 'winners' and 'losers', the political arena must provide channels where interests can be aggregated into the competitive political processes. As the next chapter will illustrate, in the 1990s few viable links were formed between Zambian economic interests and the political party system. As no party offered an agenda challenging MMD's economic reforms, the interest groups representing

1. Personal communications, James Mutale, executive director ZPA (1992–1994). Lusaka, October 14, 1996. The negative press towards the privatisation process in general and more specifically the role of ZPA was particularly evident in the *Zambia Daily Mail* which throughout 1992–1993 almost on a daily basis carried articles which in general associated privatisation with redundancies and, more specifically, questioned the sales value of the firms put up for privatisation.
2. See Chapter 2 and the discussion of the critique of the dual reform perspective.

business, labour and agriculture had few channels into the political arena. The next chapter will show that the political reform process itself weakened the position of interest groups due to the combined effects of the electoral system, organisational proliferation and executive dominance.

5

Political Liberalisation 1991–2001

The Decline of Interest Group Influence

> It is better to be a President of a non-democratic country than not to be a President of a democratic country![1]

The democratic transition in 1991 raised hopes both domestically and abroad that Zambia would develop into a consolidated democracy. However, this chapter will demonstrate that despite the conducting of multiparty elections in 1991, 1996 and 2001, a multitude of civil associations and a vocal independent press, the Zambian democracy is far from institutionalised. While the multiparty system has been maintained, the quality of political governance declined within a few years after the 1991 political transitions. One of the most remarkable features of Zambia's dual reform experiences is the decline of influence of the main economic interest groups. This chapter will show that paradoxically, the multiparty reforms weakened the influence of the main interest groups. As MMD started to consolidate its political power-base from 1993 onwards it increasingly disregarded the views of interest groups. Continued executive dominance, coupled to the organisational proliferation, and a weakly institutionalised party system, has meant that in Zambia in the 1990s the electoral channel has not functioned as a credible 'threat' to the incumbent government. As a result, throughout the 1990s the government was able ignore the voices of business, agriculture and labour within a system of multiparty rule.

The chapter first assesses the main political developments in the two election periods, 1991–1996 and 1996–2001. Secondly, it analyses the interaction between Zambian interest groups and political parties in the period 1991–2001. A concluding section summarises the analysis.

Political Developments 1991–2001

In its 1991 election manifesto MMD committed itself to engage in wide and broad-based consultations with interest associations. It also promised to create a new constitution based on the principles of consensus and the active participation of the Zambian people. Furthermore, MMD promised to de-link the government from the party structures. Promising to work on the principle of cooperation with all progressive and legally constituted organisations, the Manifesto stated that:

1. Statement made by one of Chiluba's political advisor's prior to the 1996 elections.

> MMD works on the basis of profound democratisation of inter-party relations. The MMD upholds democratic principles such as electiveness and replaceability, openness and accountability, non-subordination of the minority to the majority, and the right of the minority to defend its interests publicly if these interests should be threatened. (1991:11)

The First Election Period (1991–1996)

Despite the large electoral majority, MMD was from the beginning a very divided party as the broad 'rainbow' coalition encompassed business interests, academics, students, trade union representatives and former UNIP politicians. To establish a coherent party of the wide and dispersed coalition of interests presented the new party in government with a great challenge. The main factor uniting the MMD coalition was the quest for change and for carrying out policies in contradiction to the past practices under UNIP and Kenneth Kaunda. As argued by one observer, "[t]hose who opposed President Kaunda knew what they did not want. They were less certain about what they did want" (McPherson 1995:20). As a result, adherence to the electoral promises was complicated by a number of factors. MMD and President Chiluba had committed themselves to a leaner state apparatus and a smaller cabinet. However, the new President was under popular obligation to accommodate those who had been elected to the MMD executive who had acted as a shadow cabinet during the election campaign. Furthermore, it was necessary to accommodate all the main interests within MMD and at the same time reward the financiers of the electoral campaign. Instead of reducing the Cabinet, it was increased from 23 members under UNIP to 25 in addition to 23 deputy ministers and ministers at the provincial levels. The new MMD government from a very early beginning became associated with political practices of the Second Republic. Throughout the transition process, UNIP politicians had left the old party with varying degrees of grace as the political tides began to turn. Commenting on the transition process and the forming of the first government, Bratton argues that:

> [D]uring the selection of parliamentary candidates, the MMD headquarters often pushed local preferences aside, creating an unfortunate precedence of arbitrary, patrimonial decision-making. Top MMD officers grabbed safe seats in the Copperbelt Province, and regional MMD bosses allegedly bought party cards en masse to boost their own local followings. (1994:118)

Reflecting both the wide and dispersed support-base of the MMD and, at the same time, the new government's lack of institutional ties to the bureaucratic structures, the MMD government initially functioned as a broad and loosely structured coalition that allowed each ministry a great deal of autonomy. The first Cabinet was characterised as a technocracy, or a team of ministers committed to 'getting the job done'.[1] However, starting with the ministerial reshuffles

1. Personal communications, Aka Lewanika, Lusaka, June 1, 1995 and September 17, 1996. The emphasis on personal qualifications over political experience was also illustrated by the choice of ministers for the first Cabinet. The Ministries of Finance and Commerce were given to private businessmen, Emmaunel Kasonde and Ronald Penza, the first Minister of Health was a medical doctor, Boniface Kavimbe, and the Minister of Agriculture was a large commercial farmer, Guy Scott.

in the spring of 1993, a number of changes could be observed. According to the first Minister of Agriculture, who at this stage was dismissed from the Cabinet:

> The 1991 government was really a technocracy. Previous Permanent Secretaries were now appointed as ministers ... we were all experts in our fields. This all changed in 1993 when Chiluba set out to consolidate his power base and get rid of challenges. He [President Chiluba] then abandoned the idea of the various ministries being in control of things and abandoned the idea of ministerial management teams.[1]

The Imposition of a State of Emergency (1993)

The previous chapter argued that the government's honeymoon from open criticism voiced by economic interest associations was sustained until late 1993. The political strains of keeping the loosely structured coalition government together, however, began to make themselves felt in the spring of 1993. Increasingly, factionalism within the MMD party unfolded. The political period of grace from its political opposition and the national and international press came to an end with the decision to reinstate state of emergency laws on March 4, 1993. This decision followed the discovery in February 1993 of a plan by some members of the former ruling party (UNIP) to topple the government.[2] President Kaunda had maintained a state of emergency throughout his rule and its removal constituted one of the main political topics during MMD's 1991 electoral campaign. The re-implementation of this unpopular legislation, in the face of threats of UNIP resurgence, was opposed by both MMD and opposition Members of Parliament. In addition, the decision provoked sharp criticisms from the international press and the international donor community.[3] The state of emergency was proposed to last for three months but was lifted after nine weeks, under pressure from the international donor community (see discussion in Chapter 6). Considering the short duration of this policy measure, the most critical aspect of the short spell of state of emergency law was the manner in which the law was implemented. Reminiscent of political practices of the Second Republic, MMD used its parliamentary majority to push through this controversial piece of legislation, including verbal threats to MMD back-benchers raising critical remarks during the parliamentary debates.[4]

Power Consolidation and Emerging Executive Dominance

The conflicts deepened further in April 1993. At this time, a major ministerial reshuffle resulted in the departure of several of the 'key reform ministers' from the MMD Cabinet. Among the dismissed were the Minister of Finance,

1. Personal interview, Guy Scott. Lusaka, September 13, 1996.
2. The document, named "The Zero Option Plan", aimed at making Zambia ungovernable through acts of civil disobedience. This discovery, together with what President Chiluba referred to as a grave political and crime situation in the country, were the major reasons cited for the re-invocation of the state of emergency laws. 26 opposition members with a basis in UNIP were detained. Those arrested included the son of Kenneth Kaunda.
3. Official Verbatim Report of the Parliamentary Debates of the Second Session of the 7th National Assembly (15 January to 18 March 1993). The Parliament debated the State of Emergency 10–11th March. See also *Africa Confidential*: "Zambia: The Model Democracy Loses Its Shine", Vol. 34, No. 10, (May) 1993. On the reactions from the international donor community, see Chapter 6.
4. The State of Emergency was ratified in Parliament with 114 against 23 votes.

Emmanuel Kasonde, the Minister of Agriculture, Guy Scott, the Minister of Mines, Humphrey Mulemba, and the Minister of Education, Arthur Wina. The reshuffles brought to public attention that MMD was a deeply divided party. Increasingly, the political conflicts became reported in the local press as a struggle for control of the party between the new politicians entering the political arena in 1991 with a background in business or academia and the so-called 'seasoned veterans' who had political experience from the Second Republic.[1] Again reminiscent of political practices of the one-party era, Chiluba refused to explain to the public why these ministers were dismissed. Both the political handling of the declaration of the state of emergency and the cabinet reshuffles reflected that the MMD government did not see the need to engage in political coalition-building or to enter into public debates to explain its policies.

The April 1993 ministerial reshuffles were followed by the establishment of a new party, the National Party (NP). The NP was led by a number of the founding members of MMD who by now had either resigned from the MMD government (Aka Lewanika and Baldwin Nkumbula) or been dismissed (Humphrey Mulemba, Arthur Wina and Emmanuel Kasonde). The establishment of the NP created a new channel for the opposition and was followed by a series of defections from MMD. By November, the number of resignations of MMD elected Members of Parliament had reached 11, and the government announced that these seats were to be contested in by-elections. MMD took these elections very seriously and both the President and the vice-President toured all the contested constituencies. Again paralleling the political practices of the Second Republic, the November 1993 by-elections were characterised by a focus on ethnicity rather than policy. Furthermore, a notable facet of the ruling party's campaign was the commandeering of vehicles from the by now cash-starved parastatal companies. MMD had condemned UNIP for such practices throughout the 1991 parliamentary and presidential election campaign. However, answering the criticism raised by the independent press about MMD continuing this practice of the Second Republic, the deputy secretary of MMD argued that: "To demand that there must be a line between government and the party is academic. You will not find it anywhere else" (*The Weekly Post,* November 12, 1993). The National Party won four out of the eight contested seats.[2] By the end of November, four other prominent 'founding members' of MMD had resigned from government.

The 1993 by-elections for the first time signalled that the MMD government was regressing from its democratic agenda and reverting to policy patterns established during the one-party era. With former UNIP politicians gaining more prominent positions in the Cabinet, patterns of one-party dominance became evident. By late 1993, the initial tolerance of difference of opinion within the Cabinet was largely gone (*EIU Country Report,* 4th Quarter 1993; Nordlund 1996:132). During its election campaign, MMD had promised to run a corruption-free and transparent government. However, already in 1992 two

1. "Why the MMD cracks widened into a split", *The Weekly Post,* August 13–19 1993.
2. Most attention was given to the Matole province, where Emmanuel Kasonde was fighting to retain his seat under the NP banner. According to *Africa Confidential,* Kasonde lost his by-election bid in a contest marked by ethnic slurs and probable fraud: "Zambia: Defeat and Defections", Vol. 34, No. 25, (December 17), 1993.

ministers, Nkumbula and Lewanika, resigned from government citing frustration with the increasing levels of corruption within government as the main reason for their resignations.[1] From late 1993 onwards the reporting in the independent press increasingly focused on the issue of corruption.

In the summer of 1994, the 'generational power struggle' within MMD became a public issue when a team of young politicians within MMD launched a campaign to remove the UNIP veterans from the MMD leadership. Referring to their group as either 'the Young Turks' or 'the Progressives', a group of MMD Cabinet members and MPs presented a 'Vision Statement' aiming to move the party back onto its initial democratic path and further, to recreate an atmosphere of tolerance of criticism and difference of opinion (*Times of Zambia,* July 20, 1994). The reactions from the so-called 'old guard' paralleled the handling of political dissent in the Second Republic. Claiming that the 'Young Turks' were not true Zambians and that the issues raised were tribal rather than national, senior MMD Cabinet members, many with a long-standing political background in UNIP, invariably dismissed the dissenters as irresponsible and disgusting (*Times of Zambia,* July 21 and July 22, 1994). The conflict within MMD between 'the young guard and the old' appeared settled in favour of the latter when Chiluba in March 1995 publicly attacked discontented younger politicians for seeing older politicians as a mere obstacle to their own political ambitions (*EIU Country Report,* 2nd Quarter 1995:7). The President then issued a directive banning members of the MMD National Executive Committee from holding meetings without permission from the party secretariat and dismissed two deputy ministers identified with the 'Young Turks' group, Derrick Chitala and Dean Mung'omba, from the Cabinet.

The Return of Kenneth Kaunda

The internal conflicts within MMD displayed by the 1994 events illustrated the lack of party discipline in MMD. Perhaps indicating the weakly institutionalised parties in Zambia more generally, similar events unfolded within UNIP. In September 1994, Kenneth Kaunda let his intentions to return to national politics be publicly known (*Times of Zambia,* September 12, 1994). Kaunda made it clear that he wanted to return to the leadership of UNIP. Kaunda's return to politics divided the UNIP party between those who wanted the party to go back to the days of Kaunda and the 'modernisers' who wanted to develop an alternative economic programme and a new style of democracy under its present leadership of Kebby Musokotwane. Despite obvious disregard for democratic practices, at an extraordinary UNIP Congress in February 1995, Kebby Musokotwane lost by a clear margin to Kenneth Kaunda.[2] The return of Kenneth Kaunda seemed

1. Upon resigning from his Cabinet position, Baldwin Nkumbula called for an extraordinary MMD convention to discuss remedy measures against the growing corruption within the party (*The Weekly Post,* July 17–23, 1992).
2. According to the *New African,* when fist fights broke out between rival factions at the UNIP headquarters, paramilitary police had to disperse the crowds in what the 'modernising wing of UNIP' referred to as a well rehearsed act by Kaunda to claim back the party leadership (April, 1995:31. See also *EIU Country Report,* 1st Quarter, 1995).

to revitalise the former ruling party. In the 1995 by-elections UNIP won seats in former 'MMD territory'.[1]

By 1995, a number of incidents indicated that the political leadership of MMD had placed consolidation of political power at the centre of their political concerns. With the exit of reformers from the Cabinet, ethnic conflicts became more apparent and ministerial appointments to an increasing degree reflected President Chiluba's Bemba background (Simutanyi 1997; Bratton and Posner 1999). With Kenneth Kaunda's return, the politics of personal vendetta also reappeared (*EIU Country Report*, 2nd and 3rd Quarter 1995). Throughout 1995 and 1996, harassment of critical voices within the party and the independent press, as well as increasing checks on the freedom of civil society associations, dominated the national political arena. However, the issue that brought the actual political liberalisation process into question was the handling of the constitutional amendment process.

Power Consolidation through Constitutional Amendments

One of MMD's central promises during the 1991 election campaign was to rewrite the constitution to offer stronger protection of civil liberties and ensure the de-linkage of the party and the government. However, the process of constitutional reform did not commence until late 1993 when a 24-member review commission (The Mwanakatwe Commission) was appointed to collect views from the general public and propose a draft constitution (GRZ 1995b). The commission released its report in June 1995 and the government responded to the report with a Government White Paper that upheld many of the commission's proposals (GRZ 1995a). Among several contentious provisions contained in the commission report, and accepted in the White Paper, was a clause requiring both parents of any presidential candidate to be Zambians by birth. This provision effectively disqualified former President Kenneth Kaunda, whose parents were born in Malawi, from contesting the 1996 elections. This clause, while supported by many petitioners to the Mwanakatwe commission, was widely interpreted as an attempt by MMD to remove its most powerful potential opponent from the 1996 elections.[2] The Constitutional Review Commission's recommendation to adopt the constitution in a national referendum was, however, ignored. The government preferred instead to proceed with the immediate adoption of the constitution by the MMD controlled parliament. This decision provoked a fierce public debate involving opposition parties, civil society groups and representatives of the donor community. Arguably, the adoption of the constitution

1. 14 by-elections were held between August 29 and October 10, following defections from the various parties and deaths of several Members of Parliament. MMD won 7 seats, UNIP 3. Between 1991 and 1996 48 by-elections took place in Zambia. 8 parties contested these elections, but only MMD, UNIP and NP succeeded in winning seats. Voter turnout was generally low, around 20 per cent (Foundation for Democratic Process (FODEP): By-election reports 1992–1996; Polhemus 1997; Simutanyi 1997).

2. Another provision requiring that traditional chiefs abdicate their positions before being eligible for elected political office was similarly interpreted as an effort to disqualify UNIP's vice-presidential candidate, Senior Chief Inyambo Yeta. Further evidence that barring UNIP and Kenneth Kaunda and UNIP's candidacy was the real purpose of the clause is supported by the chants "We've defeated Kaunda" by MMD Members of Parliament following the adoption of the constitution. *The Post*, May 16, 1996.

provoked such controversy due to the issues at stake. Kaunda's return to the UNIP presidency was perceived as a real threat to MMD's continued rule. UNIP was the only party in Zambia with a largely intact grass root administrative structure. Through ownership of profitable local companies, the party was also in a position to carry out a nation-wide election campaign. The ratification of the constitution by the MMD-dominated parliament blocked Kaunda's candidacy and effectively eliminated UNIP's realistic chance of competing with the MMD in the 1996 elections (Bratton and Posner 1999). Despite the efforts and protests by non-governmental organisations, political opposition parties and the international community, the government went ahead and adopted the constitution in parliament. After a heated debate, the Parliament passed the Constitutional Amendment Bill on May 21, 1996. On May 28, the President signed the bill into law. Protest rallies against the constitution and threats by the major opposition parties to boycott the 1996 elections were followed by a series of bomb attacks in Lusaka and in the Copperbelt. Eight UNIP leaders, including the vice-presidential candidate, were detained and charged with treason and the murder of a policeman who had been killed during the bombings.

The 1996 Elections

The revision of the voters' registry was a second controversial issue in the months leading up to the 1996 general elections. Following months of delay and a tender procedure fraught with irregularities, the government awarded the contract to an Israeli-based firm (Nikuv Computers) in December 1995. Three months later, the exercise concluded with only 2.3 million registrations out of an estimated voting population of 4.6 million. By June 1996, a number of major NGOs, opposition parties, and the independent press, joined by the international donor community, were ready to conclude that the process of political liberalisation begun in 1991 had been abandoned. Following a heated discussion on the timing of the elections, the government on October 14 announced that parliamentary and presidential elections would be held on November 18. Four days later, UNIP and six smaller opposition parties declared that they would boycott both the presidential and parliamentary elections, citing the government's mismanagement of the voter registration process as their main reason. UNIP also announced that it would campaign to encourage citizens not to participate in the 1996 elections.

Despite the boycott, MMD still faced challenges from five opposition parties. MMD's election campaign was similar to the one conducted by UNIP and Kenneth Kaunda in 1991. MMD candidates enjoyed the use of government vehicles. Furthermore, fertiliser, maize and development funds were distributed to attract supporters in the rural constituencies (*The Monitor* 1996; Baylies and Szeftel 1997; *SAPEM*, October 1996:5). In a pre-election bid, the Cabinet announced that 9,000 government houses would be sold to sitting tenants (*Times of Zambia*, April 17, 1996). Reminiscent of the 1991 elections, the Foundation for Democratic Process (FODEP) found: "Glaring disparities in the allocation

Table 5.1: Parliamentary election results 1996

Party	Candidates	No of seats
MMD	150	131
Independents	99	10
NP	83	5
ZDC	141	2
AZ	11	2
NLP	83	0
UNIP*	2	0
Others	9	0
Total	**594**	**150**

* UNIP as a party boycotted the parliamentary elections; two UNIP candidates nevertheless ran on the UNIP label.
Sources: 1991/1996: Krennerich (1999), Gould 2002: 312, 2001; http://www.elections.org.zm/p-cand/par-candidates.html.

Table 5.2: Presidential election results 1996

Candidate	Total no. of votes	Percentage vote
Frederick Chiluba (MMD	913,770	72.6
Dean Mung'omba (ZDC)	160,439	12.7
Humprey Mulemba (NP)	83,875	6.7
Akashambatwa Mbikusita-Lewanika (AZ)	59,250	4.7
Chama Chakomboka (MDP)	41,471	3.3

Sources: Krennerich (1999)

of air-time and space among the main contenders in the election".[1] The independently owned newspapers, which published critical articles and editorials on the way the election exercise was carried out, were increasingly exposed to harassment by MMD supporters and the police.[2]

The election day itself proceeded peacefully. Challenged by four other presidential candidates, Chiluba won his re-election in another landslide victory with 73 per cent of the vote. In the parliamentary elections, MMD captured 131 of 150 the parliamentary seats. Zambia Democratic Congress (ZDC) won 14 per cent of the vote but only managed to secure two seats. The National Party (NP) and the Agenda for Zambia (AZ) captured five and two seats respectively. Independent candidates won 10 constituencies. The 1996 election results were clear. Judged by their outcome, the 1996 Zambian election was a triumph for the ruling party MMD, and President Chiluba wasted no time before he declared the election result an endorsement of MMD's political and economic

1. "How Some Monitors Arrived at 'Not a Free and Fair' Verdict", *The Monitor*, November 29–December 5, 1996.
2. Human Rights Watch/Africa Report claims that *The Post* was the target of twenty acts of harassment by the government or its supporters between January 1994 and October 1996. "Zambia: Elections and Human Rights in the Third Republic", December 1996:23–24.

record (*The Post,* November 21, 1996). However, as evidence of democratic consolidation, the elections were deficient. The flaws related in particular to the process leading up to the 1996 elections including harassment of the press, NGOs, and interest groups and culminated with the adoption of the constitutional amendments. Immediately after the 1996 elections, disquiet among monitoring groups and opposition parties was voiced. The complaints focused on the conduct of the elections, the electoral campaign and the legal-constitutional structures and mechanisms under which they were held. It was particularly the last issue that led most local monitoring groups to arrive at the conclusion that the elections had not been free and fair (*The Monitor*/FODEP 1996). Yet, despite the boycott and the electoral funds at MMD's disposal, observers argued that, overall, the elections in 1996 served as an indication of MMD's ability to convince voters that it should be given another five year term.[1]

Political Developments in the Second Chiluba Administration (1996–2001)

Necessitated by the substantial cuts in donor support, the re-elected MMD government began a process of regaining democratic credibility in early 1997. One of the first important moves was to discard the drafted media bill that required all media institutions to be registered with the state. Second, a number of semi-autonomous institutions of restraint were created. These included transferring the conduct of election administration from the Office of the vice-President to an independent Electoral Commission of Zambia (1996), the delinking of the Anti-Corruption Commission (ACC) from the presidency, and the creation of a permanent Human Rights Commission (1997). In addition, presidential appointment to the Drug Enforcement Commission required parliamentary approval from 1997.

The main institutional reforms aimed at strengthening democratic accountability in the post-1996 election period were pushed by the international donor community. The domestic political agenda was, however, characterised by verbal attacks against individuals and a complete lack of trust between the government, the opposition parties, media, and the NGO community. The 1996 election results were not accepted as legitimate by the Zambian opposition. In 1997 the opposition parties grouped under the National Patriotic Coalition (NPC). Encouraged by the international donor community, as most main bilateral donors had made a dialogue between the government and the opposition a condition for aid resumption, the government and the NPC started a process of dialogue. But meetings organised by the International Institute for Democracy and Electoral Assistance (IDEA) in Stockholm with representatives from all the major opposition parties and the MMD were not successful as there was no agreement on the terms of negotiation. The NPC proposals included the repeal

1. Based on a national probability sample survey of 1,182 Zambian adults conducted immediately after the November 18-elections, a team of researchers from Michigan State University and the Institute of African Studies (UNZA) concluded that most Zambian citizens endorsed the integrity of the 1996 elections. The 1996 post-election survey found that 43.2 per cent of Zambians assessed the overall performance of the MMD government as good or very good, whereas only 21.7 per cent saw it as poor or very poor (Bratton et al. 1997).

of the 1996 constitution, nullifying the 1996 elections and setting up an interim government leading to the establishment of a constitutional assembly to draft a new constitution and preparing new elections (*Times of Zambia*, June 27, 1997). None of the suggestions from IDEA, including proposals for a bill of rights, were taken up by the opposition coalition. The government, in turn, refused to discuss the proposals put forth by the opposition (*Times of Zambia*, June 30, 1997).

Despite having secured a second term in office through a comfortable electoral majority, President Chiluba and the government displayed an increasingly more uncompromising attitude towards the opposition from 1997 onwards. Political opponents, journalists, and non-governmental organisations were frequently raided by the police. The government also used economic means to silence the opposition.[1] According to Zambian media analysts, in the post-1996 election period the investigative reporting of the independent media declined due to self-censorship caused by economic threats from the MMD government through tax-harassment and the increasing costs of libel suits.[2] In August 1997, the political tensions between the government and the opposition intensified when the police opened fire on Kenneth Kaunda and Roger Chongwe at a political rally organised by the opposition in Kabwe.

The 1997 Coup d'Etat Attempt

October 28, 1997 Chiluba survived a coup attempt by two junior officers. Despite the fact that the Zambian police gained control of the radio station and arrested the soldiers after three hours, Chiluba declared a state of emergency. The MMD government immediately linked the coup to vague pronouncements by Kenneth Kaunda weeks before that an uprising was imminent. 17 high-profile members of the opposition were arrested, including ZDC's leader Dean Mung'obma. On December 25, Kenneth Kaunda was placed under house arrest for alleged participation in the October coup. The political tension continued in 1998 as the state of emergency was extended for another three months. In February 1998 the alleged coup plotters—including Mung'omba—were formally charged with treason. The government finally lifted the state of emergency laws in March 1998. June 1, Kenneth Kaunda was released from detention on condition that he retired from national politics and he immediately announced his intention to retire as President of UNIP. Dean Mung'omba and Nakatindi Wina were released shortly after when Chief Justice Japhet Banda ruled that their trial had been unreasonably delayed.

In late 1998, the political climate in Zambia appeared to have settled and opposition parties began to focus on the upcoming 2001 elections rather than the flawed 1996 elections. Shortly before the December 1998 local government

1. As an example, the Foundation for Democratic Process's (FODEP) critical report on the 1996 elections prompted the Zambia Revenue Authorities to withdraw its tax-exempt status and submit a substantial back-dated tax bill and to confiscate FODEP assets. AFRONET Communiqué May 1997. (http://www.afronet.org.za); Barraclough 1998.
2. Personal communications, M. Phiri, Zambia Independent Media Association. Lusaka, October 17, 2000.

elections the United Party for National Development (UPND) was formed. Under the leadership of Anderson Mazoka, a former director of Anglo-American Corporation, UPND gained 28 seats in the 1998 local government elections. In 1999, the Zambia Alliance for Progress (ZAP) was established, representing a novelty in contemporary Zambian politics as for the first time, an attempt was made to form a coalition. ZAP's success was limited, however. In order to join the ZAP-alliance, the parties had to resign their parliamentary seats. In the September 2000 by-elections Zambia Democratic Congress's (ZDC) seats were lost to MMD, and two opposition parties who had opted *not* to join the alliance, UNIP and UPND. Arguably, ZDC experiences served as a warning to other parties and before the 2001 elections.

The Third Term Debate

Despite Chiluba's public statements on at least six occasions indicating that he would step down at the end of his second term as required by the 1996 constitutional amendments, by late 1999 it was clear to most observers that he now harboured different thoughts. While Chiluba never officially stated that he intended to stand for a third term his actions indicated that he would very much like to. Public speculations about Chiluba's intentions increased when Chiluba in early 2000 refused to name a successor and warned his cabinet members about stating presidential ambitions, allegedly to prevent open conflict within MMD (Burnell 2003:5). After a series of MMD by-election victories in September 2000 the third term campaign intensified. By January 2001 a campaign was under way to secure the removal of the two-term limit from the constitution and from MMD's own articles regarding the presidency of the party. According to MMD, a referendum would offer the Zambian public a chance to decide whether Chiluba should be granted another term in office to finish the development projects he had initiated in 1991. While never official stating so, Chiluba appeared to support the campaign that was given ample financial support. As a further indication of the president's intentions, in the February 2001 cabinet reshuffles he removed several ministers known to oppose his third term bid.

The budget presented to Parliament in January 2001 set aside US$ 400 million for the establishment of 72 positions as District Administrators (DAs). The official reason given for the establishment of the new local government structure was to improve service delivery in the rural areas. But while the DAs were considered civil servants, they were provided with vehicles and offices outside the formal local government structures. Placed in control of the crucial Constituency Development Funds that provide much of the small-scale finance for government projects, the district administrators' privileges sharply contrasted with the working conditions of local government councillors. The district administrators were personally appointed by Chiluba and were structured to report directly to the Presidential Office. Just like the position of District Governors introduced by UNIP during the one-party era and scrapped by MMD in 1991, the District Administrators represented a politicisation of the civil service.

Despite considerable and growing opposition inside and outside the party, at a controversial party convention in April 2002, MMD voted to nominate Chiluba for a third term as president of the MMD party. Most observers assumed that this would pave the way for MMD's attempt to alter the 1996 Zambian constitution. Shortly after, the vice-President Christon Tembo and eight other cabinet dissenters were expelled from MMD for opposing the third term campaign. Some months later (August) a Tribunal found MMD's Minister of Home Affairs and the Minister of Works and Supply guilty of corruption as K 2 billion was diverted from district road funds to fund the MMD convention. In a parallel process, one third of the Members of Parliament, including 50 MMD MPs, delivered the Parliamentary Speaker notice of a motion to impeach the President. But, the motion was dismissed by the Speaker who argued that the issue could only be solved once the expulsion of the MMD Cabinet members and MPs from parliament had been finalised.

The attempt by President Chiluba and the MMD to gain yet another term in office was met with a massive, and well co-ordinated, response from the Zambian public. In February 2001 a coalition of civic organisations, including the Law Association, the Zambia Episcopal Conference and the Non-Governmental Organisation Co-ordination committee adopted the Oasis Declaration opposing the third term bid. Between February and early May 2001, a number of public demonstrations and debates took place indicating that the Zambian civil society exhibited a degree of strength, national reach and organisational capacity. When President Chiluba on May 5 announced to the public on Zambian Public TV that he had no intention of running as MMD's presidential candidate, the third term debate effectively ended. But the third term issue drained the Zambian state of considerable resources, split the ruling party, and suggested to the Zambian public and international observers that the ruling party's regard for the democratic process was, at best, shallow. As argued by Burnell (2002:1111), ensuring that a highly controversial issue was thrust into public debate, the opposition (and MMD) was distracted from an early and concerted programme of electoral registration. Further, by focusing on Chiluba personally, the opposition was diverted from targeting MMD's poor socio-economic performance (Ibid.).

The MMD's choice of Levy Patrick Mwanawasa as presidential candidate in August 2001 accentuated division in the MMD party and led to widespread speculations that Chiluba had hand-picked his successor whom he could manipulate. According to MMD's statutes, Mwanawasa should have been elected at the party's National Convention and not by the National Executive Committee, as was the case. The election of Mwanawasa as the presidential candidate resulted in the exit of MMD's influential National Secretary Michael Sata who had been in the forefront of Chiluba's "third-term" campaign from its inception.[1]

1. After resigning from the party that did not give him a chance to run for the presidency or vice-President Sata claimed that he had never supported Chiluba's 'third-term' bid, but had merely been defending the government and party position and he "was merely doing his job as the party's chief executive". *The Post*, October 15, 2001.

Shortly after leaving the MMD Sata announced that he was going to run for the presidency under the newly formed party, the Patriotic Front (PF).

The 2001 Presidential, Parliamentary and Local Government Elections

In the December 27, 2001 elections the voters had a choice between 11 presidential candidates and in several constituencies almost as many parliamentary candidates to choose from. The elections resulted in a fragmented but better-balanced parliament than in the two previous elections. MMD kept the presidency, but Levy Mwanawasa's mandate was exceedingly weak. Patrick Levy Mwanawasa of MMD was sworn in as Zambia's new president on January 2, 2002, after the most closely contested elections witnessed in the country. According to the results published by the Electoral Commission of Zambia (ECZ) Mwanawasa beat his main rival, Anderson Mazoka of United Party for National Development (UPND) by just under 34,000 votes, or by 1.9 per cent of the votes cast. Only 19.5 per cent of the registered voters voted for Mwanawasa, or approximately 10 per cent of those eligible to vote. 71.3 per cent of the votes cast were in favour of the other ten candidates, leaving Mwanawasa with the weakest electoral mandate for any previous president with 29 per cent of the total vote. The presidential contest was a three-way race between Movement for Multiparty Democracy (MMD), United Party for National Development (UPND) and Forum for Democracy and Development (FDD). The parliamentary elections reduced the MMD dominance as after the 2001 elections MMD controlled approximately 50 per cent of the seats (including the 8 seats selected by the presidency) whereas after the 1996 elections MMD controlled 87 per cent of the seats. The turnout of 67 per cent of the registered voters was higher than expected, given that the vote took place during the rainy season and that polling day was not declared a public holiday.

However, local and international election reports accused the government of failing to honour the promise to create a level playing-field for the elections. Furthermore, the voter registration level of only 55 per cent of the people eligible to vote was characterised as too low, creating the suspicion that potential voters had been deterred from registering. As the election campaign got under way, the District Administrators intervened in the electoral process to the advantage of the MMD by campaigning for the MMD candidates in the district. The DAs continued to be active campaigners for MMD despite a High Court ruling of December 4, 2001 declaring that, as civil servants, they were not permitted to engage in political activity. In addition, the international election reports concluded that the state media had been campaigning for the MMD.

Based on the electoral preparations, actual conduct and post-election handling FODEP, Afronet, Coalition 2001, the Carter Centre and the EU election monitoring team all concluded that the results should be questioned (*Monitor* December 15–21, 2001; Mulwanda 2002). Both the local and international observer teams concluded that in view of the administrative failures in the pre-election period; the biased electoral playing-field; serious flaws in the counting and tabulation procedures, together with the close outcome of the elections, they

Table 5.3: Parliamentary election results, 2001

Party	Candidates	No of seats
MMD	150	69
UPND	149	49
UNIP	144	13
FDD	146	12
HP	114	4
ZRP	138	1
PF	103	1
ZAP	17	0
AZ	16	0
NLD	17	0
SDP	7	0
Independents	84	1
Total	**1085**	**150**

Source: 2001: Electoral Commission of Zambia: http://www.elections.org.zm/results

Table 5.4: Presidential election results 2001

Candidate	Total no. of votes	Percentage vote
Levy Mwanawasa (MMD	506,694	29.2
Anderson Mazoka (UPND)	472,697	27.2
Christon Tembo (FDD)	228,861	13.2
Tilyenji Kaunda (UNIP)	175,898	10.2
Godfrey Miyanda (HP)	140,678	8.1
Benjamin Y. Mwila (ZRP)	85,472	4.9
Micahel Sata (PF)	59,172	3.2
Nevers S. Mumba (NCC	38,860	2.2
Yobert Shamapande (NLD)	9,481	0.6
Gwendoline C. Konnie (SDP)	10,253	0.6
Inonge Mbikusita-Lewanika (AZ)	9,882	0.5

Source: 2001: Electoral Commission of Zambia: http://www.elections.org.zm/results

could not be confident that the declared results represented the wishes of the Zambian electors (Meadowcroft 2002; EUEU 2002). Similar to the post-election period in 1996/97, by mid-2002 courts started hearings in a lawsuit brought by three of the losing presidential candidates in the 2001 election. The contestants claimed that the court should annul the election due to irregularities prior to the election as well as in the conduct of the elections themselves. In addition, a total of 40 losing parliamentary candidates filed petitions challenging the results of the elections. Whether or not their claims are accepted by the court, the case illustrates the same lack of trust in the electoral process amongst the opposition parties in 2001 as in 1996.[1]

1. UN Integrated Regional Information Networks, February 5, 2002. (http://alllafrica.com/stories/printable/200202050147.html)

Political Liberalisation and the Decline of Interest Groups

In 1991, Zambia re-implemented multiparty democracy. Since then, Zambia has arranged three multiparty contests and therefore seems 'on track' for democratic consolidation. However—from a promising start in 1991—Zambia did not progress in this way. Despite the adherence to a multiparty constitution, local and international observers argue that Zambia's democratisation process stagnated mid-way through Chiluba's first election period. What can explain why MMD maintained power through the 1990s, despite a dismal record in terms of economic governance and human rights? When by 1993/94 the major economic interest associations, human rights associations and churches stated that they had lost faith in MMD, why did not other parties emerge that could benefit from the societal discontent this displayed? The 2001 electoral outcome clearly indicated that the Zambian population wanted change as 71 per cent of the electorate cast their vote for an opposition candidate/party.

Chapter 4 argued that the effects of the economic reforms split some interest associations and that reduced membership as a result of economic decline further marginalised these associations' influence. In the next section, it will become evident that the process of political liberalisation *further* weakened the position of interest groups due to the combined effects of organisational proliferation, the weakly institutionalised party system, and growing executive dominance witnessed in Zambia's Third Republic.

Organisational Proliferation

The Weakening Voice of Business

From 1995 onwards, the position of business towards the MMD government changed quite markedly. The controversy surrounding the government's abortive and costly attempt to bail out the Meridian Bank BIAO in the spring of 1995 was the one issue cited by business representatives in which they started to doubt the commitment of the MMD government to economic reforms. Apart from the economic repercussions and the set-back to the economic reform programme caused by the government bail-out, the political aspects of the government's handling of the 'Meridian Bank Saga' was possibly more damaging. From business and other sources it was alleged that senior government officials may have benefited from the bank's demise (*Mail and Guardian*, July 21–28, 1995; *Profit*, June 1995). Suspicion of 'political logic' having guided the Meridian decision was expressed by most members of the business community. In an editorial article in the monthly magazine *Profit*, a very direct and damaging critique of the government's lack of transparency and accountability was presented (*Profit*, December 1995). This unusually harsh critique was followed up by ZACCI's condemnation of the government's handling of the constitutional amendment process. The government's lack of interest in consulting with the business associations as the 1996 elections approached was indicated by MMD's refusal to take part in a ZACCI-organised forum where the government and opposition parties were invited to present their economic agendas.[1] Following the criticism voiced by business, the government stopped calling the formal meetings between business and government. In the period 1996–2001 meetings became sporadic, and increasingly business representatives were met by junior ministers when they called on government.[2]

The Decline of Labour

As indicated by the discussion above (part one) in the period leading up to the 1996 elections, the political agenda in Zambia was captured by electoral and civic education NGOs and the political opposition parties. The issues concerning the constitutional amendment process and the voter registry overshadowed most economic issues. In the period 1996–2001, this situation was largely maintained due to the large number of NGOs established in the 1990s, and these associations' organisational and financial strength vis-à-vis the interest associations representing business, and labour.[3] Illustrating the way organisational proliferation marginalised labour, the trade union movement sided with the opposition in calling for the 1996 constitution to be adopted by a constitutional council (*Times of Zambia*, October 15, 1995). However, the stand of the trade unions received little media attention. According to Simutanyi:

> Given the adoption of the multiparty system in the country, the political role of the trade unions has declined. The role that used to be played by trade unions during the Second Republic is now being carried out by political opposition parties that are now taking on the state on a number of policies and interest groups have reverted to their roles as political pressure groups. (1995:210)

In addition, political pluralism also opened up for trade union proliferation and the break-up of the strong union federation established in 1971. The provision of 'one industry one union' was observed in the 1993, that replaced the 1990, Industrial Relations Act.[4] However, the clause forbidding the forming of more than one union federation came into conflict with the new Zambian Constitution guaranteeing freedom of association as well as the government's decision in 1996 to ratify the International Labour Organisation's (ILO) conventions 87 and 98 allowing for multiple trade union centres. ZCTU perceived the lifting of the 'one industry one union clause' in the new labour relations act from 1997 as being implemented in bad faith to weaken the trade union movement (Banda 1997). Under Kaunda's leadership, a strong and unified trade union movement was created with a basis in an industrial relations act guaranteeing ZCTU monopoly representation and secure finances (IR 1971). Ironically, when faced

1. The meeting was held on September 12, 1996 and all the main opposition parties were present.
2. Personal communications, Theo Bull, hotel-owner and ZACCI-member. Lusaka October 20, 2000 and July 22, 2001. The views were supported by ZACCI's acting executive director Nelson Chisenga, save for the formal consultations on the PRSP document (interviewed December 28, 2002 by Dr. E. Bwalya on request of author).
3. The financial capacity of Zambian NGOs is of course closely related to donor funding.
4. The new Industrial Relations Act of 1993, which replaced the 1990 Act, was by most observers regarded as a concession to the labour movement for its role in the transition process, as the unions managed to re-institute the clause of 'one industry one union' to maintain trade union strength (*The Post*, October 25, 1994; Simutanyi 1995).

with pluralist politics, involving competition for members, funds and attention, the trade union movement was no longer protected by a law granting it monopoly representation and funding. As argued by one informant:

> Chiluba and his contemporaries did not have to organise, they were handed everything on a silver platter. ... In sum unions must [now] learn to live without the help of the law. ... They [unions] must devise better ways to organise themselves and bargain more aggressively.[1]

Thus, by 1996, economic reforms as well as political liberalisation had reduced the influence of the trade union movement. Increasingly, the position of ZCTU was compromised by either the government or one of the unaffiliated unions accusing ZCTU of 'second Republic mentality' and inability to change with the new political and economic realities (*Financial Mail,* August 10–16, 1994). In 1995, the President of ZCTU issued a statement to the press indicating that in the absence of strong opposition parties to MMD, ZCTU would again assume the role of the opposition centre due to the experiences of workers with economic reform. In response, a representative of the MMD government accused ZCTU of living in the past, and like a dinosaur, being unable to adapt to a new policy environment (*Financial Mail,* January 10–16, 1995). The frustrations felt within the trade union movement with regard to finding its place in the new political and economic environment were expressed by a ZCTU representative:

> We have voiced our concern. We have had discussions with government prior to the liquidation of UBZ and Zambia Airways. They said the airline would not be liquidated, then something happens ... Chirwa or Shamenda [General Secretary and President of ZCTU] goes to the press. The same day one person from one of the 35 opposition parties defects to MMD and that steals the news headlines. Due to this crowded public agenda, people and our members may think we are not doing anything, but that is wrong. But we have to appreciate that the environment has changed. Before it was only UNIP and ZCTU. ... Now there are lots of NGOs and political parties. The result is that there is more competition for our voice to be heard. Before, even the law [labour legislation] was assisting us.[2]

The Reduced Role of Agricultural Interests

Contrary to business and to some extent labour, in terms of their large number and thus electoral potential, agricultural producers constituted the largest potential 'winning coalition' or electoral threat, to MMD. However, the dualism in Zambian agriculture made it impossible for agricultural producers to lobby the government in a coherent and unified manner. In the period before the 1996 and 2001 elections, the coverage of the agricultural liberalisation process in the local press indicated that the rural people had a number of channels to voice their views and concerns, despite their organisational weakness. Members of Parliament were one important channel. Debates in the parliament increasingly revolved around the problems facing the small-scale producers, the problems of maize remaining uncollected in the villages and so forth. Both in terms of reporting the parliamentary debates and its independent coverage, the local media rep-

1. Personal interview, Robinson Sikazwe, Regional Consultant, Norwegian Confederation of Trade Unions (LO). Lusaka, November 28, 1996.
2. Personal communications, Alfred Mudenda, Assistant General Secretary ZCTU. Kitwe, December 3, 1996.

resented another vital channel for the rural producers.[1] As a result of the weakness of formal associations, the press coverage focusing on more populist issues and finally, rural MPs concerned with re-election, the public attention on agricultural policies in Zambia was dominated by the concerns of the small-scale producers in the remote areas.

Agricultural liberalisation, contrary to the privatisation of the mines (postponed until 2000) and the public sector reform programme (discontinued), was sustained throughout the two Chiluba administrations, albeit with several reversals and confusing signals displayed. Largely reflecting the political importance attached to this issue, in both the 1996 election period and, again, before the 2001 elections there were numerous indications of reversals of MMD's liberal agricultural policies.[2] Throughout the 1990s the continued supply of fertiliser and hidden subsidies in the form of non-repayment of loans by small-scale producers disrupted a potential agricultural market and slowed down the restructuring process.[3] Further evidence of the importance attached to the rural vote was offered in 1996 when President Chiluba opened the National Assembly and announced a 29 billion Kwatcha debt relief scheme to farmers (*Times of Zambia*, January 20, 1996). Furthermore, addressing crowds in the Copperbelt, President Chiluba assured them that prices of mealie meal would soon drop (*The Post*, June 3, 1996). While ZNFU had been lobbying for debt relief since the 1993 agricultural season, the government announcement was nevertheless met with negative reactions. ZNFU's President accused the government of using a political gimmick by giving debt relief in an election year (*Times of Zambia*, January 23, 1996). The political dilemmas facing a government seeking re-election created a rather distorted policy agenda. As argued by the executive director of ZNFU:

> People are starting to want their subsidies back, and as the politicians do not really understand liberalisation either they are more or less promising to deliver that and thus giving out confusing signals. ... It is evident that the poorest farmers were better off before. Then they were at subsistence level plus. ... There should have been assistance in terms of rural infrastructure. However, here nothing happened. First the subsidies were removed, then from January 1993 the financial and agricultural sectors were liberalised. There is a tremendous lack of consistency in government policy. ... They are not following a policy of liberalisation, they are vote getters.[4]

Largely supporting the views of ZNFU regarding the lack of consistency in the government's agricultural policy, the Minister of Agriculture found that:

> ... there have been a lot of reversals which hamper the progress of liberalisation. The problem is that we have not been able to have a clear policy. The government itself has reversed. We have backtracked which has had a negative effect. Fertiliser is the main area of backtracking. This is all election induced. ... There was a fear in government that the small-

1. Headlines like "Peasant farmers stuck with maize *(Times of Zambia*, August 28, 1996); "Farmers panic over maize pricing" (*Times of Zambia*, June 18, 1996); "Will mealie meal shortages and queues cause panic?" (*The Post*, January 17, 1995) were an almost daily occurrence in the local press.
2. See Chapter 4.
3. Personal communications, Hans Hedlund, Lusaka, September 19, 1996; George Gray, ZNFU. Lusaka, October 20, 1996; and Frans van de Ven, Chief Technical Advisor, MAFF. Lusaka, November 27, 1996.
4. Personal interview, George Gray, ZNFU. Lusaka, October 2, 1996.

> scale farmers would be convinced by the UNIP and ZDC subsidy promises. As a result, government had to go back and duplicate mistakes from earlier years.[1]

Similar to business (ZACCI, ZAM) and to labour (ZCTU), ZNFU became more critical towards the MMD government's political record from 1995 onwards. In August 1996, Ben Kapita, the president of ZNFU took his criticism towards government a step further by forming a political party, the National Lima Party (NLP) together with the first Minister of Agriculture, Guy Scott. Officially, ZNFU did not advise their members to support any party. However, the support was given through the farmers' magazine, which stated that ZNFU welcomed the Lima Party as a party which would voice rural and agricultural producers' concerns (*The Farmer*, Vol. 1, No 10, September 1996). The view of ZNFU was made clear in the statement by its executive director, George Gray:

> We have great expectations of the Lima Party as they will be more attentive to the needs of farming. The Lima Party will bite the bullet of liberalisation and let the market run the show. They have a better understanding of the dichotomy within the farming community and they understand that credit is not the answer to the poorest. A stupid action like spending 10 per cent of government budget to bail out a bank will not be done by the Lima Party. ... We feel that this government [MMD] has had a waning commitment to agriculture.[2]

Thus, contrary to business interests as well as the labour movement, ZNFU was the only association of the three main sectoral interests considered to openly express support of an opposition party before the 1996 elections. However, possibly reflecting the perceived lack of electoral threat posed by ZNFU, the responses from MMD to this move were limited. MMD Cabinet ministers claimed that the National Lima Party only reflected the political ambitions of one man (*Times of Zambia*, January 23, 1996). Furthermore, the split of interest within the group of associations representing agricultural interests became clear when the Peasant Farmers Union (PFUZ) advised its members *not* to support the National Lima Party arguing that they were not for peasant farmers (*Times of Zambia*, November 1, 1996). In response to the criticism of partisanship, the National Association of Small-Scale and Peasant Farmers Union (NASSPFU) accused PFUZ of being a political front for the UNIP opposition, arguing that this was the reason why the latter organisation had refused to merge with NAPSSFU which was formed in 1989 (*Zambia Daily Mail,* August 31, 1996). The co-operative federation did not endorse a specific political party before the 1996 elections. But illustrating the proliferation of agricultural interests, in the 1996 elections the LIMA party failed to capture the vote of farmers.

The Missing Link between Economic Interests and the Party System

Contrary to agriculture, the trade union movement did not endorse a political party in the 1996 (nor 2001) elections. But ZCTU made it clear that it had withdrawn its support from MMD. ZCTU argued that government had deliberately

1. Personal interview, Simon Zukas (MAFF). Lusaka, December 13, 1996.
2. Personal interview, George Gray, ZNFU. Lusaka, October 2, 1996.

attempted to weaken the trade union movement (ZCTU 1996). The split within the Zambian labour movement was based in internal economic, political, as well as personality differences. The claims that the MMD government had engineered the conflicts at the 1994 Quadrennial Congress were not further supported by evidence. However, it is clear that the MMD government in the period after 1994 capitalised on the split in the trade union movement to further its own political agenda. The improved working relationship between the non-affiliated unions, and in particular MUZ, and the government, was indicated in the 1996 election campaign when President Chiluba announced that miners, contrary to other parastatal employees most notably in the transport sector, would be paid their terminal benefits prior to the privatisation of ZCCM (*Times of Zambia*, November 13, 1996).[1]

While increasingly more critical to the MMD government's will and ability to create a facilitating environment for business and economic growth in Zambia, ZACCI and ZAM officially supported Chiluba and MMD's bid for a second electoral term (*ZACCI Business Line*, Vol. 1, No. 6, August 1996; *Profit*, September 1996). Taking the opposition parties to task for their failure to outline their economic visions for Zambia at the September meeting, a member of ZACCI's executive board voiced an opinion that was repeated by most business representatives interviewed:

> ZACCI's position is that we want a clean government and policies that facilitate economic growth. We are greatly disappointed with MMD, however, we are more sceptical to everybody else. We invited all opposition parties to present their economic policies. The auditorium was packed with business people wanting to find out what parties had to offer. However, the results were meagre. Economic policies are almost absent from their agendas, and no one is campaigning on an economic issue.[2]

The statement above points to a fundamental flaw in the dual reform literature in terms of democratic developments in sub-Saharan Africa: the missing links between economic interests and the political party system. In Zambia in both the 1996 and 2001 elections, no party offered a political agenda that challenged MMD's economic reforms. As a result, interest groups had few available channels into the political arena.

Party Developments in the Third Republic

As argued above, in the two first multiparty elections MMD did significantly better than any of the contenders in both the presidential and parliamentary elections. Despite the weak foundations of the MMD party, the 1991 elections gave it a sweeping electoral mandate. UNIP was reduced to a regional party as its 25 parliamentary seats were all won in the Eastern Province. MMD had been established as a broad coalition, united by what it was against. It was therefore prone to dissent. Two years after the elections, senior MMD members and founders left the party arguing that corruption was rife, establishing the Nation-

1. At the time of writing (2003) miners are still awaiting their terminal benefits.
2. Personal interview, Mebelo Mutukwa, ZACCI. Lusaka, November 4, 1996.

al Party in 1993. A host of other parties were also formed by people associated with the first MMD government like Agenda Zambia, Zambia Democratic Congress, Liberal Progressive Front and the Lima Party. Despite being discredited after the 1991 elections, UNIP was the party with the greatest potential to become an opposition with a national support-base. But as UNIP boycotted the 1996 parliamentary and presidential elections, MMD and 8 opposition parties contested the elections. MMD won 125 out of 150 parliamentary seats and further increased its majority to 131 seats in the 1996 elections. Illustrating the limited social basis of Zambian parties, all the 8 contesting parties in the 1996 elections were headed by individuals who had been elected to parliament on an MMD ticket in 1991. Roger Chongwe of the Liberal Progressive Front (LPF) had been the first Minister of Legal Affairs, Guy Scott, who together with Ben Kapita, headed the National Lima Party (NLP) was the first Minister of Agriculture. Humphrey Mulemba, head of the National Party (NP) had been Minister of Mines in the first MMD Cabinet and before that, a member of various UNIP cabinets. Akashambetwa Mbikusita-Lewania, head of Agenda for Zambia (AZ), had been a founding member of MMD and a Minister of Science, Technology Education and Vocational Training. Dean Mung'omba and Derrick Chitala had been instrumental in the founding of MMD and served as deputy ministers in the MMD Cabinet. In the 1996 elections, they headed the Zambia Democratic Congress (ZDC). As expected with the First-Past-The-Post electoral system, the winning party was rewarded by a larger share of the seats than it obtained of the votes, and in 1996 its share of the seats actually increased while its share of the votes declined.

With hindsight, UNIP's decision to boycott the 1996 elections was a major strategic error as it now lost its avenue to national politics and confirmed its regional platform (Bratton and Posner 1999; Bratton et al. 1997; Simutanyi 1997).[1] In the period after 1996, UNIP did not regain strength. Before the 2001 elections UNIP was weakened by the internal infighting between two candidates claiming the presidency of the party. The fact that a democratically elected president of the party, Francis Nkhoma, was removed to pave the way for Tilyenji Kaunda, second son of Kenneth Kaunda, indicated that the Kaunda family to a large extent still controlled UNIP. Despite the instability that has characterised UNIP, the party maintained viable structures in most parts of the country. As a result, UNIP was the only party which successfully held primary elections to select its parliamentary candidates in the 2001 parliamentary elections.

Unlike the early opposition parties, the first parties to form in the post-1996 elections period were not formed or led by people who had been in senior positions in MMD, or active in politics in general. The National Christian Coalition (NCC) formed in 1997 and the United Party for National Development (UPND), are typical examples. NCC emerged from the Pentecostal churches led by a charismatic pastor, Neves Mumba. Until forming UPND in December 1998, Anderson Mazoka was the managing director of the Anglo-American Cor-

1. UNIP officials admitted that the 1996 boycott was a huge mistake as UNIP lost the chance to re-build their national position in the period 1996–2001. Personal communications, Robson Chongo, UNIP's Party Secretary, Freedom House (UNIP), Lusaka, October 16, 2000.

Table 5.5: Party formations 1991-2001

	Party name	Date of formation
MMD	Movement for Multiparty Democracy	1991 (January)
UNIP	United National Independence Party	1959 (October)
MDP	Movement for Democratic Process	1991(April)
LPF	Liberal Progressive Front	1993 (October)
NP	National Party	1993 (September)
ZDC	Zambia Democratic Congress	1995 (May)
NLP	The National Lima Party	1996 (August)
AZ	Agenda for Zambia	1996 (October)
UPND	United Party for National Development	1998 (November)
NCC	National Christian Coalition	1998 (July)
SDP	Social Democratic Party	1998
FDD	Forum for Development and Democracy	2001 (May)
ZRP	Zambia Republican Party	2000 (December)
PF	Patriotic Front	2001 (September)
NLD	National Leadership for Development	2000
HP	Heritage Party	2001 (April)

Source: http://:elections.org.zm/politicalparties.html

poration (AAC) in Zambia with no previous political experience. However, as the 2001 electoral race gathered momentum, a host of new political parties formed. The last party formations occurred after the April 2001 MMD convention chaired by former members of the MMD National Executive Committee or Cabinet. The parties that formed due to erosion of internal party democracy and internal splits over the third-term issue, included the Zambia Republican Party (ZRP), the Heritage Party (HP) and the Forum for Democracy and Development (FDD). Disagreements within the MMD Cabinet over the nomination of the presidential candidate led to the forming of the Patriotic Front as late as September 2001.

The parties preparing to contest the 2001 elections shared the following characteristics. First, apart from UNIP, NCC, and UPND, they all emerged from MMD. Second, all eleven parties formed behind a strong leader-figure who, more often than not, contributed the bulk of the finances the parties controlled.[1] Third, it was virtually impossible to separate the parties along ideological or programmatic lines. According to the party manifestos all parties vowed to continue the current economic policies, albeit manage them better than MMD had done for the past ten years. Fourth, the parties were based mainly in Lusaka, to the extent that few apart from the incumbent party and UNIP had party structures or membership in regions outside the capital. As a result, the parties adopted most parliamentary candidates centrally, and the candidates adopted were often not from the local area they were to represent.[2]

1. An interview with Anderson Mazoka, President of UPND, revealed that this was a concern: "Every penny [for party financing] comes from our pockets. As party leader, I have to lead by example and I have used my family's resources to build this party. This worries me. This means that by 2001 I will have spent much of my personal fortune. If I make it to government I have to recover some of it. This form of party financing will make me corrupt". Personal communications, Lusaka (Leopards Hills Rd.) October 19, 2000.
2. The analysis of the party structure in Zambia is based on Chileshe Mulenga (2001), Burnell (2001) and The Electoral Institute of Southern Africa: "Political Parties Gear for Elections in Zambia" (http://www.eisa.org.za), downloaded November 16, 2001.

Comparing Party Programmes 1996 and 2001

Of the 35 parties registered in Zambia with the intention of participating in the 1996 parliamentary and presidential elections, only some of them could be considered proper party organisations in the sense that they presented a party manifesto and could claim a certain grass roots following. These were, apart from MMD, UNIP, the National Party (NP), The Liberal Progressive Front (LPF), Zambia Democratic Congress (ZDC), the Agenda for Zambia (AZ) and the National Lima Party. Of these parties, only UNIP had a party machinery at the grass roots level. Only eight parties participated in the 48 by-elections contested between 1991 and 1996.[1]

Analysing the party programmes of the main opposition parties with regard to economic policies, few major differences could be detected.[2] The opposition parties which presented party manifestos before the 1996 elections were the Agenda for Zambia, the Liberal Progressive Front, the Movement for Multiparty Democracy, the National Lima Party, the National Party, the Zambia Democratic Congress and the United National Independence Party. All the manifestos of the major parties stated that they were in favour of a continued process of economic liberalisation. Furthermore, all parties lent their support to the process of privatisation and improvement of the agricultural sector as strategies for revamping the economy. Nevertheless, some differences could be detected. MMD was the only party to explicitly state that it was against subsidies, most other manifestos were vague on this issue. UNIP was the party that most clearly attempted to take advantage of the socio-economic effects of the economic reforms in 1996. Kenneth Kaunda also cited the economic situation as the main reason why he ended his political retirement. Furthermore, on the issue of privatisation, UNIP's position deviated most clearly from MMD's. While committed to the privatisation process, the UNIP Manifesto stated that privatisation should be regarded as a means to real economic empowerment. The UNIP Manifesto further argued that ZCCM should only be partially privatised and instead reorganised to operate in a competitive market (UNIP 1996:19). Stressing its aim of carrying out structural adjustment reforms at a different pace and in a different manner, the UNIP Manifesto stated that UNIP was committed to economic liberalisation, but not state abdication from the economic field. Similarly, both the National Party, the Zambia Democratic Congress and Agenda for Zambia argued in favour of privatisation but at a much slower speed.

The area where most opposition parties sought to capitalise on the economic critique raised against MMD was agriculture. The National Lima Party explicitly prioritised agricultural policies and presented itself as wishing primarily to become a strong agricultural lobby in parliament (NLP 1996). Both NLP and the LPF claimed to represent the farmer (NLP 1996; LPF 1996). The ZDC

different party opinions

1. The parties MMD, UNIP, NP, National Conservative Party (NCP), United Patriotic Party (UPP), National Democratic Alliance (NDA) and the United Democratic Party (UDP) contested the by-elections. Of these, only MMD, UNIP and NP managed to secure seats. FODEP By-election results 1991–1996. See also Simutanyi 1997.

2. Suggesting perhaps, as one informant argued, that all party programmes were written by the same consultants! Personal communications, Allast Mwanza, Department of Economics, University of Zambia. Lusaka, November 2, 1996.

underscored the party's belief in gradual liberalisation of agricultural markets, arguing that the government should be participating in agricultural marketing and provide facilitating structures (*The Farmer*, July 1996). Indicating perhaps a more populist approach, a member of the UNIP Central Committee revealed that his party would reduce the price of mealie meal if voted back into office (*Times of Zambia*, April 8, 1996). In sum, however, the 1996 party programmes and electoral campaigns were largely devoid of economic issues. As such, the 1996 elections were a significant departure from the Zambian policy debates in the late 1980s when opposition to the various structural reform programmes had centred around the desirability of economic reform programmes as such.

Party Proliferation before the 2001 Elections

In the 2001 election the voters had a choice between 11 presidential candidates and in several constituencies almost as many parliamentary candidates to choose from. However, based on the party manifestos presented, there was hardly any difference between the parties in terms of their policy choices and inclinations. Despite MMD's poor economic record and the popular discontent with the economic policies none of the contesting parties presented an alternative economic agenda. Minor differences only emerged on social policy preferences and the attention devoted to the moral standing of the political leadership, as well as on the promotion of Zambian participation in the economy as entrepreneurs rather than as workers. In the case of UPND, UNIP, and FDD their economic policy framework was linked to negative comments about the performance of the MMD government over the past decade. Generally the three main opposition parties offered similar policies to the once carried out by MMD but with more disclosure and transparency. The UPND Manifesto characterised the 1990s as "the lost and wasted decade" and accused the MMD of producing "budgets of despair and trickery" and of "gross mismanagement and poor planning" (UPND 2001). In its stead, UPND adopted as their guiding principle a "pro-poor development strategy that would guarantee availability of basic needs of the people". To improve industrialisation, tax incentives would be employed to stimulate investments in manufacturing. Partnerships between local and foreign investors and the creation of export processing zones were emphasised. Although these objectives and measures testified to the party's free market orientation, other proposals indicated a stronger role for the government. For agriculture UPND appeared less inclined to leave development to market forces as the Manifesto proposed to subsidise fertiliser and feeds in order to boost production and improve living conditions.

UNIP's 2001 Manifesto propounded a "free social market economy", private sector driven but with government intervention where necessary. UNIP identified the failure of MMD as being caused by "chaotic implementation of macro-economic policies", no planning, 'over-liberalisation' of the foreign exchange market, unmanageable domestic public debt and the poor performance of the stock exchange ("a white elephant in a dormant economy") and Zambia Privatisation Agency ("merely offloaded Zambian enterprises to foreigners and the ruling elite"). Like UPND's, the UNIP Manifesto indicated that a greater state involvement in agriculture was called for (UNIP 2001). FDD's vision was to "create a poverty free Zambia where people are in charge of their own development" (FDD 2001). This could be achieved through decentralisation of power, job creation by the promotion of investment, particularly in the small-scale manufacturing sector, elimination of all forms of discrimination, restoration of integrity, transparency and accountability in public affairs, constitutional reform, and by enhancing the capacity of public institutions. Emphasising the creation of a private sector development fund, a stable macro-economic environment, a tax regime facilitating economic growth, and increased competitiveness of the agricultural sector, FDD in its party manifesto emphasised market mechanisms to a greater degree than UPND and UNIP. The market orientation was further underscored by the emphasis on the need to maintain a conducive and professional relationship to Zambia's international partners.

As expected, MMD focused on the achievements of the past decade and discussed issues "beyond 2001" ((MMD 2001). The MMD Manifesto was structured almost identically to the UPND Manifesto and confirmed MMD's commitment to liberalising the economy. According to the Manifesto, MMD would maintain a liberal economic environment; continue with the empowerment programmes of enshrining property rights for domestic and business properties; provide concessions to investments with high labour content located in outlying areas engaged in agriculture, manufacturing, mining and tourism. With the support of civil society organisations, MMD also promised to engage in public works programmes to improve the social and physical infrastructure to make the areas attractive for private enterprise. Lastly, and underlining the party's commitment to trade liberalisation, the Manifesto emphasised the need to maximise the benefits of belonging to regional trade institutions. Thus, MMD's objectives did not differ significantly from UPND's, UNIP's or FDD's, but like FDD, the MMD Manifesto tended to emphasise the private sector more.

With regard to health and education policies, UPND attempted to move away from the social policy prescriptions of the international financial institutions. Hence, UPND declared that it would make education a priority and would ensure provision of free basic and secondary education. Only two political parties placed emphasis on the involvement of Zambians in wealth creation as industrialists and farmers. These were the Zambia Republican Party and the Patriotic Front. In its Manifesto ZRP stated that economic development required the involvement of Zambians in wealth creation in the industrial and agricultural sectors (ZRP 2001). PF also subscribed to this view, but also took exception to the country's excessive taxation and extremely open liberal foreign exchange regime. The PF Manifesto stated that there was need for a law in Zambia to halt capital flight. PF wanted to restrict foreign exchange dealings and promoted the use of letters of credit for businesses operating in Zambia.

The 2001 party manifestos indicate that the political opposition parties operated within a limited political and ideological space. All parties indicated a general acceptance of the structural adjustment programme. No party or politician lobbied for a return of the controlled exchange rate regime or protection of local industries. As a result, the Zambian parties represented in the 1996 and 2001 elections failed to offer the electorate distinctive choices along the lines of economic policy. The lack of alternatives presented by the opposition parties may also explain why Zambian interest associations, while clearly critical of MMD and the economic reform process, did not endorse an alternative party (apart from ZNFU) nor present an explicit anti-economic reform agenda. Lack of clearly identified issue ownership inhibited the parties' ability to attract a stable electorate and also made it easier for politicians to switch between parties.

Overall, the political party opposition in Zambia in the Third Republic has been exceedingly weak and the parties have failed to provide checks on the powers of the executive in the 10 year period. Characterised by their centring around leadership, being funded by rich individuals, and by lack of will to co-operate and work as team, they did not provide societal interests with a viable channel into the political arena. According to one observer:

> The Zambian phenomenon whereby many politicians now like to conceive of themselves as the president of a political party and envisage being the next republican president, and treat parties as personal vehicles to that end, is the second republic's most notable legacy to the contemporary party scene. (Burnell 2001:7).

Possibly the main reason for the inability of the opposition to challenge the incumbent through the electoral channel lies in the enormous prerogatives vested in the executive office.

Executive Dominance and the Effects on Interest Articulation

A defining feature of executive dominance is the failure of the incumbent to maintain a distinction between the government and the party (Carothers 2002). The discussion above has indicated that in the 1990s, multiparty democracy in Zambia failed to produce influential 'watchdogs' and counter-forces against state malpractice and corruption. Pluralist democracy has so far not challenged the hegemony and increasingly more authoritarian practices witnessed within the MMD government. Contrary to expectations in the dual reform literature, the Third Republic in Zambia witnessed an overwhelming, and growing, concentration of power in the executive office. This was witnessed by the increasing marginalisation of the parliament, courts and other institutions of constraint and the blurring of state-party lines. Due to the weakness of the MMD party vis-à-vis the position of UNIP during Zambia's one-party era, executive dominance actually increased in Zambia in the 1990s.

In addition to the MMD government's deliberate attempt to weaken the opposition in the first part of the 1996–2001 election period, the powers of the presidency also increased markedly in this period. According to the Zambian constitution, the president is the head of state and head of government, elected for a five-year term. After being elected, the president may appoint and dismiss a vice-president and cabinet members from among the MPs. According to the constitution, the Zambian president also holds the power to appoint judges and members of various agencies of constraint, such as the Electoral Commission and the Anti-Corruption Commission. Although the budget must be approved by parliament and spending is subject to audit and control by parliament, the president clearly has the upper hand.[1] Within the offices of the president there are several mini-departments, such as 'the Presidential desk of religious affairs' and 'the Presidential desk of street vendors', also budgeted according to the president's wishes.

During the one party era the UNIP government introduced a leadership code for leaders which was made part of the Republican Constitution.[2] The leadership code forbade leaders (in the party, government, local authorities and statutory corporations) to run businesses or earn extra emoluments while in office. When MMD took office in November 1991 the leadership code was scrapped and leaders were free to run or own businesses while in office (Chanda 2003:65). From the mid-1990s onwards the distinctions drawn by senior MMD members between the state and the party and between private business interests and their jobs became increasingly blurred. As argued above, MMD's disregard for party-state distinctions was witnessed as early as the 1993 by-elections. Furthermore, in both the 1996 and 2001 presidential and parliamentary campaigns, Chiluba appeared at MMD rallies providing leases for council houses and other state welfare-services. Chiluba also used the discretionary presidential fund to drum up support for the MMD by donating to churches, sports clubs, schools and health centres across the country.[3] District Administrators also enhanced the powers of the president at the local level.

The powers of the presidency were further compounded by the weak position of the parliament. With few institutional resources and their agenda very much controlled by the government, recommendations from parliamentary committees have largely been ignored by the government and constitutional ambiguities about cabinet responsibilities were very often exploited to the advantage of the government (Burnell 2003). Because the president has the power to appoint the cabinet ministers, they are in practice not responsible to parliament. Despite the democratic transition in 1991, the Zambian Parliament has remained without real powers in budgetary matters. It cannot increase the proposed sum for various ministries, nor can it change the total budget estimate (Chanda 2003).[4]

Increasing the president's already large discretionary financial powers, 'the Presidential Discretionary Fund', which was introduced for the first time in the 1998 budget, provided the president with a part of the budget that he could spend according to his own priorities. In the 1998 budget, the Parliament approved a discretionary fund of K 12 billion (US$ 5 million). In the 1999

1. See Peter Burnell's careful analyses of the role of the Zambian Parliament in the 1990s with regard to the role (and weakness) of parliamentary scrutiny (2001); legislative-executive relations (2003); and parliamentary committee reforms (2002b).
2. *The Constitution of Zambia* 1973, Part IV.
3. Press Briefing by Brigadier General Godfrey Miyanda, Heritage Party President, Comment on the Outcome of the 2001 Presidential, Parliamentary, and Local Government Elections in Zambia, held at Mulungushi International Conference Centre, Lusaka, 8 January 2002.
4. Even if appropriations have been made for certain purposes it is up to the Ministry of Finance and Economic Development to actually release the appropriations to the ministries. Ministries also have a number of opportunities to disperse funds for purposes without parliament's prior consent.

budget the government refused to announce the amount allocated the Presidential Fund raising speculations about abuse. No official criterion for disbursement was stated for the fund, commonly referred to as the 'slush fund' in the Zambian press. The sums distributed to the Office of the President, the budget vote that contains the President's discretionary fund, often far exceeded the estimates voted by Parliament, and MPs found it hard to identify recipients (Burnell 2001b).[1] Furthermore, no system of accountability was installed to ensure that the funds were used for legitimate purposes. Illustrating the lack of accountability, the vice-President told Parliament that it was not entitled to scrutinise the accounts of the Office of the President-Special Division (*Zambia Daily Mail*, February 23, 2001). A similar innovation, increasing the President's personal economic influence in the second Chiluba administration was the Presidential Housing Initiative established in 1999, supposedly duplicating the functions of the already existing National Housing Authority. The institution of District Administrators also clearly increased the powers of the president and further weakened the local government structures.

Crowding Out the Private Sector

The effects of executive dominance in terms of business's ability to influence political and economic developments were clearly evident as the first Chiluba administration started to consolidate its power before the 1996 elections. Illustrating the blurred line between private business interests and national policies, the declaration of assets by the new Members of Parliament in 1997 indicated that the assets of some of the new MPs and cabinet members included ownership of large and recently privatised companies and airlines. The Minister of Finance, Ronald Penza, was reported to conduct business with 24 government departments and parastatals through his own company (*Times of Zambia*, January 4, 1997). The President of ZACCI voiced the frustrations felt by the business community of 'business people-cum-politicians' crowding out the private sector:

> At independence, they [the government] wanted independence but did not know what to do with it. In 1991 they [the government] wanted multiparty politics and to get rid of Kenneth Kaunda, now they do not know what to do with it. This government is reverting more and more to the styles and policies of the former government. They have not created an enabling environment for business, they want to do business themselves.

With the majority of economic activity in government control, business people supportive of government were awarded government contracts. Contrary to this, business people critical to government faced harsh economic realities. Emmanuel Kasonde, MMD's first Minister of Finance, left MMD in 1993 and shortly after became the President of the National Party. His decision to rejoin MMD in 1997 was by observers linked to his private business interests which

1. In a debate in parliament an opposition MP claimed that the Auditor General's report revealed unconstitutional movements of funds from Cabinet Office to State House and the President 'who cannot be touched'. *Parliamentary Debates*, No. 112, January 22–March 18, 1999. See Burnell 2001b, footnote 37).

had suffered badly since 1993.[1] Dean Mungomba's decision in 2001 to link 'his party' ZDC to MMD was interpreted in a similar manner. In the same vein, and indicating the level of executive dominance, all the major civil society groups in Zambia emphasised the need to remain politically neutral or to work with 'the government of the day' and denied being allied with any political party. Leaders of various organisations consistently reported that "we will work with the government of the day". This attests to the continuing lack of political competition as well as to the reality that influence over policy rests on maintaining good relations with the *ruling* party.[2]

The consequence of the Zambian constitution, as well as the political developments witnessed particularly in Chiluba's second election period, is that there are today hardly any countervailing institutions in Zambia. As three consecutive elections since 1991 have shown, the electoral system reinforces the tendencies of executive dominance in Zambian politics. In the words of the Economist Intelligence Unit assessing the political developments in 2000: "MMD has evolved from a disparate and uneasy coalition of unions, churches and business people united to end Kenneth Kaunda's rule to a hierarchical patronage structure" (*EIU Country Profile*, January 2001:13). In such political environments, organised interests representing business and labour have very limited power to act as buffers against state malpractices or influence economic policies.

The Pluralist Paradox

The analysis of the domestic policy process between the Zambian government and the main domestic interest associations has indicated that MMD did enjoy a period of grace in the sense that its relationship to the main economic interest groups was characterised by low levels of conflict in the initial period after the 1991 elections. The government also enjoyed much general public support for its economic policies until the end of 1993. However, overall, the government did not aim to build consensus around the various reform measures through extensive and effective consultations with interest groups. Despite the increasingly stronger criticism appearing from 1994 onwards, the MMD government over the five-year election period introduced, and maintained, economic reforms that fundamentally altered the economic system from a state developmentalist model to an essentially liberalised, free-market system. No opposition party campaigned on an alternative economic agenda in the 1996 election campaign, nor in the 2001 elections.

Both the political and economic reform processes regressed markedly from the mid-1990s. The second electoral period was characterised by power-consolidation, not through widening the support-base, but through the use of consti-

1. In personal communications with Emmanuel Kasonde October 7, 1996, he indicated that his private business was badly affected by 'his current political status'. Kasonde had at the time been offered a position in government. However, indicating his commitment to MMD, he stated that he would consider going back into government if the current team was changed. In 1997, he renewed his MMD membership and took up the position as Director of Zambia Revenue Authorities. In January 2002, he was made Minister of Finance in Mwanawasa's Cabinet.
2. This view has been stated in numerous interviews I have conducted with representatives of Zambian civil society organisations in the period 1996–2002.

tutional manipulation and control of state resources for purposes of patronage. Ties to key interests groups were weakened rather than strengthened. Both due to the effects of the economic reforms (discussed in Chapter 4) and the way the political reform process was carried out by the two Chiluba administrations, interest associations representing labour, business, and agriculture were unable to stall the political and economic regression witnessed as MMD's reform commitment waned.

In Zambia the opening up of the political arena saw the creation of a large number of non-governmental associations ranging from welfare oriented associations to organisations seeking to influence the state on issues of human rights, democracy and press freedom. Similarly, the reintroduction of multiparty politics brought about 36 new opposition parties, some with a short life-span and none with a strong following. The effects of the associational proliferation for traditional interest groups of labour, business and agriculture was that it became increasingly more difficult to be seen and heard in the press, in public fora and thus to lobby government. The 'thinness' in terms of membership base and associational density of the economic interest groups further reduced the incentives of the government to consult and to yield to the interests pushed by any particular organisation. All associations provided only weak bases for electoral and coalitional support for the government. Contrary to expectations, the influence of interest associations representing agriculture, business and labour declined with the introduction of political liberalisation in 1991. No sectors of the economy constituted clearly identifiable 'winners', nor did they perceive themselves as such. Overall, interest groups were unable to oppose the economic reform measures seen to hurt their members' interests; they were also unable to curb the declining standards of governance displayed by the MMD government from 1993 onwards.

For economic interest associations to be able to influence policies as envisioned in the pluralist notion of 'winners' and 'losers', the political arena must provide channels in which interests can be aggregated into the competitive political processes. However, no party offered an economic agenda challenging MMD's economic reforms in the 1996 or in the 2001 elections and, as a result, the interest groups representing business, labour and agriculture had few actual channels into the political arena. Thus, contrary to the pronouncements of the most pessimistic observers of the dual reform process, interest group pressure and protest did not compel the Zambian government to increase spending in order to maintain its popularity. But the fact remains that the government throughout the 1990s increased government spending much to the detriment of the Zambian public at large. While interest groups outside the state were too weak to challenge the government, they were also marginalised and lacked political channels to curb the increasing degrees of government malpractice witnessed from 1993/94 onwards. Despite the lack of economic growth generated, and the fact that no sectors of society had emerged as clear 'winners' of the economic reform measures implemented, the MMD government was not faced with a political movement which seriously challenged its popularity or curbed is malpractices.

However, considering the lack of economic results and Zambia's past reform record, some puzzling questions remain unanswered: After five years no sector of society had emerged as 'reform winners' so why did no opposition party nor any interest group launch an alternative economic policy in the 1996 election campaign? Furthermore, if commitment to the economic reforms was shallow even within MMD, why were the reforms maintained and even accelerated before the 1996 elections? The analysis has indicated that both the processes of privatisation and agricultural liberalisation, two areas of reform which went a long way, had little domestic support. Why were these reform measures stressed more than other reform measures? The analysis of the internal policy relations between the Zambian government and the main economic stake-holder groups cannot provide completely satisfactory answers to these questions. This suggests that the answers, at least partially, must be sought in the analysis of the external relationship between the Zambian government and its international partners.

6

Aid for Reform

The Relationship between the Zambian Government and the International Donor Community

In this chapter the role of the international donor community, represented by the World Bank, the International Monetary Fund (IMF) and the largest bilateral donor governments is brought into the analysis. The first section discusses the economic and political conditionality applied through the Consultative Group meeting process in the period 1991–2001. The second section analyses the leverage of the Zambian government vis-à-vis its external partners in terms of political and economic reform implementation. A concluding section assesses the uses and effects of the donor community's conditionality instruments in Zambia's dual reform processes.

The chapter argues that, overall, the international donors had more leverage in terms of economic policy reform than it did in the case of political reforms. The negotiations between the MMD government and its external partners indicate that all major economic reforms came as a result of a distinct pressure from its external partners. However, due to the large number of conditions presented and conflicting views within the donor group, the Zambian government used its economic reform 'record' to split the external donors. As a result, the effects of the bilaterally imposed aid-sanctions in the period 1996–1998 were limited. In the second election period, the credibility of the conditionality-instruments waned in the context of declining political and economic governance witnessed by the MMD government.

Chaired by the World Bank, Consultative Group meetings appeared in the mid-1980s as a mechanism to improve co-ordination among donors and cooperation with the recipient governments in the field of macro-economic and structural policy reforms. In addition to the Roundtable meetings hosted by UNDP, the Consultative Group meeting process hosted by the World Bank intended to serve as 'pledging sessions' to help close financing gaps for the aid recipient countries. When the donors in the early 1990s included concerns of governance on their conditionality agenda, issues pertaining to accountability, the rule of law, transparency and respect for human rights were added to the Consultative Group meeting agendas. The multilateral institutions maintained the position that their operations did not interfere directly in a recipient country's internal policies. However, the inclusion of governance issues in the Consultative Group discussions brought the international finance institutions closer to the bilateral donors on the issue of political conditionality. According to the World Bank's own report on governance issues:

> In its role as Chairman of the Consultative Group (CG) meetings between donor agencies and governments, the bank has at times communicated to borrowing countries views of the donors on issues relevant to the political dimensions of governance that fall outside the Bank's mandate. (1992:xvii)

Despite a distinct 'non-political' profile, the analysis of donor-government relations in Zambia in the period 1991–2001 indicates that the international finance institutions, together with the bilateral donors, through the Consultative Group meetings advocated a policy agenda including both political and economic conditionality issues.

Political and Economic Conditionality 1991–2001

While the deteriorating economic situation was a concern in itself, the immediate issue confronting the MMD government in 1991 was the external financial situation (see Chapter 3). Due to the withdrawal of IMF and World Bank credits, Zambia had incurred arrears on its debt to the multilateral institutions. Zambia's financial credibility was at a low-point as the country was ineligible to draw on IMF funds as well as World Bank and bilateral balance-of-payments support grants. The need to restore international confidence and to increase the level of donor funding was therefore of paramount importance for the government. The emphasis placed on restoring Zambia's international financial reputation was emphasised by an advisor to the Ministry of Finance:

> Economic reform is meant to fundamentally alter a country's growth prospects. In principle, reform is not primarily a means of satisfying external creditors. But because of Zambia's poor credit standing, a practical precondition for the resumption of sustained growth is for Zambia to re-establish a reputation of responsible financial behaviours. Thus, a major objective for the reform effort has been to gain regular access to international finance as due to its debt overhang Zambia could not finance its economic imbalances independently of donor support. (McPherson 1995:14)[1]

In September 1991, shortly before the elections which brought MMD to power, the relationship between the UNIP government and its external donors was nearing the level of conflict reminiscent of the 1987–89 period. When President Kaunda in early 1991 announced that the full liberalisation of maize subsidies would be postponed until after the 1991 elections the World Bank suspended its second tranche of funding agreed to in March 1991 because Zambia had failed to meet the 60-day deadline for the reduction of its arrears. The World Bank suspension led a number of the bilateral donors to cease disbursements to Zambia at a time when donor patience with the slow pace of economic reforms was

1. Malcom McPherson was the team leader of the Harvard HIID team working as advisors within the Ministry of Finance until the spring of 1996. The Harvard advisory team within the Ministry of Finance started its operations in 1990.

wearing out. As a result, a number of bilateral donors withheld balance-of-payments support and programme aid. This was the situation shortly before MMD's electoral victory. The suspension of the aid programme meant that the new government had to convince aid donors that it was willing to make difficult and potentially unpopular political decisions. Furthermore, it meant that it was necessary to secure more donor funding than would have been necessary had UNIP continued the programme. By the end of 1990, total arrears on principal and interest payments amounted to approximately US$ 3,400 million of which about 40 per cent was owed to the World Bank and the IMF (*EIU Country Profile*, 1993/4:39). The debt to the multilateral institutions was not subject to forgiveness and 70 per cent of debt servicing was owed to the multilateral institutions (Andersson and Ndulo 1994:23).

The reality facing Zambia in the 1990s was that there were simply *no* sources to which it could turn for foreign exchange to cover its basic imports and development programmes. But as a result of Zambia's peaceful democratic transition in 1991, and the MMD government's promise to embark upon comprehensive economic reforms, an extraordinary effort was launched by the international donor community. In the absence of debt forgiveness, the World Bank designed a new policy to assist countries with non-accrual status that made it possible to process loans during a pre-clearance performance period (Kapur et al. 1997:1070). This policy measure was implemented in order to assist countries to pay their debt, and thereby be able to regain access to World Bank financial resources. In reality, the World Bank crafted a 'bridging loan' from bilateral and commercial sources. On a specific date, the bridging loan was extended to the country to clear its arrears to the World Bank and, in turn, disbursements from the World Bank's loans would repay the creditors for the bridge loan:

> Although in effect the Bank was advancing the money to clear arrears to itself, the policy was a pragmatic accommodation to the procedural complexities of a multiparty package. In the absence of debt forgiveness, the policy adopted was the only workable solution to a growing problem aggravated by the growing fraction of inflexible (principally multilateral) debt. (Kapur et al. 1997:1070)

To be eligible for such bridging loans, however, a country had to undertake an adjustment programme in agreement with the World Bank. Furthermore, a country was required to undertake a stabilisation programme endorsed and monitored by the IMF and, finally, to establish a medium term financing plan that included the clearance of arrears to all international finance institutions and make current debt payments falling due during the performance period (Ibid.). Another step taken to assist heavily indebted nations, was the creation of a facility called 'the Fifth Dimension'. Through this facility, the World Bank and bilateral donors provided additional resources to assist countries that were ineligible for other sources of World Bank finances due to outstanding arrears. Yet, similar to the World Bank bridging loan facilities introduced, to actually receive supplementary credit from the Fifth Dimension programme, a country had to be current on its debt servicing to the World Bank and have an acceptable adjustment programme in place. Against this background, the Zambian government had very little choice but to accept the policy packages and prescriptions presented to it by the external donors. As argued by the Economist Intelligence Unit:

> The reversal in donor attitudes is central to Zambia's economic recovery. ... The importance of donor approval leaves the government with its hands tied to a large extent with respect to economic policy and the fact that its economic ideology coincides with that of the Bretton Woods Institutions is less than a coincidence. (*EIU Country Report,* No. 1, 1992:6)

The political steps taken by MMD in the period shortly before and after the 1991 elections indicate that the movement was aware of this situation. In the period before the 1991 elections, informal meetings were carried out between the international donors and MMD. The level of contact and mutual understanding was reflected in MMD's successful soliciting of international funding as a social movement in the process of transition to multiparty democracy (Andreassen et al. 1992; Chiluba 1995; Ihonvbere 1996). The first Minister of Finance, Emmanuel Kasonde, also emphasised that the preparatory meetings on economic policy issues had been conducive and given the new government a head start on the economic reforms.[1] The attempts by the new MMD government to re-create good ties with its international donors began almost immediately. In December 1991, President Chiluba called the largest international donors to State House and declared that the Zambian government intended to re-establish its creditworthiness and international image by honouring the conditions laid down by the international finance institutions and bilateral donor governments (*Times of Zambia*, December 6, 1991). Within weeks of taking office, MMD reached a broad agreement with the World Bank and IMF on economic adjustment. The agreement reached was reflected in the Policy Framework Paper 1991–1993, which initially had been negotiated between the UNIP government, the IMF and World Bank (GRZ 1991a).

As the new MMD government signalled commitment to an economic restructuring programme, the IMF in 1992 devised a new lending facility, the Rights Accumulation Programme (RAP). Similarly to the World Bank facility described above, the RAP facility was designed to help a country that had technically failed to meet its obligations but was making genuine efforts to reverse the economic decline. The RAP, designed to eventually enable the country to pay back the more than US$ 1 billion in arrears owed to the IMF, meant that repayments would be postponed for three years, providing the fulfilment of the agreed structural adjustment targets. By the end of 1992, through the World Bank and IMF bridging loans, the Zambian government was therefore able to clear its non-accrual status to the multilateral institutions. In early 1992, the World Bank, as host of the Consultative Group meeting, felt that enough progress had been achieved, and confidence in the Zambian government gained, to call a Consultative Group (CG) meeting between Zambia, her main bilateral partners, the IMF, and the World Bank.

1. Personal interview, Emmanuel Kasonde, Minister of Finance 1991–1993. Lusaka, October 7, 1996.

Table 6.1: Consultative Group meetings 1991-2000

Date	Issues of debate
March, 1992 (Paris)	– the economic reform programme (main) – the drought and food security situation – the external debt situation
December, 1992 (Paris)	– inflation – government spending/fiscal balance – military spending – the implementation of a cash budget – corruption – the slow pace of privatisation – the slow pace of civil service reform
April, 1993 (Paris)	– macroeconomic stabilisation – Civil service reform – the composition of public spending, – lack of adherence social sectors – slow pace privatisation/Zambia Airways – inflation – the state of emergency – corruption
December, 1993 (Paris)	– macroeconomic stabilisation – slow pace of privatisation (ZIMCO) – improve social sector service delivery – government expenditure priorities – governance, corruption and drug trafficking
March, 1994 (Paris)	– 'renewed partnership' – the continued high interest rates – the slow progress on privatisation – the external debt situation – military spending
December, 1994 (Paris)	– the continued slow pace of privatisation – the delayed closure of ZIMCO – limited progress on the Public Sector Reform Programme – governance and corruption – poverty
December, 1995 (Bournemouth)	– privatisation of ZCCM – lack of progress on the Public Sector Reform Programme – poverty alleviation – governance issues (constitution, voter registration)
July, 1997 (Paris)	– 'renewal of partnership' – budget balance and discipline – the external debt situation – privatisation of ZCCM – Public Sector Reform Programme – poverty reduction – governance issues – aid dependency
May, 1998 (Paris)	– privatisation of ZCCM – Public Sector Reform Programme – poverty reduction – governance issues, Human Rights Issues, state of emergency – GRZ introduces: capacity building for good governance
May, 1999 (Paris)	– resumption of World Bank/IMF balance-of-payments support – privatisation of ZCCM – Public Sector Reform Programme – poverty reduction – governance issues (corruption, HR) – regional stability
July, 2000 (Lusaka)	– 'renewal of partnership' – good governance: election administration voter registration level playing field – civil society – poverty reduction

Economic Conditionality Exercised through the Consultative Group Meetings

At the March 1992 CG meeting the Zambian government presented a draft of a new policy framework paper covering the period 1992–1994, essentially the same Policy Framework Paper that UNIP had agreed to in 1991 (GRZ 1992). The policy framework paper, and the government's first budget (1992) were well received for being ambitious and courageous (*Times of Zambia*, February 6, 1992)[1]. The Consultative Group meeting further commended the government's prompt actions in the first four months of implementing the economic restructuring programme, especially the progress towards phasing out maize and fertiliser subsidies. But concerns were raised about the government's commitment to the privatisation process. The external donors urged that concrete goals be set and monitored to allow for significant progress. The positive evaluation of the external donors was, nevertheless, not followed by immediate increases in financial assistance. In view of a financing gap estimated at US$ 300 million as the meeting was concluded, the World Bank urged the bilateral donors to reallocate funding from existing programmes to balance-of-payments support.[2] The chairman of the meeting warned that:

> If we cannot respond to the needs of a country whose governance and policy record sets a standard for the region, then our own commitment to the adjustment process in Africa, and in the region, our ability to deliver in the way envisaged by the SPA [Special Programme for Africa] must be reassessed.[3]

Progress Affected by Drought

Despite the stated intentions of the MMD government in terms of economic liberalisation, as well as the actual steps taken, many of the economic targets set for 1992 were not met mainly due to the impact of the 1992 drought. Despite the missed targets, the informal Consultative Group meeting held in December 1992 indicated that the external donors judged Zambia's economic restructuring progress positively (*EIU Country Report*, No. 1, 1993:7).[4] The government's spending overruns, rampant inflation and excessive expansion of money supply were put down to the pressures caused by the drought and the civil service salary increases (*EIU Country Report*, No 1, 1993:12). While the issue of corruption as well as the slow pace of privatisation was mentioned, the main theme was inflation that ran at 165 per cent per annum in 1992. On the basis of these concerns, the Consultative Group meeting strongly urged the government to put itself on a cash budget (*Weekly Post*, January 8–14, 1993; McPherson 1995).

1993 was a year of political turmoil in Zambia. The internal political conflicts reflected a growing scepticism with regard to the democratic commitments of the MMD Cabinet as well as critique of the economic reform programme,

1. See World Bank 1992a; Norwegian Ministry of Foreign Affairs 1992; World Bank/IBRD 1992b.
2. The financing gap was closed later in the year, through additional funding and debt relief.
3. Statement by the World Bank chairman of the CG meeting, S. Denning. March 23, 1992.
4. The December CG meeting was an informal meeting scheduled to hear progress reports before the official meeting in March, where pledges of funds would be made.

particularly related to the effects of the agricultural liberalisation process. The government's *external partners*, however, praised the MMD government for its commitment and achievements in the area of economic liberalisation. At the Consultative Group meeting in April 1993, the Zambian government was commended for its exemplary handling of the 1992 drought. According to the external donors, despite the devastating drought, the government had not only met the adjustment targets, but also implemented the most effective drought programme in Southern Africa (*EIU Country Report*, 2nd Quarter 1993). The donors lauded the bold measures introduced to eliminate fertiliser subsidies, increase maize prices, decontrol interest rates, liberalise foreign exchange, and reduce budget deficits. But the gap between the targets and outcomes was again marked in the case of inflation. The Zambian government had at the March 1992 CG meeting agreed to the conditions set by the IMF and the World Bank requiring the removal of subsidies to and/or the closure of Zambia Airways.[1] Despite this promise, the Zambian government continued to subsidise the airline through 1993. A number of donors present at the CG meeting expressed concerns with the composition of the budget, where administrative expenses and subsidies to Zambia Airways still accounted for exceptionally high expenses (*Times of Zambia*, November 24, 1993; *EIU Country Report*, 4th Quarter, 1993).[2]

The following informal Consultative Group meeting in December 1993 indicated a growing concern by the donors with the apparent gap between intentions and actual implementation, particularly relating to the slow pace of privatisation and the expenditure priorities of the government. However, for the first time governance concerns overshadowed economic issues (see section below).

The Consultative Group in March 1994 displayed more positive sentiments as the donors welcomed many encouraging developments. In terms of economic liberalisation, the commitment displayed to combat inflation was especially commended as well as the enhancement of institutional capacity at the Zambia Privatisation Agency (ZPA). The continued high interest rates and the slow pace of the privatisation programme were, nevertheless, expressed concerns. Again, governance became the main issue of discontent, as all donors indicated that aid withheld, frozen or suspended would be released when the reform process on governance was moving forward with the same purpose and determination characterising the government's handling of the drought, inflationary control and budget discipline.[3] A further indication of the international finance institutions' positive evaluation of Zambia's economic performance was given when the Word Bank in May 1994 granted Zambia US$ 41 million as a contribution to the country's commercial debt buy-back scheme citing Zambia's 'exceptional

1. A major concern raised by the US delegation was the US$ 31 million restructuring plan, financed by a commercial credit from a Kuwaiti Bank, clearly violating both IMF and World Bank conditionality. USAID, 1994: "Zambia: Consultative Group Meeting. Interagency Review Paper" (December).
2. See World Bank/IBRD 1993a; World Bank/IBRD 1993b; Norwegian Ministry of Foreign Affairs 1993.
3. For the first time in the history of Zambia's Consultative Group meetings, at the March -94 meeting the financing gap was closed by a combination of increases in donor pledges and measures by the Zambian authorities to reduce foreign exchange needs.

performance' in implementing its structural adjustment programme as the main reason (*EIU Country Report*, 3rd Quarter 1994:12).

Conditionality to Forward the Process of Privatisation

More explicit conditionality measures were again witnessed at the CG meeting in Paris, December 8–9, 1994 (World Bank/IBRD 1994c; USAID 1994). The external donors initially requested the meeting to be postponed questioning the government's continued commitment to reform due to the slow progress in the area of privatisation. In particular the donors expressed concern about the government's lack of decision on the issue of Zambia Airways and the continued role of ZIMCO, perceived as stalling the privatisation effort. The donors, led by the World Bank, threatened to withhold US$ 60 million in balance-of-payments support due for the last quarter of 1994 unless the airline was restructured before the Consultative Group meeting. The domestic policy debates in Zambia (Chapter 4) indicated that the issue of Zambia Airways was a contentious issue and that the government had promised the unions that the airline and ZIMCO would not be liquidated (*Times of Zambia*, November 11, 1994). On December 3, the Minister of Finance announced the liquidation of Zambia Airways. Furthermore, the government indicated its commitment to close ZIMCO (*The Post*, December 6, 1994). The World Bank then called for an end of year CG meeting.[1] At this meeting the government reaffirmed its commitment to phase out ZIMCO by March 1995 and to continue with privatisation. These developments, coupled with good marcoeconomic performance (inflation and interest rates fell sharply in the second half of 1994 due to tight fiscal and monetary control) resulted in continued donor support. The meeting concluded that the second CG meeting scheduled for the spring was no longer necessary. As a result, the Zambian government committed itself to more frequent and informal consultations with donors in Lusaka on economic management and governance issues.

1995 was expected to be the turn-about year for Zambia's economic reform process. In early 1995, the Rights Accumulation Programme was scheduled for completion. The conclusion of the RAP was supposed to be directly followed by a new programme of policy goals agreed to with the IMF and a supply of funds through an Enhanced Structural Adjustment Facility (ESAF). The significance of an EASF was highlighted by the fact that Zambia was estimated by March 1995 to have accumulated enough credits to be entitled to a US$ 1.2 billion credit from IMF enabling the country to pay back its arrears to IMF and to continued to borrow on concessional terms (*EIU Country Report*, 3rd Quarter 1994:12). The ESAF agreement meant that Zambia's US$ 1.2 billion arrears on which Zambia had paid 8 per cent interest would be converted into a US$ 1.3 billion loan at 0.5 per cent interest with a five-and-a-half year period of grace before repayment was due (*Profit*, January 1996). This in turn would result in Zam-

1. See "Background Paper" prepared by United States' Delegation to Zambia's Consultative Group meeting. Paris, December, 1994.

bia's quota in IMF to rise, which determined the country's access to IMF financing and special drawing rights. Continued progress would bring additional support from the World Bank and the bilateral donors, in particular through increased debt rescheduling from the Paris Club.[1]

Despite the optimistic forecasts, 1995 turned out to be the most difficult year in the adjustment process since 1991. With a second drought affecting the country in May 1995, it could be said that, luck was again not on Zambia's side. However, as argued in Chapter 4, the problems encountered were also results of poor financial discipline and poor management on the part of the government. In view of the policy slippages that occurred in the first half of 1995, IMF's Executive Directory Board decided to postpone the completion of the RAP and extend it to December 1995 (IMF 1995). While the temporary break in negotiations was viewed as potentially dangerous for continued donor assistance, a permanent break was seen as unlikely. As argued by the Economist Intelligence Unit:

> It is likely that the government will be successful in getting the Fund [IMF] back to the negotiating table, not least because of the flurry of recent activity around the privatisation programme. Also in the government's favour is the fact that the IMF and other donors are extremely reluctant to see Zambia fail. Now that the Rights Accumulation Programme (RAP) is finished and most of the country's arrears to the Fund are due to be cleared, Zambia is well on the way to becoming a new model pupil in Africa. Zambia's economic recovery will be testament to effectiveness of the economic policy advice given out by the IMF and other donors. (*EIU Country Report*, 2nd Quarter 1995:5)

The statement above proved an adequate assessment of the situation. In October a team from the IMF visited Zambia to assess the range of benchmarks and economic performance criteria. The aim was to enter into the Enhanced Structural Adjustment Facility (ESAF) with the IMF, pay the US$ 1.2 billion in arrears, which in turn would pave the way for the December 1995 Consultative Group meeting. The work of the Zambian government was crowned with success in early December when the RAP was finally concluded and an ESAF agreement was signed with the IMF. The new agreement secured Zambia access to IMF funding over the next three years. The new deal with IMF quickly yielded positive results with other donors. The December 14–15, 1995 Consultative Group meeting met Zambia's positive progress with more pledges, although concern was raised over the worsening social conditions in Zambia (*Profit*, January 1996:7).[2] Donors commended Zambia for its accomplishment in terms of completing the RAP and the initiation of ESAF. The impressive progress on privatisation was also acknowledged, although donors emphasised the need to privatise ZCCM. The December Consultative Group meeting indicated that IMF and the World Bank generally were satisfied with Zambia's economic

1. The complex, technical nature of the various structural adjustment facilities and negotiations between the IMF/World Bank and the Zambian government add credence to a comment by the Director of USAID in Zambia who claimed that maybe only 4–5 people in Zambia understood the actual contents of the reform programme. Personal interview, Joseph Joe Stepanek. Lusaka, September 12, 1996. My own understanding of the issues involved is largely owed to conversations with Hendrick van der Heijden, Ministry of Finance and Håkon Hellebust, country economist at the Norwegian Embassy/NORAD.
2. See GRZ 1995d; USAID1995; SIDA 1995; Norwegian Ministry of Foreign Affairs 1995.

progress. The bilateral donors shared the conclusions of the multilateral donors in terms of Zambia's progress in the area of economic reform, but the Consultative Group meeting raised concerns on a broad range of governance issues. All pledges were made conditional on the Zambian government maintaining the momentum of the economic reform programme and achieving tangible progress on several issues of governance. Thus, reminiscent of the situation at the December meeting in 1993, governance was made a condition for continued bilateral balance-of-payments support—despite a consensus on the economic reform achievements.

A Temporary Break of Cooperation with the International Finance Institutions

Within weeks of entering into the ESAF agreement with the IMF, Zambia failed to meet six out of ten of the agreed benchmarks, as revealed by the IMF February (1996) review (IMF 1995b). According to the IMF, the two main reasons for the failure of the programme were errors in the programme design and precarious commitment of the Zambian authorities.[1] Noting the credibility problem stemming from its mixed policy performance, the Zambian government was urged to strengthen its financial policies and accelerate structural reforms. An IMF staff-monitored 'shadow programme' was set in motion temporarily and the mid-term review of the ESAF was postponed on request of the Zambian authorities in order to correct the situation. As the new ESAF programme failed almost from its inception, and encountering further problems of policy implementation in the early months of 1996, the Zambia government was under heavy pressure to meet the March 1996 benchmarks. The IMF mission visiting Zambia in February then agreed with the government to make adjustments to earlier set benchmarks. In May 1996, the MMD Cabinet endorsed the plan for privatising the copper industry. This decision indicated to the external donors a significant sign of continued commitment to the economic restructuring process. Thus, the executive directors of the IMF in July 1996 agreed that consistent satisfactory performance under the staff-monitored programme, accelerated progress with respect to privatisation of ZCCM and assurances of balance-of-payments financing indicated that the completion of the mid-term review was within reach.[2]

However, no CG meeting was called for 1996 due to the bilateral aid-freeze in the spring of 1996 following the controversy over the signing of the constitution amendments in May 1996. The bilateral freeze of balance-of-payments support affected the Zambian reserves and the uncertain situation caused by the

1. Personal communications, E. Taha, resident representative IMF, Lusaka, December 10, 1996 and Ellah Chembe resident economist, World Bank, Lusaka, September 9, 1996.
2. The corrective actions beginning in February were to provide the foundation for a staff-monitored programme for 1996. This illustrates the particular relationship between the IMF and its member countries. Contrary to other donors who may decide to suspend aid disbursements, it is only a government decision to end the relationship with the IMF that will result in a break-up of the IMF's relationship with a member country. Eligibility to draw on the IMF funds is however, contingent on a country clearing its debt arrears and meeting specific performance criteria. Thus, if benchmarks are not met, a new programme is negotiated. Failure to meet the originally set ESAF benchmarks in December 1995, therefore, meant that a new programme was negotiated with stronger measures to make up for losses and failure the next year.

delayed mid-term review of the IMF caused a postponement of World Bank balance-of-payments funds as well.[1] A representative of the Bank of Zambia described the situation:

> In May arose the problems with the bilateral donors over the constitution and we lost approximately 210 million dollars in balance-of-payments support. The problem was of course that external balance-of-payments support was built into our debt service. This created problems with our creditors and it altered our foreign exchange agreement with ZCCM. June then became a critical month. However, we were able to meet benchmarks and the programme review was scheduled for July. By that time, the issue of the election had surfaced and the bilateral donors were pressurising the World Bank not to disperse their agreed funding of 31 million, which should have been dispersed in June. In the third quarter we were expecting 45 million from the World Bank. This sum, however, was contingent upon a Fund guarantee note that the programme was on course. The World Bank was now under continued pressure from the bilaterals to withhold money and the dialogue with the international finance institutions did not go on as expected. The World Bank adopted a wait and see attitude. Then came the annual meeting of the World Bank and the IMF and during the discussions it was agreed that they would give us the 45 million, but continued funding is conditioned upon the bilaterals coming back. Otherwise our funding would be a bridge to nowhere.[2]

In June 1996 the United Nations Development Programme (UNDP) warned of the dire economic consequences that would result from aid cuts, citing capital flights and reduced foreign direct investments, rising inflation, lower domestic investments and declining ability to service external debt (*EIU Country Risk Service*, 3rd Quarter 1996:3). But the doom scenario predicted by the UNDP proved to be largely unfounded. Mainly due to the positive mid-term review conducted by the IMF, largely determined by the government's endorsement of a privatisation plan for ZCCM and improved macro-economic performance, multilateral aid was not affected by the punitive measures implemented by the bilateral donors in 1996. Denying that political criteria affected its lending, the World Bank in October released US$ 45 million in balance-of-payments support after the positive report by the IMF. As will be discussed in detail below, the continuation and increase of multilateral aid, coupled with the reduction of debt servicing, reduced the effects of the withdrawal of bilateral balance-of-payments support in 1996. Due to a good agricultural harvest, recovering from the 1995 drought, and growth in non-traditional exports, GDP rose by 6.4 per cent in 1996. In February 1997 the IMF completed its mid-term review of Zambia's economic performance and reported itself happy enough with progress to allow the country to draw on concessional funding under the ESAF agreement. This approval paved the way for a formalisation of the 1996 agreement with the Paris Club of official bilateral creditors of a 67 per cent reduction in Zambia's debt obligations. Furthermore, the approval of the IMF paved the way for a World Bank sponsored Consultative Group meeting, which had not been held since December 1995.

1. Which in April 1996 stood at US$ 135 million, down from US$ 155 in March and US$ 205 in April 1995 according to *EIU Country Report*, 3rd Quarter 1996.
2. Personal interview, Dr. Danny Kalyalia, economic advisor, Bank of Zambia. Lusaka, January 9, 1997.

Table 6.2: Policy based loans from multilateral institutions

Institution	Loan	Requirements
World Bank	1991: Economic Reform Credit (ERC)	Phase out maize subsidies, liberalising maize markets, limit bank credits, remove tariff bans, eliminate surplus civil service staff, announce privatisation policy, offer a minimum of 6 parastatal companies for sale, complete studies of Zambia Airways.
World Bank	1992: Privatisation and Industrial Reform Credit (PIRC I)	Fiscal and monetary performance, harmonise sales taxes, broaden tax base, reduce tariffs, retrench 10,000 civil service workers, enact privatisation law, offer additional 10 parastatals for sale, restructure ZIMCO.
World Bank	1993: (PIRC II)	Fiscal and monetary performance, reduce tariffs, develop plans for land markets, reform Investment Act, offer for sale 60 companies, establish Privatisation Trust Fund, study options to privatise ZCCM.
World Bank	1994: Economic and Social Adjustment Credit (ESAC I)	Redirect budget to social sectors (health and education), eliminate export ban on maize, create legal basis for land leasehold, and begin sale of state owned farms, adoption of acceptable financial plan for Zambia Airways.
World Bank	1995: Economic Recovery and Investment Project (ERIP I)	Consolidate improvements in macro-economic management, stimulate investment, reorient role of state in investment financing, reform social security system, restructure and privatise ZCCM.
World Bank	1996-97: (ESAC II)	Maintain a social sector budget of at least 35%, privatise ZCCM, implement 1995 Land Act, implement National Housing Policy of 1995, amend Employment and Industrial and Labour Relations Act, formulate policy on collaboration with NGOs in welfare service delivery.
World Bank	1998-2001: Public Sector Reform and Export Promotion Credit (PSREC)	Facilitate privatisation of ZCCM; improve performance of public service; promote private investment; strengthen delivery of social services.
World Bank /IMF	2000: Heavily Indebted Poor Countries Initiative (HIPC)	Debt relief to be spent according to a poverty reduction strategy paper (PRSP), owned by government and civil society. Quantitative benchmarks: Macroeconomic stabilisation, fiscal balance, privatisation of remaining parastatals, including Zesco, Zamtel, Zanaco.
IMF	1992-95: Rights Accumulation Programme (RAP)	Restore macroeconomic stability, eliminate arrears to international creditors, implement Economic Recovery Programme in collaboration with multinational finance institutions. Completed December 1995.
IMF	1995-97: Enhanced Structural Adjustment Facility (ESAF I)	Development of a National Poverty Reduction Action Plan; gazetting of banking regulations, re-invigorate public sector reform; privatisation of ZCCM, Zamtel, Zesco. Not completed.
IMF	1999-2001: Enhanced Structural Adjustment Facility (ESAF II)	Macro-economic and structural reform; privatisation of ZCCM, Zaltel and Zesco; implementation of public service reform; implementation of National Poverty Reduction Plan. Not Completed.
IMF	2001-2005 Poverty Reduction and Growth Facility (PRGF)	Support of poverty reduction strategy paper (PRSP), owned by government and civil society. Quantitative benchmarks: Macroeconomic stabilisation, fiscal balance, privatisation of remaining parastatals.

A Temporary Renewal of Partnership

At the July 1997 Consultative Group meeting the donors emphasised the positive development trends in the areas of macro-economic stabilisation and growth. The Zambian delegation's presentation of the privatisation plans for ZCCM and further, the plan for implementing the Public Sector Reform Programme, were received positively by the external partners (World Bank/IBRD 1997a; Norwegian Ministry of Foreign Affairs 1997; GRZ 1997b). At the Paris Consultative Group meeting Zambia's major donors resumed funding and pledged US$ 435 million for 1997 of which US$ 150 million was allocated for balance-of-payments support. As a result, the July 1997 Consultative Group meeting witnessed 'a renewal of partnership', as it was phrased by the World Bank, between the donors and the second MMD administration (IBRD/World Bank 1997b).

However, internal policy concerns again strained the relationship between the Zambian government and the international donor community. Soon after the process of bid analysis and evaluation for the privatisation of ZCCM had been initiated, the process stalled because of the new negotiating team appointed by the MMD Cabinet (see Chapter 4). Furthermore, due to an unbudgeted wage increase granted the public service in the second half of 1997, the budget went off track. The October 1997 coup d'état and the government's follow-up to the coup strained the relationship with the donors considerably. In the early parts of 1998, the Minister of Finance, nevertheless, announced that an agreement had been reached with the IMF on a second annual ESAF programme. In order to achieve its growth and poverty reduction objectives, the Minister of Finance announced that in 1998 the government would implement *seven* major programmes; the Public Sector Reform Programme, the Poverty Reduction Programme, the Health Sector Programme, the Basic Education Sector Investment Programme, the Electric Power Sector Investment Programme, and the Road Sector Investment Programme. The government would also invigorate the execution of the Agricultural Sector Investment Programme, ASIP.[1] The Budget Address also indicated that the privatisation of the mines was expected to be finalised in 1998 and that the government intended to make progress on the privatisation of the Zambia National Oil Company. This programme was outlined in a draft Policy Framework paper and Memorandum on Economic and Financial Policies discussed with the IMF and World Bank. But the document was never formally submitted to the IMF as in March the Minister of Finance was dismissed and the new Minister of Finance, Edith Nawakwi, demanded more time to review the programme (*The Post*, March 23, 1998; *Inter-Press Services* March 31, 1998).

Failed Privatisation Leads to Aid Freeze

When the government and the Kafue Consortium in February 1998 failed to finalise the transaction agreement on the main assets of ZCCM, the relationship

1. Ronald Penza's Budget Address, January 15, 1998. For further details, see Heijden 2000:53.

between the Zambian government and the donor community reached a new low point. The events surrounding the ZCCM privatisation, coinciding with other governance problems, led to a continued suspension of bilateral balance-of-payments support. As the government had failed to reach an agreement with IMF on the second annual ESAF arrangement for 1998–2001, no balance-of-payments support from the World Bank was provided either. A positive development relating to governance—the release of Kenneth Kaunda—nevertheless paved the way for a May 1998 Consultative Group meeting in Paris. While donor pledges were not in explicit terms tied to the privatisation of the mines, a number of bilateral donors and the World Bank representative indicated that the disbursement of the pledged balance-of-payments support would follow the sale of Nkana and Nchanga mines (*EIU Country Profile*, 3rd Quarterly, 1998:9). A growing sense of donor-fatigue was sensed at the 1998 CG meeting, according to the Economist Intelligence Unit: "The [Zambian] government's obvious confidence that it can outsmart donors irritates them and could backfire this time around" (Ibid.:9). The prediction proved correct. The privatisation of the mines was not completed and as a result, in 1998 Zambia did not receive any balance-of-payments support. Due to the set-backs in Zambia's economic recovery programme in 1998, it was not feasible to reach an agreement with the IMF on the second annual ESAF programme. However, towards the end of the year an agreement was reached on a new three-year ESAF programme for the period 1999–2001. In terms of structural adjustment reforms, the Zambian government promised to continue its efforts to privatise ZCCM at the earliest possible opportunity, to continue with the public service reform, to draft a National Poverty Reduction Action Plan and to improve school enrolment through the establishment of the Basic Education sub-Sector Investment Programme.

ESAF II was approved by the IMF in March 1999, paving the way for a Paris Club meeting on bilateral debt-relief in April 1999. The launching of ESAF II and the progress made with the privatisation of ZCCM led to a favourable outcome for Zambia at the May 1999 Consultative Group meeting in Paris as both bilateral and multilateral donors resumed their balance-of-payments support to the extent that balance-of-payments support exceeded debt servicing (for the first time since 1994). External resource transfers to Zambia more than doubled from 1998. But in 1999, again, the gulf between the government's economic policy statements and implementation was displayed. The tax reductions announced in the 1999 budget, the failure to collect fees and charges and another unbudgeted for wage increase for the public sector meant that the objectives of the ESAF II could not be reached.

Thus, Zambia ended the 1990s with yet another unimplemented programme agreed upon with the international donor community. The Rights Accumulation Programme (RAP 1992–1995) was implemented, albeit delayed. But the first ESAF programme 1995–1998 went 'off track' in the first months of 1996. The programme was only implemented for one year (1997), as the government failed to reach an agreement for 1998, due to the government's failure to abide by the commitment to privatise the mines. The second ESAF was launched in March 1999 but the programme was off track again by July 1999. Despite a succession of unimplemented agreements, the July 2000 Consultative Group meeting held in Lusaka pledged one billion US$ in external support and indicated that Zambia would reach the decision-point for HIPC before the end of the year on the basis of the Interim Poverty Reduction Strategy Paper (PRSP) adopted in July 2000.[1] Through the heavily indebted poor countries (HIPC) initiative Zambia was granted debt relief of US$ 3.8bn for a period of 20 years. Arguably, Zambia did not reach the HIPC debt relief due to its economic reform 'track record', but mainly because of policy changes within the international aid regime. By now the HIPC process was severely criticised for being too slow. Furthermore, it was not possible for Zambia to meet the debt repayment schedule as the RAP repayments were scheduled to start in 2001. Without multilateral debt relief Zambia would have become a defaulter almost automatically.

Despite clear limitations to effective donor co-ordination, in the early 1990s, the bilateral and multilateral donors had reached a consensus on economic policy reform. In terms of political reform, or governance issues, however, the bilateral and multilateral donors promoted very different policies, which clearly affected the donors' political leverage.

Political Conditionality Exercised through the Consultative Group Meetings

Governance issues were raised for the first time at the Consultative Group meeting between donors and the Zambian government in April 1993. The meeting represented a distinct shift in the relationship between the Zambian government and its donors. So far, the relationship had been characterised by mutual praise. This time, Zambian politicians, including the President, increasingly warned of interference in the nation's internal political affairs and stressed the need to protect the sovereignty of the nation (*EIU Country Report*, 2nd Quarter 1993; *Africa Report* Vol. 38 No. 3, 1993; *Zambia Daily Mail,* March 26, 1993). At the December 1993 Consultative Group meeting, the bilateral donors made governance issues their main issue of concern and new aid pledges were withheld pending drastic action by the Zambian government on issues of corruption and drug trafficking within high political offices. In clear terms, the delegates of the donor governments stated that continued balance-of-payments support was conditioned on decisive action regarding drug trafficking which was threatening "to turn Zambia into the Colombia of Africa" (*Times of Zambia,* December 15, 1993). Several representatives of the bilateral donor governments present criticised named members of the MMD Cabinet. In their statements, the British, American, German and Japanese representatives argued that the current levels of aid to Zambia could not be sustained unless the issue of drug trafficking was addressed immediately (World Bank/ IBRD 1993c). In his closing statement, the Minister of Finance reassured the donor community that the problems concerning drug trafficking would be dealt with by the end of January (GRZ 1993a).

At the 11th Consultative Group meeting for Zambia held on March 22–23, 1994, the 1993 conflicts appeared to be solved. According to the World Bank,

1. It happened in December 2000.

the March meeting in Paris represented a genuine renewal of partnership (World Bank/IBRD 1994b; Norwegian Ministry of Foreign Affairs 1994). The dismissal of three central members of MMD, and criminal charges raised against two, were by the donors considered as indications of firm action by the Zambian government. All donors indicated that aid withheld, frozen or suspended would be released. As a result of the good progress detected in the areas of both political and economic reforms, for the first time in the history of Zambia's Consultative Group meetings, the financing gap was closed.

The December 1994 Consultative Group meeting indicated that both the Zambian delegation and its external partners were optimistic about reform implementation in 1995. The meeting concluded that a second CG meeting in the spring, as had become the practice in the past, was no longer necessary or conducive. Instead, the government committed itself to more frequent and informal consultations with the donors in Lusaka on economic management and governance issues (World Bank/IBRD 1994c). The late part of 1995 witnessed a distinct decline in the commitment to good governance by the Zambian government linked in time to Kenneth Kaunda's return to politics, and followed by UNIP's political gains in the September 1995 by-elections. Interviews with donor representatives present in Lusaka further indicated that from mid-1995 onwards, it was increasingly more difficult to reach the President.[1]

At the December 1995 Consultative Group meeting in Bournemouth, the tensions between the external partners and government over the issue of governance once again became the main issue of debate. At this meeting, serious concerns were raised on a broad range of governance issues. Several of the external partners addressed the vital links between good governance and economic growth. The Zambian government reiterated its commitment to a constitutional process based on consensus, free and fair elections, and an independent Anti-Corruption Committee (GRZ 1995d). However, the frustrations felt by the government, and the level of conflict in the relationship between the donors and the government at this stage, was illustrated by the opening statement of the Minister of Finance:

> It is understandable why our dialogue in 1995 has focused on key points which have created difficulties. However, it is unfair, and it grossly distorts the picture, to ignore the many positive developments over the last year. (GRZ 1995d)

The sentiments expressed by the bilateral donors, who increasingly felt a sense of betrayal concerning the promises made in 1991, were no weaker. As argued in the closing remark of the head of the US delegation:

> Finally, we note that these [the constitution and the voter registry] are not issues exclusively between donors and the government of Zambia. These are issues being voiced by the people of Zambia; indeed these issues are being driven by the Zambian people. As with the Manifesto, we support the goals being voiced by the Zambian people and will look at our role as a co-operating partner in the light of progress to achieve their goals. (GRZ 1995e)

1. Personal interviews, James Polhemus; Joseph Stepanek, USAID. Lusaka, September 12, 1996; Ingrid Wetterqvist, Political and Commercial Officer, Swedish Embassy. Lusaka, September 5, 1996.

The conclusion of the Consultative Group meeting was that the meeting of Zambia's external financing requirements for 1996 was contingent upon demonstrated progress on key issues of governance in the areas of conduct of free and fair elections, governmental transparency and accountability in the use of public funds as well as some key issues of structural economic reform (*The Post*, December 19, 1995; World Bank/IBRD 1995b; GRZ 1995e). The use of political conditionality and threats of aid withdrawal had produced 'results' in 1993 when three key ministers were dismissed from cabinet positions. But on the issue of the constitution as well as the voter registration process, the government did not bow to the pressure and use of political conditionality by the external donor community. During the spring and summer of 1996, a majority of the bilateral donors announced that they were either withholding balance-of-payments support, freezing discussions on new aid grants, or cutting on-going project aid to Zambia. All bilateral donors cited the lack of progress on good governance and in particular the signing of the constitution banning Kenneth Kaunda from contesting the elections as their main reason for withholding financial support.[1]

Conflicts of Interests

As we have seen, the multilateral donors took a different view on Zambia's reform performance and for the first time since the transition a clear conflict of interests was witnessed between the bilateral and multilateral donors in the early parts of 1996. The World Bank and IMF saw the new initiatives in the privatisation of ZCCM as an indication of the MMD government's continued reform commitment. But after the constitutional changes in May 1996, the bilateral donors lobbied the World Bank through their home offices to stop the release of the first tranche of a US$ 90 million World Bank credit scheduled to be disbursed in June 1996. The IMF review mission in July, nevertheless, maintained that Zambia had met all the major economic and financial benchmarks set forth and it was not possible to withhold funds. As a compromise between the bilateral donors' governance concerns and the economic assessments conducted by the IMF, the Board of the World Bank decided to release US$ 45 million in October 1996. The remaining sum would be released in February 1997, pending a solution to the impasse between the bilateral donor community and the Zambian government related to constitutional issues and the upcoming elections.

The 1996 elections did not bring a solution to the stalemate between the domestic opposition and the government in Zambia. Furthermore, the elections did not bring an end to the chilly diplomatic climate between the external donor community and the Zambian government. In January, the MMD government commenced on a process of confidence building. The first meeting between the Zambian government and its external partners on the issue of governance was

1. The United Kingdom was the first bilateral donor to announce the suspension of US$ 10 million in balance-of-payments support shortly after the constitution was signed into law on May 28 (*ANC Network News* Harare, June 6, 1996). Norway then suspended all of its non-project aid on June 5 amounting to an annual amount of US$ 40 million. The US followed shortly after suspending 10 per cent of its aid to Zambia on July 16 (approximately US$ 3,5 million). In the weeks and months following, Japan, the Netherlands, Sweden, Denmark and Finland followed.

convened by the Zambian government in London in April 1997. Again, the Minister of Finance headed the Zambian delegation. In his speech to the meeting, he emphasised the developments in the areas of improving governance issues since the 1996 elections. The attempts to reach a dialogue with the opposition, and the institutional developments particularly with respect to the newly established autonomous electoral commission, human rights commission and the anti-corruption commission, were emphasised (GRZ 1997b). In June 1997 the International Institute for Democracy and Electoral Assistance (IDEA), convened a meeting between the opposition parties and the Zambian government in Stockholm with representatives from most of the bilateral donors as well as UNDP and the World Bank present as observers.[1] During this meeting, the parties agreed to continue the dialogue.[2] The meetings between the MMD government and the opposition were unsuccessful in terms of reaching a consensus.[3] Arguably, the main result of the aborted meetings between the government and the opposition in late June was that the government was able to claim that dialogue had been attempted but was prevented by the stubbornness and lack of imagination of the opposition (*EIU Country Report,* 3rd Quarter, 1997).

At the Consultative Group meeting in Paris in July 1997, the donors acknowledged the initiatives taken by the MMD government towards reconciling with the opposition through the London meeting and the attempts to follow up on the agreement reached in Stockholm (World Bank/IBRD 1997b; World Bank/IBRD 1997a). Expressing satisfaction with the positive developments, the meeting concluded that the ground was laid for the donors to engage in more active cooperation with the Zambian government. At the July Consultative Group meeting, the donors lifted the existing aid-freeze on Zambia by granting US$ 435 million to the country for 1997. Despite intense lobbying from opposition parties and human rights groups, including Amnesty International and Human Rights Watch/Africa, calling for a maintenance of the aid-freeze, the international donors decided that the MMD government should be rewarded for the progress towards good governance (*The Post*, July 10, 1997). And while the donor enthusiasm experienced in 1991 was largely gone, Zambia and its external donors resumed 'business as usual' in the summer of 1997. The government had maintained the economic reform programme, but refused to abide by the demands raised regarding the voter registration procedure and the constitutional amendment process. As argued by the Economist Intelligence Unit Report: "The government's risky policy stand of standing firm on these issues and waiting out the bilateral donor aid-freeze has paid off in a spectacular fashion" (*EIU Country Report*, 3rd Quarter, 1997:9).[4]

1. IDEA, or the International Institute for Democracy and Electoral Assistance, is an international organisation set up in 1995 and located in Stockholm. It is funded by 14 governments and a number of NGOs.
2. "The Stromsborg Statement on building sustainable democracy in Zambia" was signed by the opposition and the government of Zambia. The government committed itself to initiate a dialogue which would emphasise the design of the electoral process and increase the democratic capacity of Zambian institutions. IDEA 1997.
3. See the discussion in Chapter 5.
4. Confirming EIU's perspective, the Zambian Minister of Finance opened his closing statement by thanking the external donors for allowing him a good night's sleep for the first time in many months. The comment was revealed in a phone interview with Anke van der Hoeve Heek, Desk Officer, Zambia and Malawi, Dutch Ministry of Foreign Affairs, August 1, 1997.

A Break of Agreement with All Donors

All attempts at furthering the political liberalisation process and fostering dialogue and reconciliation between the MMD government and the Zambian opposition stalled in the latter part of 1997 due to the October 1997 attempted coup d'état. The government's follow-up to the coup-attempt, including the arrest of opposition leaders and allegations of torture of the detained, also affected the dialogue with Zambia's external partners. Due both to the slow progress on ZCCM's privatisation and the unresolved governance situation, the informal Consultative Group meeting planned for December 1997 was postponed. In January 1998 the World Bank again announced the postponement of the planned Consultative Group meeting, *despite* IMF's positive mid-term review completed in December 1997. This suggested that governance issues—and in particular the arrest of Kenneth Kaunda that remained high on the agenda of the bilateral donors—had become increasingly more important for the World Bank as well (*EIU Country Profile*, 1st Quarter 1998:19). At the May 1998 Consultative Group meeting in Paris the Zambian government promised reforms in the police and prison services. However, the main and overriding concerns of the donor community were the failed privatisation of ZCCM (see discussion above). Bilateral and multilateral balance-of-payments support started to arrive in 1999. As in 1997, at the May 1999 Consultative Group meeting in Paris, the concern of stability in the region was brought forth as an issue and Zambia was held out as a stable country in a region of conflict. Nevertheless, governance issues, especially human rights concerns and the high level of corruption remained high on the donors' agenda. The government presented for the first time a 'nationally owned' Capacity Building Programme for Good Governance envisioned as a basis for the donors and government to work together to systematically improve governance. The outcome of the meeting was positive for the Zambian government as donor pledges again exceeded the annual debt servicing requirements.

With the sale of the mines in March 2000, the focus of the donor community shifted almost entirely from economic policy to governance issues. Reflecting the policy changes in the international aid regime, now emphasising ownership and participation in processes of poverty reduction, in July 2000 for the first time the Consultative Group meeting was held in Lusaka. Due to pressure from the donor community, and the emphasis placed on civil society participation in the formulation of the poverty reduction strategy papers (PRSPs), the dialogue with civil society was intensified in the build-up to the July 2000 Consultative Group meeting. The CG meeting praised the Zambian government for having produced an interim PRSP and for its domestic stability and constructive role in the region's conflicts. On this basis, and impressed with the capacity of the Zambian civil society, the donors pledged US$ 1 billion pending accelerated progress in poverty reduction, continued economic reforms and a wide range of governance issues.[1] These included specific demands to increase participation in the

1. The positive influence of Zambian NGOs at the CG meeting was emphasised in personal interviews with Kikkan Haugen, Royal Norwegian Embassy, Lusaka, January 25, 2001; Besinati Mpepo, Civil Society for Poverty Reduction (CSPR) Co-ordinator, Lusaka October 10, 2002; Peter Henriot, Jesuit Centre for Theological Reflection (JCTR), Lusaka, October 7, 2002.

2001 election through an update of the voter-register; equal treatment of all parties contesting; and concerns of civil society. According to Economist Intelligence Unit's analysis, the government's main selling point was the significant impact made by civil society organisations:

> The only certain winners in the conditionality process that surrounds aid appear to be the international and national human rights organisations who have made it their business to demand governance reform and whose influence has been strengthened by their role in the Paris Club talks. (*EIU Country Report,* July 2000:13)

The 2001 presidential, parliamentary and local government elections brought forth a number of contentious issues pertaining to the MMD government's commitment to democracy and political reforms. The attempts to alter the constitution to allow Chiluba a third term in office and the establishment of the District Administrators reporting directly to the President were the issues that generated the most debate in the pre-election period. But in marked contrast to their sharp reaction to the 1996 constitutional amendment process, the international donors and the embassies in Lusaka remained quiet on the third term issue and did not play an active part in the domestic pre-election debates. After a long period marked by significant civil society driven opposition to Chiluba's third term bid, and after President Chiluba officially announced that he did not intend to seek a third term in office, the embassies of Denmark, Finland, Ireland, Netherlands, Norway, Sweden, the United Kingdom, and United States issued a statement supporting Chiluba's intent to step down. At the 2000 CG meeting the Zambian government had presented an action plan on good governance and human rights. Observing that very few of the criteria agreed to in this plan had been fulfilled, the bilateral donors within the European Union, nevertheless, agreed to release funding to support the government through the Electoral Commission for the 2001 elections. During interviews with the donors present in Zambia most were very critical to the governance record of the Zambian government. However, many feared that without donor support, the electoral process would become a sham.[1] The 2001 elections were denounced by both international and local election observers (AFRONET 2003). In his inaugural speech, Levy Mwanawasa condemned the role of the EU, strongly hinting that the donors had backed his opponent Anderson Mazoka (UPND).[2] Nevertheless, in March 2002 the European Union decided not to take any punitive actions against the Zambian government arguing that the election results had not been followed by state terrorism. As in 1997, the EU and other major bilateral donors tied their continued aid to constitutional reform, the continued fight against corruption and an improved electoral commission.[3] While less blatant than in 1996, the 2001 elections displayed the limited capacity of external actors to fur-

1. Personal interviews, Kristina Svensson, Swedish Ambassador, Lusaka July 17, 2001; Helen Millen, British High Commission, Lusaka, July 20, 2001; Anne Sofie Allarp, European Commission, Lusaka, July 24, 2001.
2. Inaugural speech by Mr. Levy Patrick Mwanawasa Wednesday 2, 2002.
3. Due to the uncertainties linked to the 2001 elections, no Consultative Group meeting was called. In July 2002, the World Bank again called a CG meeting for Zambia and its donors in Livingstone, again with poverty reduction as the main issue and civil society playing a vital role.

ther democratic processes through conditionality instruments in the absence of recipient government willingness.

Playing the External Game: The Leverage of the Zambian Government vis-à-vis Its External Partners

The 1990s should have signified a new era in donor-government relations in Zambia. A democratically elected government, committed to economic reform, set out to work closely with the international donor community in an attempt to turn the Zambian economy around. Assessing the relationship between the Zambian government and the international donor community in the Third Republic, the dynamics of the relationship appear to have passed through four stages: in the first phase, the level of enthusiasm was high, as the donor community was eager to support the new reformist government on the basis of the 1991 Manifesto. However, the relationship moved quickly to a second stage, as it soon became clear that the MMD government was very diverse. In this phase, donors sought to support the pro-reform ministers in Cabinet, still within a pro-reform partnership. Third, from 1994 onwards the relationship became characterised by hard negotiations and increasing use of conditionality instruments. This tactic was in particular evident in terms of the privatisation process, but also with regard to governance issues. Finally, in the post-election period (1996), the credibility of the conditionality instruments waned. The Zambian government adopted a more and more critical and sceptical attitude towards the donors increasingly viewing the process of policy reform as externally imposed. The international donor community also lost faith in the effectiveness of the conditionality-induced reform. The millennium shifts in the international aid regime, focusing on debt-relief and poverty reduction, emphasising civic participation and national ownership, reflect the frustrations felt with the dual conditionality policy of the 1990s.

Leverage in Economic Governance 1991–2001

The political transition in 1991 offered a new situation as the new democratically elected government indicated its intentions of reforming the economic system and working with the international donor community. As argued by the Zambian local press, for the MMD government facing an escalating economic crisis situation the question was not whether to adopt an IMF/WB approved structural adjustment programme but rather, which steps to take to meet the requirements of the IMF/World Bank policies (*Financial Mail*, April 21–27, 1992). The emphasis placed on restoring Zambia's international financial reputation was further underlined by one observer:

> Economic reform is meant to fundamentally alter a country's growth prospects. In principle, reform is not primarily a means of satisfying external creditors. But because of Zambia's poor credit standing, a practical precondition for the resumption of sustained growth is for Zambia to re-establish a reputation of responsible financial behaviours. Thus, a major objective for the reform effort has been to gain regular access to interna-

Zambian government & donor community

> tional finance as due to its debt overhang Zambia could not finance its economic imbalances independently of donor support. (McPherson 1995:14)

In retrospect, it may be argued that the initial period after the 1991 elections reflected an almost uncritical acceptance of the donor policy agenda on a number of economic issues. In a number of areas of policy reform, particularly in the area of trade reforms, the MMD government is regarded as having over-committed and carried out reforms too rapidly. As argued in Chapter 4, financial liberalisation was carried out prior to the achievement of fiscal balance. This increased the fiscal costs of stabilisation. According to the ESAF evaluation (Botchwey et al. 1998) the MMD government went ahead with its decision to liberalise the economy at an early stage against the advice of IMF.[1] Adams argues that the government hoped to signal its commitment to economic reform to the international donor community through decisive moves in the area of financial liberalisation:

> In the absence of other mechanisms to signal its commitment to reform, the government chose to accelerate the liberalisation measures, even though it distorted the logical sequence of reforms and imposed significant costs on the economy later in the stabilisation process. (Adams 1995:738)

Adam's argument appears plausible. During the UNIP era the Kaunda regime failed on a number of occasions to implement the agricultural and financial liberalisation measures strongly advocated by the external donors. These areas of reform were the ones pushed most consistently by the new MMD government almost from the start of its election period. The government used its 'honeymoon' to implement far-reaching reforms in the areas of liberalisation because these reforms would signal MMD's clear commitment to implement 'new' economic policies in contrast to the former regime. Arguably, the main reward for carrying out these reform measures was witnessed in the relationship to the international donor community. The negotiations carried out at the various Consultative Group meetings between Zambia and the external donor community indicate that the commitment displayed in the areas of financial and agricultural liberalisation was instrumental in the donor community's decision to reward the Zambian government with extraordinary levels of financial assistance in the 1992–94 period. Similarly, in 1993 when the government accepted the donors' advice of implementing a cash budgeting system, a new 'commitment barometer' was established. The adherence to the cash budget and the resulting decline in inflation, became a significant policy measure in terms of donor support. Minister of Finance Emmanuel Kasonde's statement to parliament illustrates the importance of international credibility and the centrality of attracting donor finance and support when presenting the 1993 Budget. Defending the decision to remove subsidies on maize meal and fertiliser, the Minister of Finance made no secret of the main intention behind this decision. Emphasising that the move would save the government around US$ 10 million, according to

1. This view is seconded in an earlier evaluation of the implementation of RAP (IMF 1995). Representatives of the World Bank and IMF also raised this issue in personal interviews. Ellah Chembe, World Bank. Lusaka June 6, 1995 and E. Talia, resident representative IMF. Lusaka, December 10, 1996.

the Minister of Finance, the main result would be the securing of an estimated US$ 600 million in donor support required by Zambia that year (GRZ, *Budget Address* 1993). Commenting on the fact that few of the economic targets set for 1992 had been met, the minister nevertheless, noted that:

> Our commitment to policy reform has yielded substantial benefits already. For example, we have been able to reactivate our Rights Accumulation Programme with the International Monetary Fund, which paved the way for external assistance amounting to US$ 1.5 billion. This amount is unprecedented in our history. (GRZ *Budget Address*, 1993)

Leverage in the Area of Privatisation

The issue of privatisation was raised in the meetings between the Zambian government and its external donors from the very beginning. According to observers, the urgency expressed by the donors in terms of privatisation in part reflected the lack of results on this aspect of structural reforms under Kenneth Kaunda. But it also reflected a desire to take advantage of the support and legitimacy enjoyed by MMD in the early stages of the reform period.[1] Reflecting the changes from a co-operative relationship to a conditionality based relationship, more explicit conditionality measures were utilised by the external donor community in order to push the privatisation programme forward from 1994 onwards. As argued in Chapter 4, the issue of privatisation only had a small group of influential supporters in Zambia and even the Zambian business community was divided on the issue of privatisation. Comparing the analysis of the internal policy debates on the process of privatisation to the external debate between the international donors and the government at the various Consultative Group meetings, external pressure, through a combination of 'promotion' mechanisms, and economic conditionality from the donors, played a significant role in terms of moving the process of privatisation in Zambia forward. In interviews with approximately 40 representatives of various multilateral donor organisations and representatives of bilateral governments, all respondents cited the privatisation process as either the main, or one of two main, adjustment achievements of Zambia during the period in question. The interviews also indicated that in terms of donor leverage, and thus the success of their economic conditionality policies, the progress achieved in the area of privatisation was considered the main area of success. For the first time since coming to power, in late 1994 the MMD government ran into serious conflict with the IMF when failing to meet the monetary benchmarks agreed for an advancement to an ESAF agreement in March 1995. Slippage on a number of macro-economic indicators led the international donors to question the MMD government's continued commitment to economic liberalisation. The new benchmarks negotiated with the IMF for the postponement of the ESAF agreement strongly emphasised progress in the area of parastatal reform. Incidentally, it was only when encountering these problems that the government made the policy decision that appeared to secure progress

1. Personal communications, Oliver Campbell White, Senior Public Enterprises Specialist, World Bank, Washington DC, March 11, 1997 and Hendrick van der Heijden, External Advisor, Ministry of Finance, Lusaka, October 28, 1996.

in the process of privatisation, namely to liquidate the holding company, ZIMCO. Furthermore, it was under increasing donor pressure and reduction of funds due to governance issues that the Zambian government in 1996 officially announced the date for the sale of the mines (ZCCM) which was set to February 28, 1997. The MMD government's commitment to a date for the privatisation of the mining industry in 1996 was the main reason behind the multilateral finance institutions' decision to continue financing the Zambian reform programme in 1996. It was also the prospects of the sale of the copper mines, and associated investments expected to flow from it, that induced most bilateral donors to resume their funding to Zambia at the July 1997 Consultative Group meeting. Similarly, when the Zambian government, to the donors' great dismay, failed to complete the sale of the mines in 1998, for the first time, the entire donor community cut balance-of-payments support. It was only when the sale of the mines was finalised in March 2000 that the donors resumed 'normal' dialogue with the Zambian government.

Conditionality to 'Fend Off' Internal Opposition

The debates on the issue of privatisation in the local Zambian press suggest that the Zambian government applied the threats made by the donors to withhold funds to justify the unpopular decisions on privatisation to its domestic audience. This is most clearly indicated by the government's handling of the liquidation of Zambia Airways. Before the December 1994 Consultative Group meeting, the international donor community threatened to withhold substantial amounts of their financial support unless the Zambian government committed to honouring the agreement reached with its external partners in 1992. The agreement included the eradication of subsidies to the national airline and/or the liquidation of the company. According to the external donors, the continued extra-budgetary payments allocated to the airline constituted a central problem in terms of attaining macro-economic stability. The pressure placed on the Zambian government to reach a political decision before the Consultative Group meeting was illustrated by the statement of the World Bank's vice-President for Africa, Edward Jaycox, who, when visiting Zambia in early December stated that "the [Zambian] government has a decision to make and we expect them to make it" (*EIU Country Report*, 1st Quarter 1995:10).

The question of phasing out the national airline was a problematic political issue both due to the number of jobs affected and a sense of national pride. The Minister of Finance made no secret of the fact that the threats posed by the donor community constituted the main reason for the government to suspend the airline when he told the local press that unless Zambia 'toed the line' in the case of Zambia Airways, the country would risk losing not only the US$ 160 million that the donors threatened to withdraw, but the whole economic recovery programme (*Times of Zambia,* November 29, 1994). The termination of the government holding company ZIMCO followed a similar process. The role of ZIMCO was raised as a concern by the external donors from 1994 onwards. However, as late as October 1993, the MMD government ordered the Zambia

Privatisation Agency to co-operate with ZIMCO, indicating that the political sympathies were with the parastatal holding company and not the new independent agency.[1] The World Bank, however, demanded that ZIMCO be closed down as a condition for calling the December 1994 Consultative Group meeting. In the face of threats by the donors, the Zambian delegation committed itself to closing ZIMCO by March 1995. After intense donor pressure, the Zambian government was forced in 1995 to honour this commitment and dissolve the holding company in order to maintain the level of funding from the international donors.[2] Confirming the influence of the external donor community, the first director of ZPA (who was dismissed in September 1994) claimed that his removal had been instigated by the donors who for a long time had argued that the privatisation process was moving too slowly (*Times of Zambia*, September 10, 1994).[3] The World Bank representative responsible for the privatisation exercise confirmed:

> The Bretton Woods Institutions were instrumental in ZIMCO's removal, they passed a fait accompli to the government. The point is that MMD also wanted to get rid of ZIMCO and we made it politically possible for them to do it earlier. With ZIMCO out of the way, things certainly became easier for ZPA as they had easier access to information and they were able to reduce the level of asset-stripping.[4]

Representatives on the Zambian side confirmed the level of donor pressure witnessed in the process of privatisation. According to the second director of ZPA, Steven Mwamba:

> The role of donors has been substantial. ...Without these it would have been very difficult to bring out quality work. ... I do not blame the donors for pushing, it is after all their tax payers money, they must be accountable to their people.

The MMD government's emphasis on maintaining a good relationship to the IFIs by, at least in principle, meeting the benchmarks set marks a contrast between the conduct of economic reform in the 1980s and the 1990s. Despite the macro-economic problems encountered from 1995 onwards, Zambia remained up-to-date on its external debt service payments throughout the two Chiluba administrations.[5] Debt servicing was maintained despite donors withholding balance-of-payments support. Furthermore, the government accelerated the privatisation programme, maintained the monetary reforms and the liberalised trade regime in 1996 despite a growing domestic opposition and the up-coming national elections. In the eyes of the international donor community, the progress of the economic restructuring programme therefore justified con-

1. Personal communications, James Mutale, Director ZPA 1992–94. Lusaka, October 14, 1996. This conclusion is also reflected in a report by van de Walle and Chiwele (1994:39).
2. The external pressure as a driving force behind the accelerated pace of the privatisation programme was further noted by Theo Bull, (ZACCI), Lusaka, January 15, 1997; Ian Fraser, external advisor, Zambia Privatisation Agency (ZPA), Lusaka, June 5, 1995; Dr. Felix Kani, Bank of Zambia, Lusaka, October 3, 1996. For similar analyses see *EIU Country Report,* 2nd Quarter 1995 and *Financial Times,* March 4, 1997.
3. See also personal interviews with James Mutale and Steven Mwamba, successor to the directorship, Executive Director Zambia Privatisation Agency 1994–1995. Lusaka, January 7, 1997.
4. Personal communication, Oliver Campbell White, Senior Public Enterprises Specialist, World Bank. Washington DC, March 11, 1997.
5. Although it is clear that as the RAP payments to IMF were scheduled to begin in 2000, without the multilateral debt relief through HIPC, Zambia would not have been able to service its debt.

tinued support to Zambia despite the regression witnessed in terms of democracy and good governance. It may therefore be argued that the government used adherence to the economic reform demands from the donor community as a 'trump card' before the international donors when serious conflict arose over the issues of respect for human rights and political liberties.

Leverage in Political Governance 1991–2001

The relationship between MMD and the international donor community was very positive in the first years of MMD's electoral term. The international donor community shared the political and economic visions of the new Zambian government, presented in the 1991 Manifesto. The MMD Manifesto committed the new government to accountability, to the strengthening of the legislature and the parliament vis-à-vis the cabinet, to the party from the state, to freedom of speech and association, as well as to adopting a new constitution based on the principle of consensus. On the basis of its Manifesto, the MMD was given a large electoral majority in the 1991 elections. However, the Manifesto also functioned as the basic document, or 'contract', between the new government and its external supporters, as it became a significant document in terms of securing the return of high levels of financial support from the international donor community. As a result, in the conflicts unfolding between the Zambian government and the international donor community in the period leading up to the 1996 elections, the question of adherence to the principles laid out in the 1991 Manifesto became a key issue.

In retrospect, the cabinet reshuffles and the introduction of state of emergency laws in the spring of 1993 ended the 'honeymoon' between the domestic opposition and the government. Maybe not surprisingly, the very same issues changed the relationship between the MMD government and the external donors from one of cooperation to one of conflict.

External Events Triggering Internal Policy Changes

At the airport coming home from the December 1993 Consultative Group meeting, the delegation led by the Minister of Finance told the press that they had committed themselves to attacking the problem of corruption and drug trafficking, and stated that this issue would be brought before the cabinet as soon as possible *(Times of Zambia,* December 15, 1993). However, the statement of the returning delegation contrasted sharply with comments made by the Minister of Home Affairs the previous day. When commenting on the donor ultimatum presented in Paris, Hon. Mr. Sata urged donors to stop pointing fingers at Zambia and instead present proof of their allegations of drug trafficking (*Times of Zambia,* December 14, 1993). Presented with the statement of the Minister of Home Affairs at the airport, the Deputy Minister of Planning and Development Cooperation, Hon. Mr. Mung'omba, declared that the excuse of asking for proof was no longer available, it was now time to act decisively on the issue of drug trafficking (*Times of Zambia,* December 15, 1993). The decision to address the press before officially informing the President of the events at the CG meeting created conflicts in the MMD Cabinet. Both the Minister of Health and the Deputy Development Minister were dismissed from their cabinet positions. The Minister of Finance 'survived' the reshuffles by publicly excusing himself for having made a public statement over the issue of drug trafficking and corruption before briefing the President (*Times of Zambia,* January 1, 1994). However, in an apparent response to the demands raised by the donors at the December Consultative Group meeting, the Minister of Foreign Affairs, Vernon Mwaanga, as well as the Community Development Minister, Princess Nakatindi Wina, and Deputy National Assembly Speaker, Sikota Wina, were later forced to resign their positions pending investigations on drug trafficking (*The Post*, January 7, 1994).

The form of conditionality imposed through the CG meeting process became more conflictual in governance than economic issues. This related both to the issues and type of politicians involved. These meetings involved politicians and MMD ministers with portfolios related to domestic and internal affairs. As a result, the level of conflicts intensified as these ministers increasingly regarded the donors as interfering in internal affairs. Furthermore, whereas the officials in the ministries of finance, commerce and agriculture with relative ease could ensure the implementation of conditions related to budget deficits and market liberalisation, non-political issues of democracy and accountability were largely outside their political domain (Fundanga 1996:95).

According to donor representatives in Lusaka, the late part of 1995 witnessed a distinct decline in the commitment to good governance by the Zambian government. Most saw the quality of governance as having deteriorated sharply and linked this development to Kaunda's return, as well as the stagnant economy and increasing levels of unemployment. But whereas the use of political conditionality and threats of aid withdrawal produced 'results' in 1993, when several ministers were removed from Cabinet, this time the government did not bow to donor pressure. The first informal meeting between the donors and the government in Lusaka was convened in March 1995 and the governance section discussed the constitutional review process, the electoral reform process, privatisation of the media, and the public order act. According to one participant, most important aspect was the fact that the meeting took place at all, due to the sensitivity of the issues involved in terms of national sovereignty.[1] But one donor representative suggested that the preparatory meetings had brought political conditionality to the centre of domestic policy making and that these meetings had increased, rather than solved, tensions between the partners.[2] As the work on the constitutional review process increasingly became tied to Kenneth Kaunda's return to the Presidency of UNIP, the informal gatherings between the donors and the Zambian government became more conflictual. Before the Consultative Group meeting scheduled for December 15, a preparatory meeting between the donors and the Zambian government was conducted in Lusaka (December 5, 1995). Alluding to the government's sense of frustration with the

1. Personal interview, James Polhemus, Good Governance Advisor, USAID. Lusaka, September 11, 1996.
2. "Consultative Group meeting for Zambia, Bournemouth, December 14–15, 1995". Statement prepared for the Zambia Consultative Group meeting by UNDP resident representative in Lusaka, Gary Davis. (World Bank: From vice-President and Secretary. Confidential).

increasing level of donor pressure and threats of conditionality, the Minister of Finance, Ronald Penza, stressed the economic achievements of the government and urged the donors to judge Zambia relative to other developing nations which would indicate that Zambia was indeed successful both in terms of political and economic liberalisation. When a representative of the donor community intervened that Zambia should be judged according to the Manifesto of 1991 which constituted a contract both between the government and its citizens as well as its external partners, the answer from a representative of government was given in the form of a loud laugh.[1]

While it may be argued that the change from conducive relations to mutual distrust related to a *combination* of economic slippage and reversals in the field of political liberalisation, it was first and foremost governance issues that generated the heated conflicts before the 1996 elections. Indicating the donors' degree of involvement in domestic policy processes in Zambia at the time, many donors present in Lusaka in 1996 expressed that they felt 'betrayed' by the MMD government. Focusing on the expectations present on both sides after the 1991 elections, a representative of the Japanese government, one of Zambia's largest bilateral contributors, argued that:

> Concerning the leverage of the donors, I think it was great in the beginning. We talked of a honeymoon where Zambia needed us, the government was ambitious and we were prepared to increase our aid. Somewhere down the middle of the road government thinking changed and they started saying, 'wait, this is OK but do we have to accept all advice, even unnecessary?' I think the honeymoon ended over the Nikuv contract [voter registration] which became a major turning point. This crisis was amplified by the Meridian crisis. Then everyone felt that their dream was over. That is when we started pointing fingers at one another. I think there is a crisis of expectations on both sides.[2]

The comment above underscores the level of expectations on both the Zambian and the international donor community's side after the 1991 elections. Due to the conducive relationship starting in 1991, based largely on MMD's political manifesto, the international donor community expected far more progress both in terms of adherence to democratic principles and economic reforms from Zambia than from 'the average African' country, as expressed in the Consultative Group discussions. Zambia in 1991 had represented something very different; an ambitious agenda promising an economic turn-around within the context of democratic governance procedures. The Zambian government for its part had expected that some years of fiscal austerity measures and economic hardships would present results in terms of growth, employment creation and substantially increased levels of foreign investments. As argued by a delegate at the December 1995 Consultative Group meeting: "The honeymoon between the

1. The level of resentment and conflict between the government and bilateral donors was further illustrated by the Minister of Finance's emotional response to the representative of the United Kingdom. When the UK representative raised the issue of individual malpractice within the Cabinet, the Finance Minister responded by asking whether donors ranted about corruption because they wanted Kenneth Kaunda back. According to donor representatives present, the two first of a total of five local meetings were successful. After a while, the meetings became so conflictual that the government refused to carry on with them. After December 1995, no new meetings were called. The events of the Lusaka meetings, referred to as 'mini-CG's' was revealed in personal interviews with James Polhemus and Joseph Stepanek, USAID mission in Lusaka. See also Stepanek 1999 (Chapter 7).
2. Personal interview, Mitsunori Yuuki, First Secretary, Embassy of Japan. Lusaka, August 29, 1996.

donors and government is over. Maybe we will [now] have a more realistic relationship based on trust".[1]

But, the fact that the bilateral and multilateral donors opted for different strategies clearly limited their leverage on governance issues.

Divisions among the External Partners

Following the bilateral aid-reductions due to the issues of governance, during the summer of 1996 an intense debate unfolded between the bilateral donors and the multilateral agencies of the World Bank and the IMF. Phrasing the decision of the Board as a form of compromise, the World Bank declared that their funding would be wasted unless bilateral assistance was resumed.[2] Obviously, the clout of the bilateral aid-freeze was reduced when the World Bank Board decided to release US$ 45 million in balance-of-payments support. A number of the bilateral donor representatives argued that if the large contribution of the World Bank had not been made available, things would have been different in Zambia in 1996. Many bilateral donors felt that President Chiluba would have been forced to retreat if the multilateral institutions had supported the position taken by the bilateral donor agencies.[3]

The conflicts arising between the bilateral and multilateral donor community in Zambia in 1996 also clearly illustrate the different incentives and goals facing the multilateral and bilateral aid agencies. The Articles of Agreement of the international finance institutions stated that their operations should not be based on political considerations. The introduction of the concept of governance by the World Bank in the late 1980s was therefore deliberately elaborated so as not to be defined as 'political democracy' associated with pluralism and electoral rule. However, in reality, through its role as host and convenor of the Consultative Group meetings, the World Bank also explicitly raised governance issues. The combined effects of the continued disbursements from the multilateral donors and the debt rescheduling agreements, which were not affected by the aid-freeze, meant that Zambia's overall balance-of-payments position was not severely affected by the 1996 bilateral aid-withdrawals. The figures provided by the Ministry of Finance illustrates the key role played by the continued multilateral funding for Zambia's finances following the freeze of much bilateral aid. The bilateral balance-of-payments support which amounted to US$ 22 million in 1996 was more than 80 per cent lower than in 1995 and represented less than 6 per cent of its 1992 levels. However, World Bank support in 1996 was the highest since 1992, at US$ 190 million, "enabling the Zambian government to weather the liquidity crisis engendered by the aid cuts" (*EIU Country Report,* 1st Quarter 1997:18).

1. Statement of the Irish Delegation (Brendan Rodgers): World Bank/IBRD 1995b.
2. Information on the communications between the World Bank and the bilateral shareholders and details of the October 1996 vote of the World Bank Board was conveyed in personal interviews with Meredith Scoville, Director USAID, Southern Africa Department, Washington DC, March 12, 1997; Phyllis Pomerantz, Country Director Africa Region, World Bank. Washington DC, March 10, 1997 and Charles Moen, chief economist, USAID, Lusaka, September 19, 1996.
3. However, it is unclear whether the donor representatives in Lusaka actually had the support of their own home offices as only the United States voted against this decision at the October meeting of the World Bank Board.

Table 6.3: Net aid transfers to Zambia 1991-1999 (US$ million)

	1991	1992	1993	1994	1995	1996	1997	1998	1999
Total External Assistance	926	928	623	556	559	445	422	322	445
BoP support	586	491	299	278	304	142	120	0	176
World Bank	202	165	144	148	160	121	111	0	107
Other	384	326	155	130	144	21	9	0	69
Commodity Aid	74	246	90	26	40	34	0	3	0
Drought	16	146	40	0	40	0	0	2	0
Other	58	100	50	26	0	34	0	1	0
Project Finance	266	191	234	252	215	269	302	330	269
Debt Relief	293	551	359	260	234	310	159	122	443
Total External Financing	1,219	1,479	982	816	793	755	581	444	888
Gross Debt Service	-718	-678	-522	-541	-590	-453	-376	-315	-597
Net Transfers	501	801	460	275	203	302	205	129	291

Source: GRZ: Ministry of Finance, 2000.

An additional factor facilitating the situation for the Zambian government in the midst of donor conflict, was the reduction in Zambia's net debt-service payments to an estimated US$ 399 million compared to US$ 519 million in 1995. The figures presented provide a key to understanding the limits of donor conditionality in terms of governance and the potential conflicts of interest between the principles of political liberalisation and economic liberalisation. The bilateral donor agencies presented an unusually unified and coherent policy reaction to the political actions of the MMD government. However, the fact that substantial amounts of their aid had been tied to the multilateral finance institutions and the implementation of economic rescheduling programmes, at least in the short run, rendered a purely bilateral reaction of limited effect. Representatives of the World Bank acknowledged that it had taken a rather 'soft' approach to Zambia. Answering the charges made by the bilateral donors that the international finance institutions were in fact 'too soft' on Zambia, the World Bank's principal economist for Zambia offered the following explanation:

> It is true that it is unusual that the Bank and Fund are regarded as too soft. This may be related to riding a bicycle. The phenomenon is that the economy is going along, one can make it go better by providing a little boost and when one is not too happy one can take the programme off for a while. This will reduce gear from 5 to 3 and the likely event is to bring it back even higher. However, the Zambian case is one of sensation where the bicycle cannot afford to slow down due to the incredible high debt servicing burden. The cost of an interruption is too high, the cost of reconstruction in terms of arrears complied is unsustainable. The experiences between 1985 and 1987 and also in 1991 has affected everybody and associated with that, it is not an easy thing to do as stopping [the adjustment programme] in Zambia would mean going from 5 to minus 5 and not from 5 to 3 in terms of complement of arrears. That is why we have got to be careful.[1]

1. Personal communications, John Todd, Principal Economist Macroecoomics, Southern Africa World Bank. Lusaka, January 16, 1996.

The Limits of Political Conditionality

As argued in Chapter 2, many studies point to the dilemmas of political conditionality and the potential conflicts between the application of conditionality and the building and consolidation of democratic institutions. The case of Zambia's dual reform processes in the period after 1991 reflects these general concerns. The conflicts between the need for consistency in aid flows to sustain and secure the processes of reform and the increasing application of donor conditionality witnessed from 1993 onwards, strained the relationship between the government and its external partners. The donor community, and in particular the various bilateral donors present in Lusaka, judged the declining performance of the MMD government on both political and economic reforms against the goals presented in the 1991 Manifesto. The MMD government, however, asked to be judged in comparison with other developing nations as well as Zambia's previous economic and political record.[1] Echoing the sense of betrayal felt among the international donors, a number of government officials who had been part of designing and implementing the reform programme, expressed anger towards the external donors as they felt MMD was being judged much more harshly than Kenneth Kaunda had been during his 27 years in office.

The Zambian government refused to bow to the demands raised by both the international donors and the local opposition on postponing the debate of' the Constitution to the next electoral term, and scraping the use of the voter registry and instead letting people vote on the basis of their National Registration Cards. Choosing to abide, in principle, by the conditions set as regards economic reforms, yet refusing to abide by the political conditionality ties, the Zambian government presented the bilateral donor community with a dilemma. Their use of political conditionality and withdrawal of balance-of-payments support had not produced the intended political response from the MMD government. By continuing and extending the withholding of financial support, the bilateral donors faced the dilemma of causing the structural adjustment programme to default at a time when the benefits of the privatisation of the mines was in sight. In the press, as well as in the negotiations with the external donors, the Zambian government indicated that it saw its commitment to carrying out an economic reform programme as more important than the process of political liberalisation. Increasingly, government representatives presented the issue as one in which Zambia had committed itself to carrying out an economic reform programme. From the perspective of the government, it was the bilateral donor community who had changed their agenda along the way by deciding to also include issues of governance. From 1996 onwards, members of the MMD government have criticised the external actors for introducing new hurdles, for 'blackmailing the government to follow an external dictate' and for 'interfering with Zambia's principle rights as a sovereign nation' (*The Post*, April 9, 1996; *The Post,* June 19, 1996; *Times of Zambia*, May 21, 1996). The multilateral institutions have

1. In his opening statement to the December 1995 Consultative Group meeting, this was the Minister of Finance's main argument, which was repeated by various members of the MMD government throughout the 1996 election campaign (*The Post*, August 13, 1996).

been portrayed as the real partners of Zambia due to their main focus on the economic reform process.

The conduct of the 1996 elections, and the fact that the multilateral finance institutions insisted that Zambia's 'economic house was in order', to a certain extent shifted the burden of responsibility from the Zambian government to the bilateral donors. Given the tension between the short-term goals of debt reimbursement and the longer-term goal of sustained economic development, the rhetorical question of ownership of the debt problem provided no clear answer in the case of Zambia. The statement by the chief economic advisor at the Swedish embassy illustrated the conflicts and dilemmas involved for all parties:

> The whole situation is a bit absurd. The Bretton Woods Institutions are of course very keen that we as bilateral donors pay Zambia's debt, we are in reality paying to them. As a result, they tend to take a much more positive view assessing the economic situation than the bilateral donors tend to do. They [the multilateral donors] naturally want to see Zambia on its feet, however, it is we that pay the credits and as a result, they gloss over economic realities. In addition, we have an additional criterion for evaluating the results, as we also have put in political conditionalities... Everybody will have to pave in, who is in the driver's seat is difficult to say.[1]

The quote highlights a number of the conflicting motivations and incentives facing the bilateral and multilateral donors. The emphasis on debt repayment by its member governments has made the multilateral institutions prone to defensive lending. Furthermore, the multilateral institutions have invested much intellectual prestige in the African adjustment programmes. Bilateral donors in the West are increasingly facing domestic parliaments demanding a stronger emphasis on democratic development and thus, political conditionality issues. In sum, in terms of political reforms, the international donor community was not able to reverse the regressive trends witnessed, in particular, from 1995 onwards. The influential position acquired by the World Bank witnessed throughout sub-Saharan Africa in the 1990s was also clearly reflected in the case of Zambia. However, despite the strong co-ordination function, in the areas of governance stressed by the World Bank, relating to institution-building to ensure accountability, transparency, and the limit of corrupt practices, a positive influence of the donors was not detected. The combined effects of the continued disbursements from the multilateral donors and the debt rescheduling agreements, which were not affected by the aid-freeze, reduced the impact of the bilateral aid-freeze as illustrated by table 6.3. Thus, the aid-freeze in the 1996–98 period represents a clear parallel to the situation in the 1980s when continued bilateral funding diluted the impact of the multilateral donors' aid cancellations.

The application of political conditionality hinges on the credibility of the sanctions imposed. In the case of Zambia, when the government refused to comply with the demands set, the logic of conditionality implied that donors would withdraw, reduce or suspend their aid. However, despite a surprisingly unified bilateral donor response to the political decisions of the Zambian government, aid was resumed after temporary reduction in 1994, 1997, 1999 and again after the 2001 elections. Zambia's precarious debt situation, coupled to the so-called

1. Personal interview, Christer Ågren, Economic Advisor, Swedish Embassy. Lusaka, September 12, 1996.

'disbursement imperative' made a real and sustained withdrawal of aid appear unlikely. Thus, instead, the application of political conditionality backfired on the donor community. Analysing the issues chosen in 1995/96 shows they were not as conducive for the use of conditionality as many of the bilateral donors in Zambia emphasised. The bilateral donors placed themselves in a corner by using political conditionality to force through changes in the conduct of the constitutional process without much thought about what would happen if the donor demands were not accepted. The donors had deprived themselves of a retreat policy. The Zambian government on its part was pressured to demonstrate before the population at large that this was a legitimately elected parliament and sovereign nation. As a result, the decision to place specific demands on amendments to the constitution left each side with limited space for manoeuvre and a resumption of the dialogue was exceedingly complicated. As indicated by the events taking place after the 1996 elections in Zambia, the donor community's implicit acceptance of election results, despite irregularities, placed both the donors and the opposition in a trap: The donor community had lost its bargaining power and the recipient government could use the legitimisation given by the donors to suppress internal opposition.

In Zambia, the concern for the economic reform programme won over the principle of political liberalisation and democratic consolidation. For the IMF and the World Bank, arguably, the key credibility point was the continuation of the process of privatisation and the continued adherence to a stable macroeconomic framework. For the multilateral institutions, Zambia's proven ability to carry through a conditionality programme in the context of political turmoil became a crucial determining factor for continued support. Due to the great stakes placed on cultivating the country as a success story of structural adjustment by both the multilateral and bilateral donor agencies, withdrawal of multilateral funding was not likely unless Zambia started to slide on its debt-service obligations. If the government was to stop meeting its debt-service commitments, and thus, risk the collapse of the ESAF agreement with IMF, a real financial crisis would be looming. As argued by the Economist Intelligence Unit: "It remains the case that the donor community in general, and the Bretton Woods Institutions in particular, need Zambia to look successful as an example to the rest of the continent of the workability of structural adjustment (*EIU Country Report*, 4th Quarter, 1996:4).

Ownership versus Conditionality

The study of conditionality based aid to Zambia in the 1990s suggests that a range of conflicting interests within the international donor community complicated the conduct of unified action when a waning commitment to reform was witnessed. Throughout the 1990s, bilateral donors emphasised political rights and gave much attention to democratic reform in their aid allocations. In Zambia, the bilateral donors' focus on policy reform and issues of governance led them to reduce aid allocations at a time when the multilateral donors claimed that the government's good economic reform record qualified for increases in donor funding. Towards the second general elections in 1996, the bilateral donors started to openly question the multilateral institutions' judgement of Zambia's economic policy record as well. The numerous different, and often inconsistent, motivations of the various donor agencies diluted the impact of the conditionality measures implemented. As a result, the Zambian government to an extent succeeded, as in the 1980s, in pitting the various donor agencies against each other.

The Zambian case study suggests that the actual effects of donor conditionality and monitoring through disbursements in tranches based on evaluation of specific targets and benchmarks was not sufficient to ensure real and sustained budgetary discipline. Referring back to the situation in the Ministry of Agriculture Food and Fisheries in 1994 when the funding allocated for the purchasing of maize as a buyer of last resort was not forthcoming as it had been spent beforehand, the former Minister of Agriculture Simon Zukas stated that:

> [T]his government is in receivership, and IMF is the real creditor. This has dictated the pace on the structural adjustment programme, and if you do not bother with [adjustment] criteria there will be problems. However, these guys [the international finance institutions] look at revenue, they do not see what happens at the ministerial level. The point is that the budget which we spend months preparing and debating is a useless document as it does not get supplied. There is complete compression. Salaries gets dispersed, but ministerial programmes do not get funding in order for government to meet the benchmarks.[1]

Similar sentiments were expressed regarding lack of budgetary discipline despite seeming to adhere to a cash budget and the macro-economic benchmarks set by the donors. The problems of lack of budgetary discipline also affected the bilateral donors. As argued by the economic advisor of the German government:

> Coming to 1997 it is our view that the budget situation is not a sane one, budget discipline is not being observed. Through our bilateral cooperation project we have been supporting Lusaka Sewage Company for more than a decade. However, this last year the Zambian government has not paid their water bill, as this payment was suppressed in order to balance the budget. But a budget is not in balance if you do not pay your bills, it is like shopping and refusing to pay and claim you have saved money. ... The simple idea that if you do not have money you cannot spend is not adhered to.[2]

With hindsight, the commitment to both the political and economic processes of reform waned within the MMD government mid-way through the first electoral term. For a number of reasons, Zambia returned to the 'politics of the past', in which the performance at CG meetings entailed making promises with no intentions of sticking to them. Both in the 1980s and 1990s, Zambia's political and economic development policies appear driven by donor funding rather than domestically formulated development concerns. The privatisation of the mines that dragged out for a decade illustrates both the effects and limits of donor conditionality in the absence of a firm and strong government commitment to the reform measures.

1. Personal interview, Simon Zukas, Minister of Agriculture 1993–1996. Lusaka, December 13, 1996. See Chapter 5 for a discussion of these issues.
2. Personal interview, Axel Zeidler, First Secretary, Embassy of the Federal Republic of Germany. Lusaka, January 15, 1997.

Conditionality and the Partial Reform Syndrome

New evidence on aid effectiveness indicates that aid transfers to date have been ineffective both in promoting growth and in inducing policy reform except in good policy environments. The Zambian case supports these findings. In the 1980s, the Bretton Woods Institutions reduced and eventually suspended their aid to Zambia as they felt that Zambia's economic policy response was inadequate. Yet, bilateral donors maintained a high level of support, and even increased it. In the 1990s the positions were reversed as over several years the Bretton Woods Institutions expanded—and subsequently largely maintained—their aid, while bilateral donors curtailed their assistance and phased out their balance of payment support because of what they perceived to be inadequate political governance. In the event, the efforts by Zambia's divided donor coalition to induce the government of Zambia to strengthen its economic and political governance were not successful. Over time, the MMD government's commitment to both political and economic reforms waned and donor finances and donor conditionality proved unable to stem the waning reform commitment witnessed from 1995 onwards. Reflecting continuity rather than a shift of practices, arguably, a partial reform syndrome was maintained and supported by the inability of donors to apply the conditionality instruments in a coherent manner. Considering Zambia's dire economic situation in 1991 and the complete run-down of the country's foreign reserves and food reserves, it may be appropriate to ask whether the large civil service, as well as the loss-making mines and national airline, could have been supported in the absence of increased balance-of-payments support from the donor community. A number of Zambian businessmen suggested that the abundance of aid in the 1991–1994 period in fact *hindered* real economic adjustment as the high aid levels made it possible for the MMD government to postpone difficult decisions.

The 'non-reform paradox' of more and more conditions leading to less and less effective conditionality was clearly illustrated in the much delayed processes of privatising the mines and reforming the public sector (Gordon 1993; Collier 1997). These processes were half-heartedly pursued by the two Chiluba-administrations in order to fulfil Consultative Group meeting demands rather than because these reforms were part of a domestically formulated development strategy. The Zambian case study indicates an absence of genuine policy learning and that commitment to reform was at best thin and confined to a few political leaders. The shallow support-base for reform explained why the reform processes and commitment to these processes regressed with only a few changes in the Cabinet. The process of aid, and in particular adjustment aid, shows that the Zambian government was essentially a passive participant and the larger population completely absent.

On the basis of the political impasse between the donors and the Zambian government in 1996, the words of President Chiluba in his book published in 1995 sound like a tale from a different country and continent:

> So, far from the external financial relationship being in contradiction with democratisation in Zambia, the international sources of funds are, for the time being showing a will-

> ingness to support the trends of democracy. ... In a sense these international institutions' own reputation is at stake in a country like Zambia, for they have an interest in seeing the success of an economic and political trend which they and their chief backers among the Western governments have explicitly encouraged. (1995:140–141)

President Chiluba's remarks underscore the ideals shared by the MMD government and its external partners at the outset in 1991. Indeed, the relationship between the government of Zambia and the international donor community both during the transition in 1991 and in the first years of MMD rule was very conducive. The visions of the new Zambian government, as presented in the MMD 1991 Manifesto, were shared by the external donors. However, the honeymoon between the Zambian government and its external partners came to an end in 1995, primarily due to governance issues. While, in theory, political and economic liberalisation were regarded as mutually reinforcing processes, in reality they were seen as conflicting and open to manipulation as the second elections approached.

From the perspective of policy change, this analysis has indicated that the role and influence of the external donor community was instrumental. Similar to the developments within the process of privatisation, other areas of the Zambian economic reform agenda follow a pattern of a formal agreement being reached between the government and its international partners, although, little or no progress is witnessed until pressure is put on government before the upcoming Consultative Group meeting. The correlation between discussions at the Consultative Group meeting and domestic policy action was also evident in the areas of inflationary control, the implementation of the cash budget and revenue collection. However, while the government moved fast to implement the financial and agricultural liberalisation measures, the progress of privatisation was very slow until 1995. Similarly, it was only after considerable donor pressure that the government in 1995 put emphasis on social sector reforms and service delivery. The public sector reform programme was postponed. Only in 1996 did the Zambian government make a decision to accelerate the pace of the privatisation of the mining industry in the face of increasing criticism from the donor community on issues of slipping financial discipline and governance. By strongly 'marketing' its commitment and capacity in the area of privatisation, arguably, the government 'gambled' that their (temporary) cancellation of the public sector reform programme in 1996 and again in 1998 would go unnoticed, despite this reform being a core element of the structural adjustment programme on which the ESAF agreement was contingent.

The objectives of the economic reform agreements between the Zambian government and its donors were articulated in Policy Framework Papers that were drawn up collaborately between the Zambian government and the staff of the World Bank and IMF. Yet, underscoring the limited domestic ownership of the reform processes, when completed these documents were submitted to the executive directors of WB and IMF. They would typically not be submitted to the Zambian parliament, nor would they be published.[1] Similarly, during the

1. See Heijden (2000). The Policy Framework Paper was published in Zambia for the first time in 1999–2001 and was also placed on the IMF website.

two MMD administrations, a number of commissions and special institutions were created as part of the structural adjustment agreements with the international donors, such as the data monitoring committee with the Ministry of Finance, and the external debt working group within the Bank of Zambia. However, much of the work of these committees was directed towards monitoring progress related to the IMF benchmarks, much less to providing internal policy advice (Heijden 2000). In light of the substantial aid and the aid agreements reached between Zambia and its external partners in the period 1991–2001, a long-serving external advisor to the Zambian government concludes:

> It is surprising that the donor community provided as much assistance as it did in the nineties, particularly in light of the perennial frustrations of donors when seeing mutually agreed-upon objectives either not being adequately pursued or achieved by government. Macro-economically, the impact of aid was nothing more than reducing the rate of economic and social decline in Zambia—the effectiveness could have been much higher if donor co-ordination had focused on fewer and more central conditionalities. (Ibid.: Ch. 4:67)

7

Political and Economic Liberalisation in Zambia 1991–2001

The time has come to conclude the analysis of Zambia's political and economic reform processes in the 1990s. After the 1991 transitionary elections, Zambia appeared ready to embark on a new economic and political development trajectory as the elected government promised to work with its international partners to implement growth oriented economic policies. After a decade of reforms, what can be concluded about Zambia's dual reform processes? In this concluding chapter the main findings of the analysis of Zambia's dual reforms 1991–2001 are presented and discussed in a comparative perspective. The first section summarises the main findings of Zambia's economic and political liberalisation 1991–2001. Secondly, the policy negotiations between the MMD government and the domestic interest groups, and between the government and its external partners are presented. The final section discusses the endurance of neo-patrimonial aspects of rule in the context of political and economic reform.

Political and Economic Reforms 1991–2001

The Economic Reform Record of the MMD Government

The economic policy changes implemented in the first years after the 1991 elections were expected to signify a major shift in Zambia's economic policy regime. However, the analysis of economic reform implementation has shown that the notion of discontinuity from the policies of the Kaunda era should not be overstated. A degree of continuity in terms of uneven implementation and limited commitment to policy reform has been witnessed since the mid-1990s. After almost a decade of continuous structural adjustment programmes, the record of Zambian policy reforms in the 1990s is complex and mixed. On the one hand, during the 1990s the foundations were laid for a shift from a state oriented to a market based economy. Most importantly, despite several exogenous shocks and uneven implementation, none of the reform measures implemented have been reversed. On the other hand, several key reforms were not implemented, including civil service reform, and the privatisation of the copper industry. The MMD government displayed genuine commitment to liberalisation and stabilisation with the implementation of the cash budget, the establishment of Zambia Revenue Authorities and the freeing of exchange controls as significant examples. However, commitment to structural reforms and a long-term strategy of growth was not displayed. Commitment to a long-term strategy of growth would have included a proactive position on the mines from the very beginning as well as a strategy to enhance tourism and non-traditional agriculture (Rakner et al. 2001). A strategy of growth would also have entailed restructuring the public service. In the second election period (1996–2001) public service reforms came to a complete stop despite the fact that these reforms had constituted a major part of every aid agreement between the Zambian government and the World Bank and IMF in the period 1991–2001. Similarly, investments in agriculture and tourism depended on investment capital, which, apart from donor funds, only could have come from a reinvigorated, privatised mining industry. But the privatisation of the mines was only finalised in 2000, after a process that left the mines with huge debts and the government with very little credibility. The main assets of Zambia Consolidated Coppermines (ZCCM) were finally sold to Anglo-American Corporation in March 2000; only to be handed back to the Zambian government two years later as Anglo-American Corporation in January 2002 announced its intention to terminate its main mining operations in Zambia.[1]

Over time, the MMD government's commitment to economic liberalisation, and the economic agreements entered into with its international partners, waned. Almost all the major reform processes were implemented in the first election period. The second Chiluba administration witnessed little progress in terms of economic policy reform. From the mid-1990s onwards, MMD's increased domestic borrowing indicated a waning commitment to fiscal discipline. Largely ignoring the cash-budget, supplementary budgets increased the spending of the Presidential Office in particular. Furthermore, numerous government interventions in agricultural marketing suggest that the government's stated commitment to agricultural liberalisation in reality was shallow, particularly during times of elections. But reform commitment should be disaggregated (van de Walle 2001; Rakner et al. 2001). Commitment to economic reform varied across issues as well as across parts of the MMD Cabinet throughout the 1990s. Public debates in Zambia suggest that the MMD government was never united on the issue of privatisation. The reactions to agricultural liberalisation from various ministers suggest that few in the MMD government had considered the implications of agricultural reforms. Similarly, there was very limited support in government for public sector reform throughout the two election periods.

In his analysis of economic reform implementation in sub-Saharan Africa, van de Walle (2001) notes that across the continent policy makers are still not convinced of the virtues of economic reform. Van de Walle identifies a marked ideological resistance to economic reforms despite the fact that African governments have sought to implement these reforms for close to three decades. Experiences with economic reform implementation in Zambia in the 1990s fit this general picture. In many ways, it is surprising that after ten years in office, and despite MMD's majority in parliament, only a partial and fragile consensus has emerged on the appropriateness of the (limited) policy changes that have taken

1. These conclusions are partly based on Rakner, van de Walle and Mulaisho (2001) and Bräutigam, Rakner and Taylor (2002).

place. The civil service, parastatal companies, the parliament, the MMD party and cabinet still display a marked resistance to economic reform. By 2001 it could not be argued that liberal economic reforms had strong support in the Zambian government. To illustrate, in February 2001, President Chiluba told a meeting in Ndola that the government would contest the sale of the remaining large parastatals, because the government considered these firms to be vital to the security of the country (*EIU*, May 2001:10). The sale of the remaining parastatals figured centrally in both the second Enhanced Structural Adjustment Facility (ESAF II) and the Heavily Indebted Poor Country Initiative (HIPC) agreements between the MMD government and the international financial institutions. As a result, IMF requested government to confirm its policies of privatisation. At this point, the Zambian Minister of Finance restated Zambia's commitment to privatisation in a letter to IMF (*The Post*, March 30, 2001). However, in the period after the 2001 elections, opposition to privatisation has intensified. After a heated parliamentary session, President Mwanawasa recently told the international donors that Zambia at this point in time would not go ahead with the sale of the remaining parastatals (*The Post*, January 14, 2003). Much of the public scepticism is related to the way the MMD government handled the sale of the main economic assets, Zambia Consolidated Copper Mines.

Despite MMD's pro-reform election manifesto, its electoral majority, and a donor community eager to support 'an African reform success', economic reforms in Zambia in the 1991–2001 period can only be characterised as partially implemented. Towards the closing of the millennium, public sentiments both in Zambia and the OECD countries turned against many of the economic reform measures promoted by the international financial institutions. Yet, most of the reforms considered to have caused Zambia's negative growth rate in the 1990s (and 1980s) either were not implemented at all or in a partial and haphazard manner. The partial implementation and waning commitment to reform witnessed in the process of economic liberalisation were also seen in the area of democratic reform.

MMD's Democratic Reform Record 1991–2001

The 1991 democratic transitions were expected to enhance the powers of societal interest groups and the legislative branch of government. These reforms were also expected to strengthen the influence of institutions promoting horizontal accountability, such as courts, auditor-generals, and anti-corruption units. Thus, the democratic reforms were envisioned to reduce the powers of the executive office. But, as in the case of economic reform implementations the analysis of political reforms in Zambia 1991–2001 has suggested that the discontinuity from the policies of the Kaunda era should not be overstated. While multiparty elections were held in 1991, 1996 and 2001, the quality of political governance in Zambia declined within a few years after the 1991 transition. The MMD government's commitment to democratic reforms waned in 1993 linked to the power struggles within the party that saw veteran politicians from the UNIP era gradually seize power. As MMD started to consolidate its power-base and Kenneth Kaunda re-entered Zambian national politics, regard for civic liberties, basic human rights and democratic principles declined. The conducting of the important second elections in 1996 proved that MMD was willing to undermine its opponents by undemocratic means. The 2001 elections again showed that the Chiluba government attempted to compromise the rule of law when a campaign to allow Chiluba a third term as president was set in motion. Unlike the 1996 constitutional amendment process that denied Kenneth Kaunda the possibility of contesting the presidential elections, in 2001 the constitution was not altered. Nevertheless, the third term debate and the conducting of the 2001 electoral campaign underline the weakly institutionalised character of Zambia's multiparty democracy.

After a decade of continued multiparty democracy and three consecutive presidential and parliamentary elections, the Zambian democracy is far from consolidated. Contrary to expectations, in the 1990s, the separation between the incumbent party (MMD) and the government became increasingly more blurred. Despite the stated intention in 1991 to reduce the powers of the presidency, the powers of the executive office increased. Indications of increased executive dominance were witnessed in the establishment of the presidential discretionary fund in 1998 and the institution of District Administrators in 2000. Moreover, ten years of political liberalisation did not bring about opposition parties capable of challenging the ruling party or offering the voters an alternative to the policies carried out by the MMD government. The capacity of the political opposition and civic associations to shape the political agenda was limited further.

Observers of Zambia's democratic development have characterised the governance practices of the MMD government as a reversal to the policies of the one-party state (Joseph 1999; Burnell 2001). Such observations miss the novelty of current governance debates taking place in Zambia and across sub-Saharan Africa. Now political leaders increasingly feel obliged to frame their political ambitions and motives within the parameters of multiparty democracy. In the 1990s, elections were held in Zambia, but provisions for a so-called level playing-field were not in place in 1991, 1996 or in 2001. The politicisation of the constitution as witnessed in 1996 and partly in 2001 represents the exact opposite of institutionalisation of democracy—a process implying that institutions are maintained even if the incumbent is negatively affected. However, as with economic liberalisation, it cannot be argued that the political liberalisation process was reversed to the extent that multiparty politics was discontinued. As with economic reform, democratic governance in Zambia in the 1990s has remained in a 'grey zone', a situation of partial reform (Carothers 2002).

Reform Implementation as Two-Level Games between Domestic and External Actors

Research carried out by the World Bank has shown that the rates of return for World Bank projects are correlated with the indices of political and civil rights collected by Freedom House (Pritchett 1998). The Zambian experiences witnessed over the last decade support this general finding. The original reformist cabinet of the MMD was committed to both economic and political reform, and the commitment to political reform and at least part of the economic reform process waned at the same time. The new politicians who replaced the original reformist cabinet have viewed both economic and political reform with much less enthusiasm. From the mid-1990s onwards, economic policy making by the MMD government became subordinated to political objectives, most notably, winning the 1996 and 2001 elections. Yet, despite the lack of economic growth generated, and the fact that no sectors of society had emerged as clear 'winners' of the economic reform measures implemented, neither the 1996 nor 2001 elections witnessed a party or politicians lobbying for a return of the controlled exchange rate regime or protection of local industry. As a result, both the 1996 and 2001 elections represented a significant departure from the Zambian policy debates in the 1980s when opposition to the various structural reform programmes had centred around the desirability of economic reform programmes as such.

The political and economic liberalisation in Zambia has been analysed as a two-level game between three sets of actors: domestic interest groups, the government, and the international donor community. Based in pluralist theory, the two-level game perspective envisioned the domestic game between the government and the domestic interest groups representing key sectors of the economy to largely determine the negotiations in the international policy game between the government and its main international partners (Putnam 1988).

The Domestic Policy Game and the Decline of Interest Group Influence

In the early 1990s a new theoretical perspective emerged arguing that economic and political reforms could be implemented simultaneously. The dual reform perspective assigned a vital role to civil society associations, arguing that participation by social groups would ensure ownership, credibility and sustainability of the reform processes. Emerging research began to suggest that growth-enhancing relationships between business and government would be facilitated by political liberalisation. With a theoretical foundation in public choice literature, the dual reform perspective saw successful reforms as a process of creating winners of economic reforms before potential losers were able to mobilise against the reforms. Critical voices, however, argued that the economic reform process would be undermined by the political reform process as the democratic powers of societal groups would force democratically elected governments to cancel economic reforms. Furthermore, as democracy implied the transfer of powers from the executive to the legislative branch of government, the autonomy of the executive to design and implement economic policies would be reduced.

The analysis of political and economic reforms in Zambia in the 1990s has shown that, contrary to expectations, the influence of interest associations representing key sectors of the economy declined with the introduction of political liberalisation in 1991 due to the combined effects of economic and political liberalisation. In each case, the unions, farmers and business associations had to adjust to the transition of the regime from state corporatism to a form of pluralism. However, the circumstances around their reduced political influence were unique to each sector.

The Declining Role of Labour

Zambia's labour unions were considered the potentially most important association due to their historical role as a major oppositional force under the previous regime and because of their ties to the government through the President. However, MMD deliberately adopted a non-consultative line with the unions. Chiluba's trade union background provided MMD with initial support and extensive knowledge of the union movement. The reduction in formal sector employment from 400,000 to 150,000 and the constant reduction in civil service employment and benefits go a long way to explain the weakened position of labour. In addition, MMD deliberately ignored ZCTU. Split into two trade union congresses since 1998, the Zambian trade unions are no longer influential in contemporary Zambian policy debates. Perhaps more surprising than the effects of economic liberalisation on trade union strength was the fact that the process of political liberalisation served to weaken the position of labour. The great number of new political parties and outspoken NGOs emerging after the political changes in 1991 resulted in a 'crowded' public arena which made it difficult for labour to publicise their position and views.

The Limited Role of Business

The business sector was envisioned to be among the main 'winners' of the dual reform processes, both due to the strong presence of former businessmen in the new parliament and cabinet, and their marginalisation under the former regime. Despite the government's harsh response to other critics, the government did not respond with repression to the views of business. Generally, however, the government did not respond to business at all. The Zambian business sector lacked institutional capacity and strength to maintain measurable pressure on the government. The area of economic liberalisation that the MMD government implemented in a relatively consistent manner was trade liberalisation. Comparative research indicates that in the short run, trade liberalisation seldom makes local industry more competitive; as the Zambian case illustrates, without time to adjust, businesses simply fail (Bräutigam et al. 2002:542). The expected winners from trade liberalisation are export oriented businesses. As witnessed in the Zambian case, few local businesses were in this position at the time the adjustment process was initiated. The effects of political pluralism with respect to business echo the experiences of labour: with a membership comprising less than 20 per cent of those in formal employment, electoral policies contributed to MMD's neglect of business interests. The interests of private business, therefore, did not constitute an electoral threat or useful political allies for President Chiluba and the MMD government. The increasing executive dominance and the blurring of state-party lines hurt business in particular, as most businesses simply could not afford to be seen as too critical to government. In the Zambian case, the weakness of the private sector vis-à-vis the state bureaucracy, and the fact that the reforms did not provide new 'winners', meant that a growth coalition could not be created. The second Chiluba administration saw the virtual collapse of both the economy and the relations between government and business.

The Lack of Agricultural 'Winners'

In Zambia, as in sub-Saharan Africa as a whole, both academic scholars and donors expected agricultural producers, particularly small-scale farmers, to be among the main 'winners' of the economic restructuring measures. But no large sector of agriculture emerged as 'winners' of the reform processes and thus, as potential constituencies of support for the government. Neither the Zambian National Farmers Union, the Zambian Co-operative Federation nor the new peasants and farming associations emerging after 1991 could claim to represent a broad segment of agricultural producers. Due to the weakness of associations, the opposition to agricultural policies was not primarily mounted by the interest groups, but by more distant and populist sources like the press and MPs representing rural constituencies. As the speakers on behalf of agricultural producers did not necessarily represent the bulk of the producers, there were few incentives for consultations for the Zambian government.

The implementation of economic reforms in Zambia in the 1991–2001 period reveals the problems of generating winners of reform policies within Africa's weak economic and institutional structures. More than any other sector, agriculture underscores the barriers economic reforms come up against in generating a political support-base (Herbst 1993; Callaghy and Ravenhill 1993; Sandberg 1990). The Zambian case fits a scenario reported from across sub-Saharan Africa. Echoing experiences in the Second Republic (Sandberg 1990) and Ghana (Herbst 1993), because of poor infrastructure in the rural areas the potential benefits of liberalised prices did not benefit rural producers who were unable to reach a market with their produce.

Reforms, but No Winners?

Few studies have focused directly on business associations in Africa, but those that have have generally come to pessimistic conclusions on the potential for forming growth coalitions (Bräutigam et al. 2002). The business community's ambivalent responses to economic reforms, as well as its weakness of organisation were noted in the case of Ghana (Herbst 1993:54–5) and Nigeria and Tanzania (Heilman and Lucas 1997). The experiences of the Zambian business community with dual reforms in the 1990s support these analyses. The weakness of the private sector vis-à-vis the state bureaucracy meant that the growth coalition envisioned in the early 1990s could not be sustained. The Zambian interest associations' limited institutional capacity reduced their ability to maintain measurable pressure on the government. Echoing findings from comparative case-analyses by, among others, Moore and Hamalai (1993) and Herbst

(1993), an important factor further undermining the collective strength of business was the fact that the business sector in Zambia, similar to labour, was unable to provide unified support for or opposition to the economic reform measures.

The Zambian case demonstrates the ability of democratically elected governments to implement thoroughgoing economic reforms despite the protests from centrally placed interest groups, including unions. The ability of democratically elected governments to implement economic reforms despite the protests from centrally placed unions has also been noted in comparative studies from Poland (Nelson 1994b; Kochanowicz 1994), Peru and Argentina (Roberts 1995), Mexico and Argentina (Gibson 1997), Brazil (Geddes 1994a), as well as other sub-Saharan African nations (Herbst 1993; Leith and Lofchie 1993). However, the split experienced by the Zambian union movement along the lines of public and private sector unions serves as a rather unique example of how dual processes of political and economic liberalisation may undermine formerly key civil society associations.

Reform Paradoxes

The Zambian experiences with simultaneous political and economic liberalisation highlight a flaw in the dual reform literature that, based in pluralist theory, assumes that certain groups will emerge as reform 'winners' and others as 'losers'.[1] Firstly, neither Zambian business, labour nor agricultural interests could be considered (or indeed, considered themselves) to be 'winners' in the reform process. While some reform measures possibly benefited a sector as a whole, other measures hurt some sectoral interests and benefited others. As a result, no sector has emerged that could be characterised as a new constituency in favour of the economic reform policies. Secondly, the racial dimension challenges the expectation that reform winners can become political constituencies for the government (Taylor 2003). In Zambia the groups that benefited most from the reforms implemented since the early 1990s were the politically least useful—Asian and white farmers and business owners who are few in number and historically favoured by the former colonial policies. By questioning the assumption that political liberalisation will enhance the position and influence of economic interest groups, this case study connects with an emerging literature arguing that interest groups have not played a determining role in undermining economic reforms. This literature has tended to dismiss the focus on interest groups and argue that in general, the interest group perspective has overstated the role of associational groups in Third World countries (van de Walle 2001; Geddes 1995). However, deviating somewhat from this argument, the analysis of Zambian dual reform processes in the 1990s has found that, paradoxically, Zambian interest groups had some real influence under the former one-party structures and that this influence has been reduced as a result of the combined processes of political and economic liberalisation.

1. This argument was first developed in Rakner (2001).

For economic interest associations to influence policies as envisioned in the pluralist notion of 'winners' and 'losers', the political arena must provide channels through which interests can be aggregated into the competitive political processes. In Zambia no links were formed between economic interests and the party system. Party formation and politics centred around issues of personalities and individual ambitions. The majority of the parties established in Zambia between the 1991 and 2001 elections formed behind a leader-figure who usually contributed the bulk of the finances the party was in control of. The various parties could not be separated along ideological or programmatic lines. Despite the growing opposition to economic reforms, all parties in the 1996 and 2001 election campaigns vowed to continue the current economic policies, albeit manage these policies better than MMD. As a result, the Zambian parties represented in the 1996 and 2001 elections failed to offer the electorate distinctive choices concerning the dimension of economic policy (Rakner and Svåsand 2003). The lack of alternatives presented by the opposition parties, and the large number of parties, may explain why Zambian interest associations did not endorse an alternative party to MMD. Thus, while pluralism in Zambia challenged the state corporatist ties between the government and certain interest associations, this opening did not provide interest associations with new channels into the political system.

Autonomy—From Whom?

Contrary to the most pessimistic observers of dual reform processes, interest group pressure and protest did not compel the Zambian government to increase spending in order to maintain its popularity. Yet, throughout the 1990s the MMD government increased public spending, largely to the detriment of the Zambian population. Most of the excess spending went to the ministries of defence, foreign services and the office of the president. Zambian interest groups were too weak to challenge the MMD government's economic policies. They were also too marginalised and lacking in political channels to stop the regression in MMD's governance practices witnessed from late 1993 onwards. The analysis of Zambia adds credence to comparative analyses of, among others, Bates and Krueger (1993), Geddes (1994b, 1995) and van de Walle (2001) arguing that interest groups in developing countries often are too weak to actually hinder reform implementation if the political leadership is committed to reform. As argued by Geddes (1995), it is not autonomy from interest groups that contributes to better economic performance but autonomy from politically motivated pressure to distribute the resources needed for effective policymaking and implementation. According to Geddes, the biggest, most articulate and politically influential losers from the transition to a more market oriented economy are government officials, ruling party cadres, cronies of rulers and the close allies of these (Geddes 1995:113). Illustrating Geddes' point, the power of vested interests within the state economy in Zambia has proven to be much more successful in terms of preventing reforms that could reduce their economic power than societal interest groups. According to this perspective, democratisation may not in itself remove the biggest political obstacle to reform, namely the government itself. While MMD moved quickly and relatively persistently to liberalise the agricultural sector reforms, reforms within the area of privatisation and the public sector took much longer, or were not adhered to at all. The incentive of reducing the power of UNIP through weakening the co-operative federations to a large extent explains MMD's persistent removal of subsidies to the peasant farmers through the agricultural co-operatives. This analysis further suggests that the continued existence of the state holding company, ZIMCO, served as the major stumbling block for the privatisation process in the initial phases. Thus, supporting the findings in comparative case-studies, in Zambia vested interests within the former state-bureaucracy have been more powerful in terms of blocking economic reforms than interest associations representing sector interests such as labour and business.

When no sectors of the Zambian society emerged as 'reform-winners' why did no political party launch an alternative economic campaign in the 1996 or 2001 elections? Similarly, why was the policy of trade liberalisation maintained and accelerated in the context of increasing domestic opposition, with Zambia being one of the first countries in the region to adopt the COMESA Free Trade Agreement in October 2000? In part, these answers should be sought in the 'policy game' between the Zambia government and its external partners.

The External Game between Zambia and the Donors

The positive correlation between political and economic liberalisation based in (parts of) the public choice literature was also adopted by the international donor community in the 1990s. Presenting their new 'dual conditionality agenda', the international donor community supported the dual reform processes through a combination of positive and negative conditionality mechanisms. In the early 1990s, the international donors provided substantial amounts of financial assistance in the initial phase of reform to soften implementation 'shocks' associated with structural adjustment programmes. At the same time, financial aid was granted to institutions and associations in order to promote and strengthen the new-found democracies. A statement by the American political scientist Larry Diamond reflects the expectations of what the international donor community could do in order to enhance both processes of political and economic reform:

> Just as economic conditionality can be aided by timely and well crafted international assistance, so can political development. In fact, political development is a much more flexible process than economic development and it is also cheaper financially. By helping to train legislators and their staff, party officials, lawyers, judges, journalists, civic groups, trade union organizers, and election administrators, we can help 'jump-start' the process of democratic development. (1991:12)

Economic and Political Conditionality 1991–2001

In Zambia, the external actors played a central role in the dual reform processes. The analysis further points to the increasingly important role of the Consultative Group meeting as an external 'parliament' or sanctioning force. The discussions and agreements at the various Consultative Group meetings to a large extent guided the internal policy debates and the reform implementation process.

The Zambian case supports these findings showing that aid transfers to date have been ineffective both in promoting growth and in inducing policy reform except in good policy environments (Burnside and Dollar 1997; Killick 1998; Devajaran et al. 2001). Throughout the 1980s, the UNIP government rejected policy reform. The cut-off from IFI finances following the cancellation of reform agreements in 1983 and 1987 was, however, largely offset by bilateral aid flows. From a position in the 1980s as a classic 'non-reformer', the reformist government that came to power in 1991 was rewarded with substantial increases in aid. But MMD's commitment to reform waned despite external support and in part because the reforms achieved so little in terms of stemming the continued economic decline. Due to both their intellectual and financial impact, the international donor community played a central role in Zambia's economic policy development in the 1990s. Financial aid was instrumental for implementing some policy reforms and sustaining other reform measures. However, the donors, as well as the Zambian government, failed to express a coherent strategy of economic growth (Rakner et al. 2001). A donor promoted strategy of growth would have placed the mining industry at the centre of negotiations with the MMD government much earlier than 1997. Instead, in the 1990s both the government and the external donors made fiscal austerity an end in itself and a measure of reform commitment. As a result, macro-economic stabilisation in Zambia today is threatened, as there has been no growth to support continued austerity. Similar to the experiences of the 1980s, donor conditionality proved unable to stem the waning reform commitment witnessed in the last half of the 1990s. The specific targeting of certain reform elements and the technically formulated benchmarks offered wide room for manoeuvre for the Zambian authorities. The government indicated commitment to various elements of the policy reform package. Yet, ownership of the reform process remained weak and policy implementation appeared justified with reference to generating aid funds rather than a domestically argued development strategy. Reflecting continuity rather than a shift in donor-government relations, a partial reform syndrome was supported by the inability of donors to apply the conditionality instruments in a coherent manner.

Aid or Reforms?

The Zambian case illustrates that the international donor community's range of conflicting interests made unified action difficult when a waning commitment to reform was witnessed. A major aim of the operations of the IMF and the World Bank is to enable indebted nations to repay their debts. In the case of Zambia, large amounts of the balance-of-payments support generated by the donor community in the period 1991–2001 were used to service old debts to the same donor institutions. Both the Zambian government and the international finance institutions had an incentive to exaggerate the results of the reform effort in order to maintain a constant flow of financial aid. In addition, the multilateral donors had high financial and intellectual stakes involved in the conduct of policy reform processes in Africa. A mixed, or even slipping, policy performance was, therefore, not easily dismissed as the costs involved in entering yet another aid agreement six months ahead were considered high. The bilateral donors, on the other hand, tended to take a somewhat different view of the political and economic reform processes in the 1990s. Most bilateral donors emphasised political reforms as a condition for financial support. Answering to their local constituencies and tax payers, the bilateral donors became increasingly wary of supporting undemocratic Third World governments. From 1995 onwards, Zambia's bilateral donors showed an increasing willingness to exercise political conditionality over such issues as corruption, drug-related activities and struggles over constitutional revisions. Pointing to the progress made on basic reforms, and the need to support a government that had gone some distance on reform, the multilateral donors continued to view Zambia's economic reform record positively, making the bilateral threat of aid withdrawal less credible.

Thus, underscoring the notion of continuity from the Kaunda era, in the 1990s donor differences have continued to dilute the impact of both political and economic conditionality. In the 1980s, the Bretton Woods Institutions reduced and eventually suspended their aid to Zambia as they felt that Zambia's economic policy response was inadequate. However, bilateral donors maintained a high level of support, and even increased it. In the 1990s the positions were reversed: for several years the Bretton Woods Institutions expanded—and subsequently largely maintained—their aid, while bilateral donors curtailed their assistance and phased out their balance-of-payments support due to what they perceived as poor political governance. In the event, Zambia's divided donor coalition was not successful in trying to induce the Zambian government to improve economic and political governance. As argued by a long serving advisor to the Zambia government in the 1990s ... "[E]xternal assistance provided to Zambia did not supplement Zambia's own savings effort but substituted for it" (Heijden 2000, Ch. 1:11).

Dual Conditionality Revisited

Van de Walle recognises a common pattern of reform implementation across sub-Saharan Africa, 'the partial reform syndrome'. According to van de Walle, the partial reform syndrome is characterised by: a) a donor role in the adjustment processes accepted as institutionalised, b) prolonged non-reform resulting in the erosion of state capacity, and c) a specific state economy that has tended to recentralise the powers of presidents (van de Walle 2001:61–62). Zambia's dual reform experiences in the 1900s largely confirm this perspective. A decade of economic reforms in Zambia produced few winners in terms of employment creation and reduced levels of poverty. While all opposition parties criticised the government's economic policies and the main interest groups were only lukewarm in their support, no interest group or opposition party offered any alternative economic strategies to the structural adjustment programme. Both the 1996 and 2001 general elections indicated that an externally approved structural adjustment programme had become a necessity for the survival of a political regime. After decades of playing divide and rule among various agents of the international donor community, in the 1990s, the high degree of donor cohesion made it very difficult for the government to champion a course very different to the policy prescriptions of the donor community. The economic conditionality restricted the domestic politicians' ideological room for manoeuvre. Large parts of economic policy making had become 'externalised' through the specifically set benchmarks. The restriction also applied to the political opposition and interest groups. All Zambian parties took the liberal economic reform as given.

Returning to the initial question of whether processes of economic and political liberalisation are mutually reinforcing, the findings of the Zambian analysis add credence to the critical dissent raised by a number of African scholars. These scholars have argued that the donors, by insisting on the implementation of political and economic reforms, have created a contradictory position. On the one hand, the criteria of transparency and accountability feature prominently in the external funders' vocabulary. On the other hand, broad areas of government decision making are appropriated to the arena of donor-recipient dialogue and conditionality. This again may imply that government officials primarily see their accountability to lie with the donor agencies (Mkandawire 1996; van Arkadie and Mule 1996). Arguably, processes of political and economic liberalisation are compatible only if a majority of the population accepts the need for a continued economic reform programme.

The case of Zambia has, nevertheless, spelled out the limits to the powers of the international donor community despite their overwhelming economic leverage. The study confirmed findings appearing in the comparative literature indicating that conditionality may be too blunt an instrument to oversee democratic developments, as well as to ensure the financial discipline associated with economic growth (Mosley et al. 1991; Collier 1997; Killick 1996, 1998; Nelson and Eglington 1992, van de Walle 2001). The Zambian case also brings forth the implicit conflicts between political and economic liberalisation, reflected in the old debate of 'trade offs' between political and economic reforms and the different positions of the various agencies of the 'aid regime'. Due to a combination of developmental needs and huge foreign debt, Zambia's economic performance had by the 1990s become a shared responsibility among the internal and external actors. It was known to all parties that the worst case scenario in terms of donor reactions would be a short interruption in the disbursal flows. This would again result in the build-up of larger arrears. Essentially, therefore, it was in the interests of the multilateral donors, as the main creditors, to maintain the economic restructuring programme.

The dual conditionality agenda opened up for a new level of implicit conflict: Which aspects of the reform agenda should be considered most important?

Zambia became one of the first serious test cases of whether political and economic liberalisation could be regarded as mutually reinforcing. Arguably, concerns with the economic reform agenda took the centre stage in both 1996 and 2001. For the IMF, the key credibility point was the continuation of the privatisation process and the continued maintenance of a stable macro-economic framework. When the Zambian government refused to bow to the pressures of the international donors and domestic opposition at large, the bilateral donor community faced a dilemma. The risk associated with the collapse of the structural adjustment programme at a time when the benefits of the privatisation of the mines were in sight, was considered overwhelming. Having tied large aspects of their aid portfolios and decision-making powers to the multilateral institutions, the bilateral donors too, let the concern for the economic reform programme win over the principle of political liberalisation and democratic consolidation.

Executive Dominance and the Sustainability of Patronage Politics

With a basis in pluralist theory, the combination of an enhanced position of domestic civil society actors and the international donor community was expected to challenge the power monopoly of the Zambian government. Yet, neither Zambia's external actors, nor its domestic interest groups, were able to significantly curb the monopolistic powers of the executive branch of the government. Contrary to the theoretical presumptions presented at the outset, the MMD government appeared as the main 'winner' of the two-level game in terms of power-consolidation. Overall, in the 1990s the MMD government did not implement reforms that seriously challenged its political power base or its own political survival. Reforms that were considered harmful, like the process of privatisation and the public sector reform programme, were postponed and even abandoned. In terms of privatisation, it is evident that only the privatisation of the mining conglomerate would have significantly affected the national economy. This issue was postponed to the very end of the second electoral term. In contrast, agricultural liberalisation and trade liberalisation did not at the outset constitute a threat to important MMD constituencies, and were consequently carried out immediately to signal the government's reform commitment vis-à-vis its external partners.

The Zambian case confirms the notion of reforming governments carefully crafting their position between two major concerns: obtaining financial assistance from the external donor community is necessary for the regime's continued survival yet governments must also ensure domestic appeasement based on a variety of institutional structures and political tactics. The MMD government's sequencing of the economic reform measures corresponded to its internal political interests. The political processes around the 1996 and 2001 elections indicated that domestic policy concern was at the heart of the government's interests. Thus, in the two-level game of economic and political liberalisation played out between donors, the MMD government and key economic interest groups, the executive branch of government enhanced its power and influence through implementing the economic reforms (partly) as requested by its external partners. By doing so, the government regained access to international finance capital, which had largely been denied the country since the mid-1980s. The external donor community was trapped in a dilemma of its own conditionality. Presented with a choice of whether to assist the continuance of the economic reform programme, or to facilitate its breakdown by insisting on democratic decision making procedures being adhered to, the donors chose economic reforms. Despite the level of influence and leverage of the donors in terms of economic policy reforms as documented by this study, the national political leadership constituted the most unified team. In Zambia, as in many other African countries, the 'new' politicians coming to power on a pluralist political agenda in 1991 proved to be seasoned veterans of the old style of politics.

Neo-Patrimonialism—The Defining Feature of African Politics?

Bratton and van de Walle, among others, have depicted neo-patrimonialism as the institutional hallmark of African politics (1997). The authors have argued that three stable, informal institutional structures have facilitated and strengthened the neo-patrimonial patterns of rule in post-independence African politics: the continued adherence to presidentialism, implying that regardless of regime form, large segments of political control remain located within the executive office; the continued presence of clientelism as a means for maintaining governmental power; and finally, the excessive employment of state resources for purposes of political gain. Contrary to the theoretical assumptions set forth, the analysis of the first decade of the Zambian Third Republic has shown that these features of political rule did not diminish with the introduction of political and economic liberalisation.

In its 1991 election campaign, MMD promised to reduce the power of the presidency by reducing the size of the Cabinet, enhancing the influence of the parliament, and further, to separate the powers of the party from those of the government. However, almost from their inception, these goals were disregarded. In order to reward the large number of people who had contributed to MMD's electoral victory in 1991, the size of the MMD Cabinet increased from the UNIP era. The new Cabinet further included a broad mixture of old UNIP politicians, businessmen and newcomers to politics, with little experience from national politics, associated with the one-party era. Reflecting on the political processes that had evolved over the five year period in Zambian politics, on July 20, 1996, several founders of the Movement for Multiparty Democracy observed the sixth anniversary of the Garden House meeting that led to the creation of the party MMD. A number of former members of the MMD Cabinet were present at the gathering. The main speakers claimed that MMD had met few of its original objectives and that the party had been hijacked away from its founders. Noting the similarities between the situation confronting the people of Zambia and the political opposition in 1990 and 1996, one speaker claimed that MMD had reinstated the one-party system in almost all ways other than in name. Another speaker found that the original pluralist basis of MMD was hijacked because some politicians in the original MMD Cabinet had a better appreciation of power and politics than others among MMD's organisers. Those with a better appreciation of power had moved quickly to remove potential rivals for the party presidency from the Cabinet. Criticising the original multiparty movement for not having scrutinised those coming into the party in 1991, the speaker noted that in addition to a patriotic elite, the MMD had taken in a parasitic elite.[1]

The political struggles played out within MMD from mid-1993 onwards reflected conflicts within MMD between 'veteran' politicians from the UNIP era and politicians with no background in UNIP, some with a strong commitment to the political ideals spelled out in the 1991 MMD Manifesto. Starting in late 1993, growing claims of corrupt practices, excessive state funding for MMD's election campaigning, and politicians-cum-businessmen enriching themselves on the basis of their political portfolios, were reported. Entering 1995, a number of incidents indicated that the political leadership of MMD had placed consolidation of political power at the centre of their political concerns. Interestingly, by doing so, the government indicated that they perceived a return of the political practices of the UNIP era to be the best way to secure continued leadership. Gradually, the reform-minded ministers who had taken part in the writing of the MMD Manifesto at the Garden House Hotel had been replaced. By 1995, the 'old timers', who had held key political positions in the Second Republic, appeared to be in charge of the MMD party and the government.

The handling of the constitutional amendment process in 1996 deviated from the promises made by MMD in 1991 when it was stated that the constitution would be adopted following wide public consultations. In the second election period, the power of the executive office increased markedly as the MMD government used the opportunity provided by the 1997 coup-attempt to silence the opposition. The creation of a presidential discretionary fund outside parliamentary scrutiny; various special desks in the Presidential Office; and large supplementary payments to the Presidential Office made the executive office 'a government within government'. Increasingly, political decisions were taken by President Chiluba without prior consultations even in his Cabinet. Thus, in Zambia various forms of neo-patrimonial rule were adapted to both policies of economic liberalisation and formal democratic openings. The Zambian case supports comparative findings from the African continent. The Zambian scenario, where the new democracy survived but where the elected rulers reverted to manipulating political rules and institutions in order to consolidate their personal hold on power, appears common. As phrased by Bratton and van de Walle: "In these states, big-man democracy is emerging, in which the formal trappings of democracy coexist with neo-patrimonial political practice" (1997:233). The political developments witnessed in Zambia, as well as around the sub-Saharan African continent, serve as an important reminder of the long

1. The sixth anniversary of the Garden House Hotel Conference that resulted in the establishment of the Movement for Multiparty Democracy was convened at the Garden House Hotel, July 20, 1996. A written report of the meeting was provided by Jim Polhemus, USAID.

term perspective required to build political and economic institutions capable of sustaining democratic forms of rule and viable economic reform processes.

In Zambia formal interest groups were weakened as a result of both political and economic processes of reform. A wide variety of political tactics, including attempts at co-opting segments of the trade unions, side-lining formal institutions and appealing to the general masses, were employed with relative success by the MMD government. Echoing experiences from across sub-Saharan Africa, the case of Zambia indicates that when organisational interests and institutional forms of representation are weakened, the stage may be cleared for direct, unmediated mobilisation by neo-patrimonial leaders. Continued economic reform and electoral victories in the absence of tangible economic growth were made possible by the lack of formal institutions with capacity to influence the government's decision making.

Do Institutions Matter?

The neo-patrimonial perspective portrays African politics as being radically different from politics elsewhere. From this perspective, it is deemed futile to analyse African political developments by means of general theories of democratisation and formal institutions. Chabal and Daloz argue that political actors maintain 'politics of disorder' to obtain the means needed to sustain neo-patrimonialism and thus are biased against the western style legal and administrative institutions (Chabal and Daloz 1999). In their view, formal institutions are means to sustain political domination, partly moulded (defined and redefined, established and abolished at will) to support the 'real' political game of neo-patrimonialism and clientelism, and partly to conceal this true nature of politics.

The Zambian case study suggests that political leaders manipulate formal institutions to their own advantage. Thus, the neo-patrimonial perspective is a useful reminder about assuming that political institutions will function in the same way independent of context. However, the conclusion should not be drawn that African polities are of a completely different nature than for instance European or Latin American ones, and therefore cannot be analysed by similar approaches. This claim exaggerates the contrasts between regions. Although there are important unique contextual conditions and characteristics of African societies, the same can be said for other regions of the world. The Zambian findings, and other sub-Saharan country cases, are supported by analyses emerging from Latin American and Eastern European experiences with dual reform processes (Hellman 1998; Roberts 1995; Gibson 1997; Schamis 1999).

Hellman notes that in the case of Eastern Europe, the main obstacle to sustained, institutional economic reforms appears to be the 'initial reform winners', i.e. those groups benefiting from the immediate liberalisation, rather than the anticipated losers (1998). Echoing the Zambian case, studies based on Latin American experiences have also suggested that governments implementing liberal economic reforms have been able to maintain political support (Schamis 1999; Snyder 1999; Burgess 1999; Roberts 1995). Studies of political and economic processes of reform in Argentina and Peru suggest that economic reform implementation has strengthened rather than weakened the populist political practices of these regimes. According to Roberts (1995), populist leaders like Fujimoro and Menem were able to divide the labour movement by targeting co-operative unions for selective wage increases, control over social welfare funds, political appointments and legal privileges. In these country cases, political de-institutionalistion appears to have been employed as a conscious strategy of personalist leaders, enabling them to establish un-mediated relationships with atomised mass followings. The failure of representative institutions like political parties, labour unions and autonomous institutions to mediate between citizens and the state has, thereby, paved the way for the direct mobilisation of heterogeneous masses, synonymous with populism. Thus, analyses based on Latin American, Eastern European and African empirical data have in recent years concluded that the question of whether democracy hinders or facilitates economic reform policies may not be the most conducive research agenda. It is suggested that within a formal multiparty system, a range of other forms of rule may be facilitated under processes of economic reform (van de Walle 2001, Geddes 1995; Roberts 1995; Burgess 1999; Hellman 1998).

Institutionalisation of Partial Reforms

The analysis has indicated that reforms in Zambia in the 1990s, both political and economic, had a strong external component, as international credibility and renewal of aid funds were considered the most important political tasks of the MMD government in 1991. In 1996, fear of not being re-elected, and thus losing access to political and financial resources, prompted the Zambian leadership to risk its newly gained international reputation and support in order to secure its own political survival in the domestic arena. In the 1996–2001 period the leverage of the donors diminished in terms of both political and economic reform. The fact that conditionality instruments were employed with no results clearly weakened the credibility of the donors' conditionality instruments. After a short period of euphoric optimism about what political and economic reforms in Zambia could accomplish in terms of poverty reduction and societal participation, it can be argued that, both Zambia's donors and Zambian policy-makers have since the mid-1990s come to regard both political and economic liberalisation as enduring processes that can be circumvented, but not completely abandoned. The weak capacity of opposition parties as well as civil society in Zambia, and the fact that these forces have been weakened by the reform processes set in motion, indicate that the long term process of consolidating and institutionalising the processes of reform may still be far down the road. Both the 1996 and 2001 elections were characterised by malpractices, indicating that the quality of the electoral process has been given relatively low priority by the Zambian government. Furthermore, the weakness of Zambia's vertical and horizontal institutions of restraint—including the party system, the electoral process, civil society, media, courts, central banks and other special agencies of restraint—is embedded in excessive power concentration in the political system. In the light of the December 2001 election results, the size of the opposition group should augur for more lively parliamentary sessions than at any time in the past. However, it is not likely that the new balance in the Zambian Parliament will entirely change Zambian politics. In the new Mwanawasa administration, almost all of the ruling party's MPs are enjoying the fruits of office as either a minister or a deputy minister. The numerous defections from the opposition parties to the MMD in the first part of the election period underline the weak foundations of the Zambian democracy and party system.

Appendix 1: Informant Interviews

1. Allarp, Anne Sofie, European Commission. Lusaka, July 24, 2001.
2. Banda, A.K., Director, Policy Planning, Ministry of Agriculture, Food and Fisheries (MAFF). Lusaka, November 27, 1996.
3. Banda, Moses, Manager, Economic Expansion in Outlying Areas. Lusaka, June 7, 1995.
4. Beardmore, Richard, World Bank Resident Representative. Lusaka, October 1, 1996.
5. Bratton, Mike, Professor, Department of Political Science, Michigan State University. Lusaka, June 3, 1995.
6. Bull, Theo, Private businessman, member of Zambia Association of Chambers of Commerce and Industry (ZACCI). Lusaka, January 15, 1997; October 20, 2000; July 22, 2001.
7. Bwalya, K.E. Ng'angu, Dr., District Chairman, Forum for Development and Democracy (FDD). Lusaka, July 29, 2001.
8. Bwalya, Bobby M., Chairman, Electoral Commission of Zambia (ECZ). Lusaka, July 30, 2001.
9. Chamvera, I., President, Zambia Association of Chambers of Commerce and Industry (ZACCI). Lusaka, October 14, 1996.
10. Chanda, Donald, Special Assistant to Kenneth Kaunda on Press and Public Relations (1995–1997), United National Independence Party (UNIP). Lusaka, October 10, 2002.
11. Chembe, Ellah, Resident Economist, World Bank. Lusaka, June 6, 1995; September 9, 1996; January 16, 1997.
12. Chembe, Martin, Director, Department of Information and Public Relations, Zambia Congress of Trade Unions (ZCTU). Kitwe, December 5, 1996.
13. Chinene, Vernon, Dean, School of Agricultural Sciences, University of Zambia, November 6, 1996.
14. Chirwa, Alec, General Secretary, Zambia Congress of Trade Unions (ZCTU) (1991–2002). Kitwe, December 2, 1996.
15. Chiwele, Dennis, Dr., Institute of African Studies. Lusaka, June 2, 1995; September 9, 1996.
16. Chongo, Robson, Party Secretary, United National Independence Party (UNIP). Lusaka, October 16, 2000.
17. Chruickshank, Stuart, Technical Director, Zambia Privatisation Agency (ZPA). Lusaka, October 7, 1996.
18. Dahlin, Elisabeth, First Secretary, Political and Commercial Officer, Swedish Embassy. Lusaka, May 30, 1995, June 5, 1995.
19. Fraser, Ian, Advisor Zambia Privatisation Agency (ZPA). Lusaka, June 5, 1995; January 8, 1997; March 21, 2001.
20. Gaustadsæther, Torbjørn, Charge d'affairs, Norwegian Embassy. Lusaka, May 29, 1995; October 1, 1996.
21. Gordon, David, Director, US Policy Program, Overseas Development Council (ODC). Washington DC, March 10, 1997.
22. Gray, George, Executive Director, Zambia National Farmers Union (ZNFU). Lusaka, October 2, 1996.
23. Haugen, Kikkan. Second Secretary, Norwegian Embassy. Lusaka, January 14, 1997; January 25, 2001.
24. Hawes, Frank, Democracy and Governance Advisor, US Agency for International Development. Lusaka, July 26, 2001.
25. Hedlund, Hans, Dr., Programme Co-ordinator Economic Expansion in Outlying Areas. Lusaka, September 19, 1996.

26. Heek, van der Hoeve, Anke, Desk Officer, Zambia, Malawi, Dutch Ministry of Foreign Affairs. August 1, 1997 (Phone interview).
27. Heijden, Hendrik van der, External Financing Advisor, Ministry of Finance and Economic Development (MOF). Lusaka, October 28, 1996; December 9, 1996; January 15, 1997.
28. Hellebust, Håkon, Country Economist, First Secretary, Norwegian Embassy. Lusaka, August 27, 1996; October 29, 1996.
29. Henriot, Peter, Jesuit Centre for Theological Reflection (JCTR). Lusaka, November 26, 1996; October 7, 2002.
30. Hill, Catharine, External Advisor, Ministry of Finance and Economic Development (MOF) and team leader, Harvard Macro-Economic Advisory Group. Lusaka, December 12, 1996; January 9, 1997.
31. Holm, Gunnar, Norwegian Ministry Foreign Affairs Zambia Desk (Oslo). December 2, 1997 (phone interview).
32. Jensen, Mads Sandøy, Danish Ambassador. Lusaka, July 26, 2001.
33. Jere, Elisabeth, Managing Director, Social Impact Division, Zambia Privatisation Agency (ZPA). Lusaka, December 6, 1996.
34. Kalyalya, Denny, Dr., Economic Advisor, Bank of Zambia (BOZ). Lusaka, January 9, 1997.
35. Kani, Felix C., Director of Economics, Bank of Zambia (BOZ). Lusaka, October 3, 1996.
36. Kasonde, Emmanuel, Minister of Finance (1991–1993, 2001–2003). Lusaka, October 7, 1996.
37. Kasumbu, Ignatius, Assistant General Secretary (Business), Zambia Congress of Trade Unions (ZCTU). Kitwe, December 6, 1996.
38. Keller, Robert, Advisor, Swedish Embassy. Lusaka, September 12, 1996.
39. Kunda, Kalila C., Executive Director, Foundation for Democratic Process (FODEP). Lusaka, October 17, 2000.
40. Laan, Cornia van der, Economic Advisor, Dutch Embassy. Lusaka, January 9, 1997.
41. Lewanika, Aka, Member of Parliament (1991–1993), Movement for Multiparty Democracy, National Party (1993–1996), Agenda for Zambia (1996–2001), Cabinet Minister (Science and Technology) (1991–1992). Lusaka, June 1, 1995; September 17, 1996; October 20, 2000.
42. Liato, Austin C., vice-President, Zambia Congress of Trade Unions (ZCTU). Lusaka, November 5, 1996.
43. Lieser, Derd, Dr., Friedrich Ebert Stiftung. Lusaka, September 2, 1996.
44. Litungu, Robert, Investment Analyst (until 1995), Zambia Industrial and Mining Corporation (ZIMCO). Lusaka, January 15, 1997.
45. Luhila, Frede, Executive Director, Programme Against Malnutrition (PAM). Lusaka, November 8, 1996.
46. Lungu, Zondani, Controller of Commercial Operations, Assistant General Manager, Zambia Co-operative Federation (ZCF). Lusaka, January 7, 1997.
47. Malembo, Patrick, Ministry of Finance and Economic Development. Lusaka, October 16, 2000.
48. Manda, Irene, Research Department, National Assembly of Zambia. Lusaka, October 3, 1996.
49. Masupha, Alfred, General Manager, Kaleya Smallholder Company, Board Member Zambia Federation of Employers (ZFE). Lusaka, October 18, 1996.
50. Matibini, Patrick, Zambia Law Association. Lusaka January 23, 2001.
51. Matoka, Cecilia, Women in Agriculture. Lusaka, November 26, 1996.
52. Mkandawire, Abel, Board Chairman Zambia Privatisation Agency (ZPA) and vice Chairman, Zambia Association of Chambers of Commerce and Industry (ZACCI), Lusaka, January 8, 1997.

53. Mazoka, A., Dr., President, United Party for National Development (UPND). Lusaka, October 19, 2000.
54. Mealins, Helen, Department of International Development (DFID), British High Commission. Lusaka, July 20, 2001.
55. Mehl, Josephine S., Executive Director, Tourism Council of Zambia (TCZ). Lusaka, October 11, 2002.
56. Moen, Charles, Chief Economist, United States Agency for International Development (USAID). Lusaka, September 19, 1996.
57. Molver, Ian, Managing Director, Lohnro Agribusiness (Cotton), Board Member, ZACCI and Zambia Revenue Authority (ZRA). Lusaka, December 6, 1996.
58. Moser, Gary, The International Monetary Fund (IMF). Washington DC, March 12, 1997.
59. Mosunda, Winnie, Co-ordinator, Women in Development Unit, United Nations Development Programme (UNDP). Lusaka, May 31, 1995.
60. Mpepo, Besinati, Co-ordinator, Civil Society for Poverty Reduction (CSPR). Lusaka, October 10, 2002.
61. Mtamboh, Ernest, Commonwealth Development Corporation (CDC), Lusaka, September 6, 1996.
62. Mubanga, Justin C. Principal Economist (Macroeconomic Policy Unit), Department of Planning and Economic Management, Ministry of Finance and National Planning. Lusaka, October 10, 2002.
63. Muchimba, C.B., Research and Information Officer, Mine Workers Union of Zambia (MUZ). Kitwe, December 5 1996.
64. Mudenda, Alfred, Assistant General Secretary (Administrations), Zambia Congress of Trade Unions (ZCTU). Kitwe, December 3, 1996.
65. Mudenda, Gilbert, Economic Consultant, Institute for Policy Studies. Lusaka, June 5, 1996.
66. Mulaisho, Dominic, Director, Bank of Zambia (1991–1995). Lusaka, October 10 1996; October 18, 2000.
67. Mulenga, P.E., Director of Organisation, Zambia Congress of Trade Unions (ZCTU). Lusaka, October 21, 1996.
68. Mulonda, Phelim, Regional Secretary, Civil Servants Union of Zambia (CSUZ), District Chairman, Zambia Congress of Trade Unions (ZCTU). Lusaka, October 14, 1996.
69. Mumba, Neves, President, National Christian Coalition (NCC). Lusaka, July 26, 2001.
70. Muneku, Austin C., Research Economist, Zambia Congress of Trade Unions (ZCTU). Lusaka, October 18, 1996; December 5, 1996.
71. Murray. Michael, First Secretary, British High Commission. Lusaka, December 17, 1996.
72. Musokotwane, Situmbeko, Advisor, Ministry of Finance and National Planning. Lusaka, October 11, 2002.
73. Musonda, Grace, Office Manager, Public Sector Reform Programme, United Nation Development Program (UNDP). Lusaka, October 8, 1996.
74. Mutale, James, Director, Zambia Privatisation Agency (ZPA) (1992–1994). Lusaka, October 14, 1996.
75. Mutale, Stella M., Senior Economist (Macroeconomic Policy Unit), Department of Planning and Economic Management, Ministry of Finance and National Planning. Lusaka, October 10, 2002.
76. Mutukwa, Mebelo, Managing Director, Pangea Partners Zambia Ltd., Chairman, Fiscal and Monetary Committee Zambia Association of Chambers of Commerce and Industry (ZACCI). Lusaka, November 4, 1996.
77. Mwamba, Nkonga, Dr., Director, Macro-Economic Development, Ministry of Finance and Economic Development (MOF). Lusaka, November 27, 1996.

78. Mwamba, Steven C., Director, Directorate of State Owned Enterprises (Ministry of Finance), Executive Director, Zambia Privatisation Agency (ZPA) 1994–1995. Lusaka, January 7, 1997.
79. Mwanajiti, Ngande, Executive Director AFRONET (The Inter-African Network for Human Rights and Development). Lusaka, January 13, 1997; October 17, 2000.
80. Mwaanga, Vernon, Minister and Chief Government Spokesman, Member of Parliament, Movement for Multiparty Democracy (MMD). Lusaka, August 2, 2001.
81. Mwanza, Allast, Dr., Department of Economics, University of Zambia. Lusaka, September 9 1996; November 2, 1996.
82. Mwape, Bright, Managing Director, *The Post*. Lusaka, January 6, 1996.
83. Mwene, Ben, Professor, Secretary to the Treasury, Ministry of Finance and Development (MOF). Lusaka, December 19, 1996; January 13, 1997.
84. Mwikisa, B., Department of Economics, University of Zambia (UNZA). Lusaka, October 19, 2000.
85. Nakalonga, M., Chief Executive, Economic Association of Zambia (EAZ). Lusaka, October 8, 1996.
86. Ndalamei, Likolo, Senior Economist, Research Department, Bank of Zambia (BOZ). Lusaka, October 3, 1996.
87. Ngoma, Gertrud, Ministry o Finance and Economic Development (MOF). Lusaka, November 5, 1996.
88. Ngoma, P.A., Deputy Minister, Office of the President and Member of Parliament (MMD) (2001–). Lusaka, October 1, 2002.
89. Nketani, Bursch, Personnel Director, Barclays Bank of Zambia, Member Zambia Federation of Employers (ZFE). Lusaka, October 21, 1996.
90. Nonde, B., Deputy Executive Director, Zambia Federation of Employers (ZFE). Lusaka, October 29, 1996.
91. Nyamazana, E., Dr., World Bank Resident Economist. Lusaka, October 16, 2000.
92. O'Donnell, Mark, Chairman, Zambia Association of Manufacturers (ZAM). Lusaka, November 4, 1996.
93. Phiri, Gideon, Chief Executive, Zambia Association of Chambers of Commerce and Industry (ZACCI). Lusaka, September 13 1996; October 2, 1996.
94. Phiri, M., Zambia Independent Media Association (ZIMA). Lusaka, October 17, 2000
95. Phiri, Roger, Assistant General Secretary, Peasant Farmers Union of Zambia. Lusaka, October 10, 1996.
96. Polhemus, James, Good Governance Advisor, United States Agency for International Development (USAID). Lusaka, September 11, 1996; November 1, 1996.
97. Pomerantz, Phyllis R., Country Director, Africa Region, World Bank. Washington DC, March 10, 1997.
98. Saasa, Oliver, Director, Institute of African Studies, University of Zambia. Lusaka, October 21, 1996.
99. Sakala, Bethel Nakaponda, Development Services Coordinator, Zambia Co-operative Federation (ZCF). Lusaka, January 7, 1997.
100. Sandala, Charles, President, National Association of Peasant and Small Scale Farmers Union (NAPSSFU). Lusaka, December 10, 1996.
101. Sannes, Arne, First Secretary (Agriculture), Norwegian Embassy. Lusaka, October 29, 1996.
102. Saurvik, Arne, First Secretary, Norwegian Embassy. Lusaka, September 6, 1996.
103. Sawaya, Emile, Principal Private Development Specialist, Southern African Department, World Bank. Washington DC, March 10, 1997.

104. Schultheiss, Michael, Resident Director Zambia Office, Friedrich Ebert Stiftung (FES). Lusaka, October 10, 2002.
105. Scorcsci, Birgitta, Women in Development Unit, Norwegian Embassy for Development Cooperation (NORAD). Lusaka, May 30, 1995.
106. Scott, Guy, Minister of Agriculture (MMD) (1991–1993). Lusaka, September 13, 1996.
107. Scoville, Meredith, US Agency for International Development (USAID), Director Southern Africa Department. Washington DC, March 12, 1997.
108. Seshamane, V., Dr., Department of Economics, University of Zambia (UNZA). Lusaka October 25, 1996; October 19, 2000.
109. Sichinga, A.C., Permanent Secretary, Ministry of Agriculture, Food and Fisheries (MAFF). Lusaka, January 16. 1997.
110. Sichone, Lucy, Director, Zambia Civic Education Association. Lusaka, January 16, 1997.
111. Siemba, Moses, Deputy Executive Director, Zambia Association of Chambers of Commerce and Industry (ZACCI). Lusaka, November 4, 1996.
112. Sikazwe, Emily, Executive Director, Women for Change. Lusaka, June 1, 1995; July 24, 2001.
113. Sikazwe, Robinson, Regional Consultant (Africa), Norwegian Confederation of Trade Unions (LO). Lusaka, November 28, 1996.
114. Simutanyi, Neo, Institute of African Studies, University of Zambia. Lusaka, September 2, 1996.
115. Stepanek Joseph, Director, US Agency for International Development (USAID). Lusaka, September 12, 1996.
116. Svendsen, Helge, Second Secretary, Business and Energy Sector, Norwegian Embassy. Lusaka, September 4, 1996.
117. Svensson, Kristina, Swedish Ambassador. Lusaka, July 17, 2001.
118. Taha, E., Resident Representative, International Monetary Fund (IMF). Lusaka, December 10, 1996.
119. Todd, John, Principal Economist Macroeconomics, Southern Africa, World Bank. Lusaka, January 16, 1996; Washington DC, March 11, 1997.
120. Ven, Frans van de, Chief Technical Advisor, Ministry of Agriculture Food and Fisheries (MAFF), Food Security Division. Lusaka, November 27, 1996; December 13, 1996.
121. Walker, Emily, vice-President, Zambia Co-operative Federation (ZCF) and Zambia Grain Growers Association. Lusaka, December 12, 1996.
122. Wamulume, Bataba, vice-President, Railway Workers Union of Zambia. Lusaka, October 18, 1996.
123. Wetterqvist, Ingrid, Political and Commercial Officer, Swedish Embassy. Lusaka, September 5, 1996.
124. White, Oliver C. Campbell, Senior Public Enterprises Specialist, World Bank. Washington DC, March 11, 1997.
125. Yesi, Abdon, Foundation for a Democratic Process (FODEP). Lusaka, January 14,1997.
126. Yuuki, Mitsunori, First Secretary, Embassy of Japan. Lusaka, August 29, 1996.
127. Zeidler, Axel, First Secretary, Embassy of the Federal Republic of Germany. Lusaka, January 15, 1997.
128. Zukas, Simon, Minister of Agriculture Food and Fisheries (MAFF) (1993–1996), Chairman, Forum for Development and Democracy (FDD) (2001–). Lusaka, December 13, 1996; July 26, 2001.
129. Ågren, Christer, Economic Advisor, Swedish Embassy. Lusaka, September 12, 1996.

Appendix 2: Chronology of Major Political Dev

1991

October

MMD wins the Presidential and Parliamentary ele

The inauguration of the Third Republic under th

1992

January

President Chiluba declares Zambia a Christian nation.

May

A pressure group, Caucasus for National Unity, is created within MMD and as a result, all Caucasus members are asked to leave the party.

July

United Democratic Party is formed by MMD Cabinet member, Enoch Kavindele.

Kaunda announces that he will resign from national politics.

August

500 striking bank workers dismissed. ZCTU criticised for being too close to MMD.

MMD ministers Baldwin Nkumbula and Aka Lewanika resign from the MMD Cabinet citing growing corruption within the government as reason for their departure.

November

UDP is dissolved and its leader, Enoch Kavindele, rejoins MMD and is immediately appointed to MMD Party Finance Committee.

1993

February

The 'Zero Option Plan' to overthrow the MMD government discovered.

26 opposition members with a basis in UNIP are detained, among them, the son of Kenneth Kaunda.

March

President Chiluba announces the reintroduction of state of emergency laws. Lifted after 82 days (May 1993).

April

Major ministerial reshuffles. 'Key reform ministers', Emmanuel Kasonde (finance), Guy Scott (agriculture), Arthur Wina (education) and Humphrey Mulemba (mines) are dismissed from Cabinet. No official explanation offered.

June

Roger Chongwe removed from Ministry of Legal Affairs, assumed to be connected to his criticism of the state of emergency.

August

Pastoral letter "Hear the cry of the poor" issued by the Catholic churches criticising the social consequences of the government's economic policies.

The National Party registered.

November

8 by-elections in which the National Party captures 4 seats.

Mwanakatwe constitutional commission established.

December

Bilateral donors threaten to withhold balance-of-payment support unless something is done about drug trafficking.

ZCTU and government rift is made public.

of ministers attending the December 1993 Consultative Group Meeting, in-ng the Minister of Health (Kavimbe) and Deputy Minister of Finance ung'omba) are dismissed from Cabinet.

ign Affairs Minister (Vernon Mwaanga), Community Development and Social Welfare Minister (Nakatindi Wina) and Deputy Speaker of Parliament (Sikota Wina) resign their positions due to repeated allegations of drug trafficking by the named ministers.

April

The managing director (Fred M'membe) and a reporter of *The Post* newspaper are arrested charged with defaming the President. The legal action does not result in a conviction.

July

Chiluba publicly criticises MMD's economic policies, arguing that unless the problems within the agricultural sector are solved, MMD will not be able to win the upcoming elections.

'The Young Turks', a group of young dissenters within MMD present their vision statement in which the governance record as well as economic policies of the MMD government are criticised.

August

Amendment of the Land Bill, intended to transform land from customary to tenure, is rejected by the National Assembly.

September

Kenneth Kaunda announces his return to national politics, citing opposition to the economic policies of MMD as the main reason for ending his retirement.

October

ZCTU's quadrennial congress at Livingstone. 5 unions leave the labour congress after losing the contested elections for leadership positions.

December

The trade union leadership claims that MMD has failed workers more than Kenneth Kaunda and UNIP ever did.

1995

January

The Post newspaper claims President Chiluba is not a true Zambian.

February

Kenneth Kaunda replaces Kebby Musokotwane as President of UNIP.

March

Frictions within MMD between the 'Young Turks' led by Derrick Chitala and 'the old guard' led by Michael Sata, are made public in Zambian newspapers.

June

Mwanakatwe Constitutional Review Commission releases its report.

Derrick Chitala, and Dean Mung'omba of the 'Young Turks' are expelled from MMD.

August

Baldwin Nkumbula, the President of the National Party and former Minister of Sports in the MMD government, is killed in a car accident implicating President Chiluba's son, Castro Chiluba. The independent press links Chiluba to Nkumbula's death.

September

Zambia Democratic Congress (ZDC) formed by Derrick Chitala and Dean Mung'omba.

Government issues a White Paper on the procedure for adopting the new draft constitution, rejecting recommendations of the Constitutional Review Commission that the draft be adopted through a constitutional assembly and a national referendum.

October

In 8 by-elections, UNIP, reinvigorated by Kaunda's return, wins 3 seats. The National Party fails to win any seats.

Incidents of harassment of non-governmental organisations and their leaders increase. 17 Catholic priests are arrested together with three other civil society leaders for campaigning against the constitutional amendment process.

November

An Israeli firm, Nikuev Computers, is offered the contract for the voter registration process.

1996

February

The first bilateral donors announce partial withdrawal of aid citing the governance situation as their main reason.

3 journalists from *The Post* are arrested and jailed on charges of libel and contempt for Parliament by the Speaker of the House. Released without charges after three weeks by a High Court ruling.

March

The Minister of Finance, Ronald Penza, announces that MMD is suspending the implementation of the public sector reform programme.

Amendments to the Public Order Act enacted by Parliament (Chapter 4) to require 14 days prior notice when requesting police permission to hold public gatherings.

May

The Government White Paper on the new Constitution is ratified by the National Assembly and signed into law by President Chiluba on May 28.

June

8 opposition party leaders, including UNIP's vice-presidential candidate, are arrested charged with treason after a spate of bombings in Lusaka and the Copperbelt (the 'Black mamba' group).

October

The government announces the second national and presidential elections in the Third Republic to take place on November 18.

UNIP and 6 smaller opposition parties announce that they will boycott the presidential and parliamentary elections due to the constitution and the voter registration process.

November

MMD wins 60 per cent of the national vote in the parliamentary elections. President Chiluba wins 71 per cent of the vote in the presidential elections. A number of local and international election monitoring groups characterise the elections as flawed due to the voter registration and constitutional amendment barring Kaunda from contesting. Some local monitoring groups, focusing on the actual voting process endorse the elections as free and fair. The voter turnout is low.

The Committee for a Clean Campaign (CCC) and ZIMT have their offices searched by the police and their leaders are taken into custody.

1997

January

Lusaka high-court judge Kabazo Chanda is suspended. Chanda had publicly criticised the Constitutional Amendment Act of 1996, and he overruled the sentence on two *Post* journalists.

February

Under the Public Order Act, police forcibly break up a UNIP demonstration in Ndola, teargas is used.

March

Substantial and long term EU funding granted, including balance-of-payments support.

A permanent human rights commission is established, but the decision is criticised by the opposition and main civil society groups as an attempt to please donors and not a genuine commitment to human rights by the MMD government.

Amendments to strengthen the Electoral Commission of Zambia (ECZ) are tabled.

An Anti-Corruption Commission is established.

The opposition's dispute of Frederick Chiluba's nationality is rejected by the Supreme Court.

June

Talks between Zambian government, the opposition and donors are initiated by International Institute of Democracy and Electoral Assistance (IDEA), Sweden.

The National Party, the main parliamentary opposition to MMD is undermined by Emmanuel Kasonde's decision to rejoin the MMD.

The controversial bill to register media is shelved by the government.

July

Fresh bilateral grants secured at the Paris Consultative Group meeting despite lobbying by opposition parties and Amnesty International.

August

Two opposition members, Roger Chongwe and Kenneth Kaunda are shot at by the police while attending a political rally.

September

Civil Servants Union of Zambia launches a nation-wide strike to protest that pay increases awarded have not been paid. Government maintains that there is no funding for pay increases.

October

A drunken army captain (Captain Solo) tries to overthrow the government, prompting the government to impose a state of emergency. Chiluba accuses opposition of being involved and 17 members of the opposition are arrested, ZDC's leader Dean Mung'obma included.

November

Dean Mung'omba and Nakatindi Wina arrested for alleged involvement in the October coup.

December

Kenneth Kaunda placed under house arrest for alleged participation in the October coup.

1998

January

State of emergency extended for another three months. Princess Nakatindi Wina arrested in connection with the October 1997 coup attempt.

The Human Rights Commission releases its report upholding allegations of torture against the arrested opposition members.

Godfrey Miyanda—who until now has been regarded as the most likely candidate to replace Chiluba as the leader of MMD—is moved from the vice-presidency to Ministry of Education.

February

The alleged coup plotters—including Mung'omba—are formally charged with treason.

Eight bombs explode around Lusaka.

The Post editor and journalists are arrested in connection with article comparing Zambian and Angolan security forces.

March

State of emergency lifted after marked donor criticism of it being prolonged.

Ronald Penza sacked from Ministry of Finance, replaced by Edith Nawakwi.

ZCTU launches mass industrial action against the civil service wage reform. The Minister of Labour, Newstead Zimba threatens to de-register ZCTU.

May

Zambia Alliance for Progress (ZAP) established as party, includes NCC, ZDC, AZ, LPF and the Lima party. It is not a merger as all parties continue to exist and leadership rotates among the parties. UNIP and UPND do not join the opposition alliance.

June

Kenneth Kaunda released from detention and he announces his intention to retire from national politics.

Trial of 80 people accused by government of involvement in the 1997 coup begins.

National Christian Coalition (NCC) forms as party.

December

Local government elections, less than half of the eligible voters are registered; of these 27 per cent cast their vote. UNIP and Kenneth Kaunda campaign prior to the elections, and the new party United Party for National Development (UPND) is formed shortly before the local elections. Under the leadership of Anderson Mazoka, UPND gains 28 seats, 64 independents are elected (mostly former MMD members).

Mung'omba and Nakatindi Wina are released. Chief Justice Japhet Banda rules that their trial had been unreasonably delayed.

High Court ruling confirms that Chiluba is a Zambian citizen.

High Court ruling on the 1996 elections accepts the claim of widespread electoral malpratice, but this is not considered to have affected the overall results.

1999

May

New political party launched, the Zambia Alliance for Progress, emerging from National Patriotic Alliance, again comprising a host of smaller parties.

A number of *Post* journalists, including the chief editor Fred M'embe, are charged with espionage, following a story comparing Angolan and Zambian military strategies and strengths. They are later released.

June

Zambia Alliance for Progress is not allowed to register as a political party because the alliance has members that are organised as parties.

August

Zambia Democratic Congress is dissolved to enable its members to join ZAP. In the subsequent by-elections, ZDC's seats are won by UPND (3), MMD (5) and UNIP (3).

September

59 soldiers found guilty in treason trials and are sentenced to death.

MMD members start clamouring for Chiluba to stand for a third term.

October

The South African President Thabo Mbeki visits Chiluba and tries to persuade him to step down after his second term.

November

Chiluba exposes Ben Mwila's financial difficulties to the press. At the November 10 cabinet reshuffle, Mwila is marginalised to Minister of the Environment.

Kenneth Kaunda's son Wezi Kaunda assassinated.

2000

January

When budget is presented for parliament, US$ 400 million is set aside for the establishment of 72 positions as District Administrators, to be personally appointed by Chiluba. The rationale given is to improve service delivery. The DAs are to have control of a Constituency Development Fund, providing much of the small-scale finance for government projects.

March

Under the Public Order Act, police violently break up demonstrations by women activists protesting the police's failure to stop the murders of nine teenage girls. Emily Sikazwe, chairperson of Women for Change, and a journalist from Radio Phoenix are beaten by the police.

Kenneth Kaunda retires from Zambian politics and resigns as president of UNIP.

May

Chiluba announces publicly that no one in MMD should campaign as presidential candidate as he fears that the party will not survive an open leadership contest.

Francis Nkhoma is elected the new leader of UNIP, replacing Kenneth Kaunda.

Under the Public Order Act 200 junior doctors are detained and arrested for demonstrating without permission.

July

Ben Mwila is expelled from MMD.

The Public Order Act is used to arrest and detain an opposition Member of Parliament (UPND) for holding a public meeting without a permit.

August

The Human Rights Commission, participants from civil society, and universities recommend that the Public Order Act be amended to remove clauses impeding political freedoms.

September

The Republican Party, under the leadership of Ben Mwila, performs badly in the September by-elections. The by-elections indicate that none of the main opposition parties have a national following. MMD wins all 8 by-elections in 4 provinces.

Over 20 non-governmental organisations formed a coalition to monitor the 2001 elections (Coalition 2001).

2001

January

UNIP Central Committee appoints Tilyenji Kaunda as UNIPs presidential candidate.

February

A coalition of civic organisations, including the Law Association, the Zambia Episcopal Conference and the Non-Governmental Organisation Co-ordination Committee adopts the Oasis Declaration opposing President Chiluba's third term bid.

March

In a joint statement, the foreign missions in Lusaka of Denmark, Finland, Ireland, Netherlands, Norway, Sweden, the United Kingdom and the US express their support for Chiluba's earlier intention of stepping down at the expiry of his second term in office.

April

MMD convention in Kabwe reappoints Chiluba as the party's President and MMD's presidential candidate in the 2001 elections.

Rally in Lusaka condemning 'the third term bid' gathers 15,000 people.

May

Chiluba announces on Zambian television that he will not stand for a third term as MMD's presidential candidate. He, nevertheless, sacks ministers opposed to his third term. Several of the sacked ministers form a new party, Forum for Democracy and Development (FDD).

One third of MPs sign a declaration seeking to impeach Chiluba.

The Civil Servants Union of Zambia launches a strike demanding pay increases of 100 to 250 per cent.

June

Voter registration begins.

July

Paul Tembo, former vice-President, now FDD member, is assassinated on the day he is due in the High Court to testify in a tribunal investigating government corruption.

Forum for Development and Democracy (FDD) formally launched.

Civil servants strike ends shortly before the OAU summit.

Zambia hosts the OAU summit. OAU is recreated as the African Union (AU).

August

Levy Mwanawasa (vice-President 1991–1993) is named as MMD's presidential candidate.

A tribunal finds Home Affairs Minister and Works and Supply Minister guilty of corruption for having diverted road funds to finance the April MMD convention.

Radio Phoenix is closed down due to late payment of its licence. *The Post* editor Fred Membe is arrested.

October

Dean Mung'omba announces that ZAP will support MMD in the upcoming elections.

Parliament reconvened for the first time since March.

December

Presidential, parliamentary, and local government elections (December 27). MMD retains control of the presidency, but its share of the parliamentary seats declines to 46 per cent. Lewy Mwanawasa, the MMD presidential candidate, wins a (disputed) electoral victory with a weak mandate, 29.2 per cent of the votes, just 2 per cent more than his closest challenger, Anderson Mazoka of UPND. The remainder of the votes is divided between nine other candidates. The elections are characterised as 'unsafe' and 'unfree' by international and local election observers.

Appendix 3: Chronology of Major Economic Developments 1991–2001

1991

November

First comprehensive set of Zambia's external debt data produced.

December

Priority programme to rehabilitate infrastructure commenced.

MMD announces that the responsibility for the privatisation process is to be handed over to the Ministry of Commerce Trade and Industry from ZIMCO.

Substantial reductions of maize meal and fertiliser subsidies announced.

1992

January

Non-traditional exporters allowed 100 per cent foreign exchange retention.

Official exchange rate devalued by 30 per cent (155 per cent through 1992).

Subsidies on maize meal removed.

Programme to reduce military expenditure in real terms over the period 1992–1994 announced.

Commitment to limiting net borrowing from the banking system by government to zero announced.

Subsidies, loans and loan guarantees eliminated for all parastatals, except Zambia Airways and ZCCM.

Debt Management Task Force created within Ministry of Finance to co-ordinate all issues related to external debt.

Zambia's arrears to the World Bank cleared.

February

An agreement reached between the Zambian government, the IMF and the World Bank on a Policy Framework Paper 1992–1994, focusing on subsidy removals, privatisation of the parastatal enterprises and liberalisation of markets.

March

First evidence of major failure of maize crop due to drought. Efforts to mobilise increased donor support started.

Controls on exports of petroleum eliminated.

June

Subsidies on maize meal (roller meal) removed.

Controls on all prices eased, most eliminated.

Fertiliser market opened up for full competition.

Pan-territorial pricing for maize eliminated, pricing to reflect differential transport costs.

July

Privatisation Bill passed in Parliament. Zambia Privatisation Agency (ZPA) established.

Legislation enacted to increase autonomy of Local Councils.

Investment Act amended to make incentives automatic and transparent.

The IMF approves of a restructured Rights Accumulation Programme (RAP) enabling a clearance of Zambia's arrears to the IMF.

August

Agreement with Paris Club on rescheduling of bilateral debt on enhanced Toronto terms. Rescheduling and debt cancellation reduces Zambia's external debt burden by US$ 1.5 billion.

September

First phase of government redundancy programme. 12,000 contract daily employees within civil service are made redundant.

October

Bureau de change system for foreign exchange introduced.

Open General License System changed from a positive to a negative list.

Report of Tax Policy Task Force recommending sweeping changes in the tax system.

December

Joint MoF/BoZ Data Monitoring Committee established.

Exchange rates unified (with ZCCM selling at the market exchange rate).

First tranche of 19 state companies offered for sale.

1993

January

Cash budget introduced.

Weekly treasury bill tender commenced.

Announcement that Exchange Control Act will be repealed.

Budget heads established for defence and security forces.

Elimination of import and export licenses announced, import license levy abolished.

Special fund set up to accelerate road rehabilitation

March

All bilateral (Paris Club) agreements finalised. Negotiations on interest rate reductions and additional debt write-off produce savings of $ 100 million.

June

Import and export licenses eliminated.

Establishment of Zambia Revenue Authority (ZRA).

July

Formal establishment of the Lusaka Stock Exchange (LUSE).

Markets for maize and fertiliser opened to full competition.

November

Commencement of Public Sector Reform Programme (PSRP).

1994

January

Exchange controls removed.

Manufacturing-in-bond permitted.

Duty drawback extended to include third party exporters.

Monitoring of ministries' commitments commenced.

Provision for countervailing duties if unfair trade practices can be proved.

April

Zambia Revenue Authority commences operations.

Privatisation Fund account established.

June

Retirement package for civil servants determined.

August

Mineral Tax Act revoked and replaced by Mineral Royalty Tax Act (bringing Zambia into line with international norms).

September

Commercial debt buy-back operation (ongoing since 1992) completed. Approximately US$ 652 million in debt eradicated.

October

Proposed Land Act converting customary tenure to leasehold is deferred by Parliament pending further consultations.

December

Zambia Airways and United Bus Company (UBZ) put into receivership.

The government announces that ZIMCO will be dissolved by March 31, 1995.

1995

January

Conversion of most commercial banks' statutory reserve deposits to medium term government debt as a means of reducing the interest rate spread.

Adjustment of personal income tax limits to overcome 'bracket creep'.

Fuel levy increased to finance Road Funds (further increased in 1996 Budget).

February

Meridian Bank supported by the BOZ and the government after a major run on its deposits.

March

ZIMCO put into voluntary liquidation.

May

Sale by public flotation of shares of Chilanga Cement to the general public.

Meridian Bank and African Commercial Bank put into receivership.

Mid-term review of ESAF delayed to December.

July

Value added tax (VAT) introduced, sales tax repealed.

Sale of Zambia Sugar Company Ltd.

Revised Land Act passed by Parliament, enabling unused land to be purchased by new investors (Land Act 1995).

August

Temporary revenue measures introduced to close budget deficit created in first half of budget year: increased excise duty on petroleum (from 30 to 45 per cent), rate on withholding tax (from 10 to 25 per cent), excise tax on electricity (from 3 to 10 per cent), and excise sugar tax (from 10 to 20 per cent).

September

Cash budget moved from daily observance to monthly observance.

Road license taxes increased.

December

The IMF recognizes Zambia's successful completion of the Rights Accumulation Programme (RAP) and approves of a three year Enhanced Structural Adjustment Facility (ESAF).

1996

January

Customs duty exemptions, including government purchases, eliminated. Customs duty tariffs reduced on most goods by 15 per cent.

February

IMF finds a number of year end benchmarks (6 out of 10) to have been missed by the Zambian government. As the March ESAF targets will not be met, a delay of ESAF is proposed.

A tentative agreement reached with the Paris Club on Naples terms being applied to Zambia's external debt obligations. The agreement implies a 67 per cent debt cancellation, pending the IMF's mid-term review evaluation.

April
Bank of Zambia (BOZ) allows ZCCM to retain 100 per cent of its foreign exchange receipts to supply the market directly.
May
Cabinet endorses plan and timetable for ZCCM's privatisation and announces the proceeds of sales to commence on February 28, 1997.
June
ZCCM Board approves of the ZCCM privatisation plan.
Increased parliamentary gratuities passed in Parliament.
July
Parliamentary gratuities withdrawn by President Chiluba.
Zambia passes IMF's mid-term review of ESAF's first year.
October
World Bank Board releases first tranche of US$ 90 million structural adjustment facility.

1997
January
The Budget Address announces a reduction in VAT rate from 20 to 17.5 per cent.
Government announces in Zambian press that it will not privatise Zambia's utility companies due to their central role in the economy.
February
Closing date for tender for the privatisation of ZCCM in unbundled units.
Zambia passes IMF's mid-term review of ESAF. The 1996 Paris Club agreement on debt rescheduling on Naples terms formalised.
July
Consultative Group Meeting. In part due to Zambia's mediating role in the Congo conflict, government persuades donors to end the aid boycott instituted in mid-1996. Donors promise US$ 150 million in balance-of-payments support as well as US$ 285 for general financing. However, bilateral donors stress that disbursements are conditional on governance reform.
The Zambian government announces the resumption of the Public Sector Reform Programme.
September
Government bans importation of wheat flour.
Dunlop announces its intention to terminate its operations in Zambia.
November
The Kafue Consortium presents a bid for major ZCCM units.

1998
February
Finance Minister Ronald Penza is replaced by Edith Nawakwi.
Government and Kafue Consortium fail to finalise the transaction agreement for the transfer of the main assets of ZCCM. The Kafue Consortium withdraws from negotiations.
March
A new and lower bid is presented by the Kafue Consortium. The bid is again rejected by the government.
May
Consultative Group Meeting. Donors pledge US$ 530 million for balance-of-payments support, but make disbursement contingent on the sale of ZCCM and governance

issues. World Bank postpones its balance-of-payments support to Zambia on economic performance grounds, reflecting the postponement of ZCCM's privatisation.

Minister of Finance announces the government's intention for the Food Reserve Agency to import fertiliser to cover the seasonal needs, signalling a reversal of MMD's previous position.

November

Ex-Finance Minister Ronald Penza assassinated in his Lusaka home.

December

Directors of Anglo-American Corporation ratify a Memorandum of Understanding on the sale of ZCCM asset packages.

1999

January

Civil servants granted 30 per cent wage increases.

March

Implementation of ESAF II, IMF approves government programme.

Anglo-American Corporation announces its intention to buy the major assets of ZCCM.

May

Consultative Group Meeting. Due to regional concerns, most bilateral donors express a willingness to disburse balance-of-payments funds. Increasing corruption and the human rights situation are held to be pressing issues, but the general outcome is positive

June

Katele Kalumba appointed Minister of Finance.

2000

January

In his budget address, the Minister of Finance (Katele Kalumba) announces that the government intends to emphasise the growth potential of the tourism sector through a range of tax concessions.

March

Sale of ZCCM to Anglo-American completed, prompting donors to release balance-of-payments support.

April

Government bans Food Reserve Agency (FRA) from distributing farming inputs due to lack of finance.

President Chiluba promises public sector workers a minimum wage of ZK 200,000 per month.

July

Interim Poverty Reduction Strategy Paper (PRSP) adopted.

The Consultative Group meeting is held in Lusaka for the first time. Conditionality shifts from privatisation to good governance. Donors pledge US$ 1 billion pending increased participation in following year's election through an update of the voter-register, equal treatment of all parties contesting, concerns of civil society.

October

The COMESA Free Trade Agreement comes into effect.

November

The parliamentary committee for economic affairs delivers its report on the privatisation of ZCCM. The report is rejected by the MMD majority in parliament.

December

Zambia is judged by the World Bank and IMF to have reached the decision point of the Heavily Indebted Poor Countries (HIPC) initiative. Zambia is granted debt relief totalling US$ 3.8bn for a period of 20 years.

2001

February

President Chiluba announces that the government will contest the sales of most of the remaining parastatals.

March

Minister of Finance publicly states Zambia's continued commitment to privatisation in an open letter to IMF.

Zambian Manufacturing Association (ZAM) presents a formal complaint to COMESA due to new labelling required by Zimbabwe government. Complaint later dismissed.

April

IMF completes second review of Zambia's Poverty Reduction and Growth Facility (PRGF) and approves release of third annual disbursement.

July

UN Development Programme (UNDP) releases its Human Development Report indicating that Zambia is the only country in the world with a worse human development index than it had in 1975.

October

National conference on Zambia's Poverty Reduction Strategy Paper (PRSP). Minister of Finance concedes that his government's liberal economic reforms have increased poverty in Zambia.

2002

January

Anglo-America Corporation announces its intent to sell, transfer or close Konkola Copper Mines, Zambia's single biggest mining company, due to prohibitive mine development costs and low copper prices.

Bibliography

Adams, C., 1995: "Fiscal adjustment, financial liberalisation, and the dynamics of inflation: Some evidence from Zambia", *World Development*, Vol. 23, No. 5:735–50.

AFRONET, 2003: "Elections in Zambia: A question of people, law and governance". Position Paper Series, January/February.

Agenda for Zambia (AZ), 1996: *Manifesto 1996–2001*.

Ake, C., 1996: *Democracy and Development in Africa*. Washington DC: The Brookings Institution.

—, 1991: "Rethinking African Democracy", *Journal of Democracy*, Vol. 2, No. 1.

Akwetey, E.O., 1994: *Trade Unions and Democratisation. A Comparative Study of Ghana and Zambia*. Unpublished PhD thesis, University of Stockholm.

Alesina, A. 1989: "Politics and business cycles in industrial democracies", in *Economic Policy*, Vol. 2.

Allen, C., 1998: "The machinery of external control", *Review of African Political Economy*, 25(75):5–9.

Amundsen, I., S. Gloppen, L. Rakner and L. Svåsand, 2001: "Democratic political institutions in Africa: A framework of analysis". Paper prepared for delivery at the Norwegian Annual Political Science Conference, Hønefoss 10–12 January.

Andersson, P. and M. Ndulo, 1994: "Hyperinflation, stabilisation and the new economic recovery program" Mimeo. Department of Economics, University of Gothenburg.

Andreassen, B.A., G. Geisler and A. Tostensen, 1992: *Setting a Standard for Africa? Lessons from the Zambian 1991 Elections*. Bergen: Chr. Michelsen Institute Report Series R:5.

van Arkadie, B. and H. Mule, 1996: "Some comments on recent developments in donor conditionality" in Havnevik, K. and B. van Arkadie (eds), *Domination or Dialogue? Experiences and Prospects for African Development Cooperation*. Uppsala: The Scandinavian Institute of African Studies, pp. 71–89.

Banda, D.A., 1997: "The trade union situation in Zambia. An overview of the law, practice and the way forward". Lusaka: Friedrich Ebert Stiftung.

Banda, D. and A. Muneku, 1996: "The impact of structural adjustment programmes on the labour market and unionisation in Zambia" (Unpublished mimeo). Kitwe and Lusaka: ZCTU/Fredrich Ebert Stiftung.

Bank of Zambia (BOZ), *Annual Reports* 1992–2000. Lusaka.

Barraclough, C., 1998: "Trouble in Lusaka", *Institutional Investor International Edition*, Vol. 23, No. 12 (December).

Barya, J.B., 1993: "The new political conditionality of aid: An independent view from Africa", *IDS Bulletin*, Vol. 24, No. 1.

Bates, R., 1994: "The impulse to reform in Africa", in Widner, J. (ed.), *Economic Change and Political Liberalization in sub-Saharan Africa*. Baltimore: The Johns Hopkins University Press.

—, 1989: *Beyond the Miracle of the Market. The Political Economy of Agrarian Development in Kenya*. Cambridge: Cambridge University Press.

—, 1981: *Markets and States in Tropical Africa*. Berkeley and Los Angeles: University of California Press.

—, 1976: *Rural Responses to Industrialization. A Study of Village Zambia*. New Haven: Yale University Press.

—, 1971: *Unions, Parties and Political Development. A Study of Mineworkers in Zambia.* New Haven: Yale University Press.

Bates, R. and P. Collier, 1993: "The politics and economics of policy reform in Zambia", in Bates, R. and A. Krueger (eds), *Political and Economic Interactions in Economic Policy Reform.* Oxford and Cambridge: Blackwell, pp. 387–443.

Bates, R. and A. Krueger (eds), 1993: *Political and Economic Interactions in Economic Policy Reform.* Oxford and Cambridge: Blackwell.

Bayart, J.F., 1993: *The State in Africa: The Politics of the Belly.* New York: Longman.

Baylies, C., 1980: "The state and the growth of indigenous capital: Zambia's economic reforms and their aftermath", in Finchman, R. and J. Markakis (eds), *The Evolving Structure of Zambian Society.* Edinburgh: Centre for African Studies.

Baylies, C. and M. Szeftel, 1997: 'The 1996 Zambian Elections: Still Awaiting Democratic Consolidation', *Review of African Political Economy,* 24(71):113–28.

—, 1992: "The rise and fall of multiparty politics in Zambia", *Review of African Political Economy,* No. 54:75–91.

—, 1984: "Elections in the one-party state 1973–1980" in Gertzel, C., C. Baylies and M. Szeftel (eds), *The Dynamics of the One-Party State in Zambia.* Manchester: Manchester University Press.

—, 1982: "The rise of a Zambian capitalist class in the 1970s", *Journal of Southern African Studies,* 8:2 (April):187–213.

Berg, E., 1997: "Dilemmas in donor aid strategies", in Gwin, C. and J.M. Nelson (eds), *Perspectives on Aid and Development.* Washington DC: Overseas Development Council (ODC), Policy Essay No. 22:79–98.

Berger, E., 1974: *Labour, Race and Colonial Rule: The Copperbelt from 1924 to Independence.* Oxford: Claredon Press.

Berry, S. 1993: *No Condition is Permanent. The Social Dynamics of Agrarian Change in Sub-Saharan Africa.* Wisconsin: University of Wisconsin Press.

—, 1993a: "Understanding agricultural policy in Africa: The contributions of Robert Bates", *World Development,* Vol. 21, No. 6:1055–62.

Beveridge, A. and A. Oberschall, 1979: *African Businessmen and Development in Zambia.* Princeton: Princeton University Press.

Bienen, H., 1990, "The politics of trade liberalization in Africa", *Economic Development and Cultural Change,* 38:4 (July):711–32.

Bienen, H. and J. Herbst, 1996: "The relationship between political and economic reform in Africa", *Comparative Politics,* Vol. 29, No. 1 (October):23–42.

Bienen H. and N. van de Walle, 1991: *Of Time and Power. Leadership Duration in the Modern World.* Stanford: Stanford University Press.

Bonnick, G.G., 1997: *Zambia Country Assistance Review. Turning and Economy Around.* Washington DC: World Bank Operations Evaluation Study.

Botchwey, K., P. Collier, J.W. Gunning and K. Hamada, 1998: "External evaluation of the ESAF. Report by a group of independent experts". Washington DC: International Monetary Fund.

Bratton, M., 1994: "Economic crisis and political realignment in Zambia", in Widner, J. (ed.), *Economic Change and Political Liberalization in Sub-Saharan Africa.* Baltimore: The Johns Hopkins Press.

—, 1992: "Zambia Starts Over", *Journal of Democracy,* 3(2):81–94.

Bratton, M., P. Alderfer and N. Simutanyi, 1997: *Political participation in Zambia 1991–1996: Trends, determinants and USAID program implications.* Zambia Democratic Governance Project, Special Study No. 5. East Lansing: Michigan State University.

Bratton, M. and D. Posner, 1999: "A First Look at Second Elections in Africa with Illustrations from Zambia", in Joseph, R. (ed.), *State, Conflict and Democracy in Africa.* Boulder: Lynne Rienner Publishers, pp. 377–409.

Bratton, M. and N. van de Walle, 1997: *Democratic Experiments in Africa. Regime Transitions in Comparative Perspective.* Cambridge: Cambridge University Press.

—, 1992: "Popular protest and reform in Africa", *Comparative Politics,* Vol. 24, No. 4, (July).

Bräutigam, D., 2000: *Aid Dependence and Governance.* EGDI 200:1. Stockholm: Expert Group on Development Issues.

—, 1991: *Governance and Democracy: A Review.* World Bank Policy Research Working Paper (WPS 815), Washington DC.

Bräutigam, D., L. Rakner and S. Taylor, 2002: "Business associations and growth coalitions in sub-Saharan Africa", *Journal of Modern African Studies*, Vol. 40, No. 4:519–47.

Bresser Pereira, L. Carlos, J.M. Marawall and A. Przeworski, 1993*: Economic Reforms in New Democracies: A Social-Democratic Approach.* Cambridge: Cambridge University Press.

Buhlungu, S. and G. Adler (eds), 1997: "Labour and liberalisation in Zambia", *South African Labour Bulletin*, Vol. 21, No. 2 (June):48–64.

Bull, T., 1999: "The mines-where are we now?", *Profit Magazine*, Lusaka, April.

—, 1998: "An incredible country", *Profit Magazine*, Lusaka, July.

—, 1996: "Boom, doom or merely gloom?", *The World Today,* Vol. 52, No. 10, (October).

Burdette, M., 1988: *Zambia Between Two Worlds.* Boulder: Westview Press.

Burnell, P., 2003: "Legislative-executive relations in Zambia: Parliamentary reform on the agenda", *Journal of Contemporary African Studies*, Vol. 21, No. 1:1–22.

—, 2002: "Zambia's 2001 elections: The tyranny of small decisions, 'non-decisions' and 'not decisions'", *Third World Quarterly*, Vol. 23, No. 6:1103–20.

—, 2002b: "Parliamentary Committees in Zambia's Third Republic: Partial reforms; unfinished agenda", *Journal of Southern African Studies*, Vol. 28, No. 2 (June):291–313.

—, 2001: "The party system and party politics in Zambia: Continuities past, present and future", *African Affairs,* 100:239–63.

—, 2001b: "Financial indiscipline in Zambia's Third Republic: The role of parliamentary scrutiny", *The Journal of Legislative Studies*, Vol. 7, No. 3 (Autumn):34–64.

Burgess, K., 1999: "Loyalty Dilemmas and Market Reform: Party-Union Alliances under Stress in Mexico, Spain and Venezuela", *World Politics*, No. 52:105–34.

Burnside, C. and D. Dollar, 1997: "Aid, policies, and growth", in *Policy Research Working Paper* No. 1777 (June). Washington DC: World Bank.

Callaghy, T., 2001: "Networks and governance in Africa: Innovation in the debt regime", in Callaghy, T., R. Kassimir and R. Latham (eds), *Intervention and Transnationalism in Africa: Global Networks of Power.* Cambridge: Cambridge University Press, pp. 115–48.

—, 1994: "Civil society, democracy and economic change in Africa: A dissenting opinion about resurgent societies", in Chazan, N. et al. (eds), *Civil Society and the State in Africa.* Boulder: Lynne Rienner Publishers.

—, 1990: "Lost between state and market. The politics of economic adjustment in Ghana, Zambia and Nigeria', in Nelson, J.M., *Economic Crisis and Policy Choice. The Politics of Adjustment in the Third World.* Princeton: Princeton University Press.

Callaghy, T. and J. Ravenhill (eds), 1993: *Hemmed In: Responses to Africa's Economic Decline.* New York: Columbia University Press.

Cammack, P., 1997: *Capitalism and Democracy in the Third World. The Doctrine for Political Development.* London: Leicester University Press.

Carothers, T., 2002: "The end of the transition paradigm", *Journal of Democracy,* Vol. 13, No. 1:1–21.

Carroll, Thomas F., 1992: *Intermediary NGO's: The Supporting Link in Grassroot Development.* Hartford: Kumarian Press.

Carter Center, 2002: "Election Observation Mission 2001, Interim Statement", *Southern African Human Rights Review,* Issue No. 9 (February).

Catholic Commission on Justice and Peace, 1997: "Social dimensions of the 1997 Budget of the Government of the Republic of Zambia". Lusaka: (February).

—, 1993: "Hear the cry of the poor", Pastoral Letter.

Central Statistical Office (CSO), 1997: *Zambia in Figures.* Lusaka: Government Printers.

—, 1995: *Zambia in Figures.* Lusaka: Government Printers.

Chabal P. and J.P. Daloz, 1999: *Africa Works. Disorder as Political Instrument.* The International African Institute, Oxford: James Currey/Bloomington and Indiana University Press.

Chanda, A., 2003: National Integrity Systems. Transparency International Study Report, Zambia.

Chazan, N., 1994: "Engaging the state: Associational life in Sub-Saharan Africa", Migdal, J.S., A. Kohli and V. Shue (eds), *State Power and Social Forces: Domination and Transformation in the Third World.* Cambridge: Cambridge University Press.

Chazan, N., J.W. Haberson and D. Rotchild (eds), 1994: *Civil Society and the State in Africa.* Boulder: Lynne Rienner Publishers.

Chazan, N., R. Mortimer, J. Ravenhill and D.Rothchild, 1988: *Politics and Society in Contemporary Africa.* Boulder: Lynne Rienner Publishers (Second edition 1992).

Cheru, F., 1996: "New social movements: Democratic struggles and human rights in Africa", in Mittelman, J.H. (ed.), *Globalization: Critical Reflections.* Boulder: Lynne Rienner Publishers.

Chiluba, F.J.T., 1995: *Democracy. The Challenge of Change.* Lusaka: Multimedia Publications.

Chua, A., 2003: *World on Fire. How Exporting Free Market Democracy Breeds Hatred and Global Instability.* New York: Doubleday.

Clapham, C., 1997: "Opposition in Tropical Africa", *Government and Opposition,* Vol. 32. No. 4:541–56.

—, 1985: *Third World Politics: An Introduction.* Madison: University of Wisconsin Press.

Clark, J., 1991: *Democratizing Development: The Role of Voluntary Organizations.* London: Earthscan.

The Constitution of Zambia, 1973.

Coleman, F., 1971: *The Northern Rhodesia Copperbelt 1892–1962.* Manchester: Manchester University Press.

Collier, P., 1997: "The failure of conditionality", in Gwin, C. and J.M. Nelson (eds), *Perspectives on Aid and Development.* Washington DC: Overseas Development Council, Policy Essay No. 22:51–79.

Collier, D. and S. Levitsky, 1997: "Democracy with adjectives: Conceptual innovation in comparative perspective", *World Politics,* Vol. 49, No. 3 (April):430–51.

Coperstake, J. and K. Wellard (eds), 1993: *Non-Governmental Organizations and the State in Africa.* London: Routledge.

Cornia, G.A. and G. Helleiner (eds), 1994: *From Adjustment to Development in Africa: Conflict, Controversy, Convergence, Consensus?* London: Macmillan Press.

Cornia, G.A, R. Jolly and F. Stewart, 1987: *Adjustment with a Human Face.* Oxford: Oxford University Press.

Decalo, S., 1998: *The Stable Minority. Civilian Rule in Africa,* Gainesville: FAP Books.

—, 1997: "On statistical correlates of democratization and prospects of democratization in Africa: Some issues for construction, inference and prediction", in Vanhanen, T., *Prospects for Democracy: A Study of 172 Countries,* London: Routledge.

—, 1992: "The process, prospects and constraints of democratization in Africa", *African Affairs,* Vol. 91, No. 362:7–35.

Devajaran, S., D. Dollar and T. Holmgren, 2001: *Aid and Reform in Africa: Lessons from Ten Country Cases.* Washington DC: The World Bank.

Diamond, L., 2002: "Elections without democracy", *Journal of Democracy,* Vol. 13, No. 2:21–36.

—, 1996: "Is the third wave over?", *Journal of Democracy,* Vol. 7, No. 3, (July):20–37.

—, 1992: "Economic development and democracy reconsidered", *American Behavioural Scientist,* Vol. 35, No. 4/5.

—, 1991: *An American Foreign Policy for Democracy.* Washington DC: Progressive Policy Institute, Policy Report No. 11 (July).

Diamond, L., J. Linz and S.M. Lipset, 1990: *Politics in Developing Countries. Comparing Experiences with Democracy.* Boulder: Lynne Rienner Publishers.

Diamond, L. and M.F. Plattner (eds), 1995: *Economic Reform and Democracy.* Baltimore: The Johns Hopkins University Press.

Dijkstra, A.G., 2002: "The effectiveness of policy conditionality: Eight country experiences", *Development and Change,* Vol. 33(2).

van Donge, J.K., 1998: "Reflections on donors, opposition and popular will in the 1996 Zambian general elections", *Journal of Modern African Studies,* Vol. 36, No. 1, (March):71–101.

—, 1995: "Zambia and Chiluba: Enduring patterns of political culture", in Wiseman, J. (ed.), *Democracy and Political Change in Sub-Saharan Africa.* London: Routledge.

Electoral Commission of Zambia (ECZ), 2001: "Electoral Commission of Zambia. Election report on the Presidential, Parliamentary and Local Government Elections 2001", http://www.elections.org.zm/results

—, 1996: *Presidential and Parliamentary General Elections 1996.* Lusaka (November 25).

Engberg-Pedersen, P., 1995: *Limits of Adjustment in Africa: The Effects of Economic Liberalisation 1986–1994.* London: Zed Books.

Epstein, A.L., 1958: *Politics in an Urban African Community.* Manchester: Manchester University Press.

European Union Electoral Unit (EUEU), 2002: "Support to the democratic election process in Zambia: First, Second and Final Interim Statements", http://www.elections.org.zm/results.

Forum for Development and Democracy (FDD), 2001: *Election Manifesto 2001.* Lusaka.

Foundation for Democratic Process (FODEP), 2002: *Election Monitoring Report.* January.

—, 1996: *Zambia's 18 November 1996 Presidential and Parliamentary Elections: Final Election Monitoring Report.* Lusaka.

—, 1992–1996: *By-election reports.* Lusaka.

Fundanga, Caleb M., 1996: "Practical effects of economic and political conditionality in recipient administration", in Havnevik, K. and B. van Arkadie (eds), *Domination or*

Dialogue? Experiences and Prospects for African Development Cooperation. Uppsala: The Scandinavian Institute of African Studies, pp. 89–98.

Geddes, B., 1995: "The politics of economic liberalization", *Latin American Research Review,* Vol. 30, No. 2:195–214.

—, 1994a: *Politician's Dilemma: Building State Capacity in Latin America.* Berkeley: University of California Press.

—, 1994b: "Challenging the conventional wisdom", *Journal of Democracy,* Vol. 5, No. 4:104–19.

van der Geest, W. (ed.), 1994: *Negotiation Structural Adjustment in Africa.* London: James Currey.

Gertzel, C., 1979: "Industrial relations in Zambia to 1975", in Damachi, U., D. Seibel and L. Trachtman (eds), *Industrial Relations in Africa.* New York: St. Martins Press.

Gertzel, C., C. Baylies and M. Szeftel (eds), 1984: *The Dynamics of the One-Party State in Zambia.* Manchester: Manchester University Press.

Gibbon, P., 1993: "The World Bank and the new politics of aid", in Sørensen, G., *Political Conditionality. The European Journal of Development Research,* Vol. 5, No. 1.

—, 1992: "Structural Adjustment and Pressures towards Multipartyism in sub-Saharan Africa", in Bangura, Y., P. Gibbon and A. Ofstad (eds), *Authoritarianism, Democracy and Adjustment. The Politics of Economic Reform in Africa.* Seminar proceedings No. 26. Uppsala: The Scandinavian Institute of African Studies, pp. 127–168.

Gibson, E., 1997: "The populist road to market reform: Policy and electoral coalitions in Mexico and Argentina", *World Politics,* Vol. 49, No. 3, (April):339–70.

Giliomee, H. and C. Simpkins (eds), 1999*: The Awkward Embrace. One Party Domination and Democracy.* Amsterdam: Harwood.

Gordon, D., 1996: "Sustaining economic reform under political liberalization in Africa: Issues and implications", *World Development,* Vol. 24, No. 9:1527–37.

—, 1993: "Debt, conditionality, and reform: The international relations of economic policy restructuring in sub-Saharan Africa", in Callaghy, T. and J. Ravenhill (eds), *Hemmed In. Responses to Africa's Economic Decline.* New York: Columbia University Press, pp. 90–130.

Gould, J., 2002: "Contesting democracy. The 1996 elections in Zambia", in Cowen, M. and L. Laakso (eds), *Multi-Party Elections in Africa.* New York: Palgrave, pp. 299–323.

Government of the Republic of Zambia (GRZ): 1991/92, 1992/931993/94, 1994/95, 1995/96, 1996/97, 1997/98, 1998/99, 1999/2000, 2000/01. *Budget Addresses by the Minister of Finance.* Lusaka.

—, 2000: "Net Aid Transfers to Zambia 1991–2001". Mimeo.

—, 1997a: "Opening and Closing Statement by the Minister of Finance at Zambia's Consultative Group meeting" (Paris, July 9–10).

—, 1997b: "Address by the Honourable Ronald S. Penza, Minister of Finance and Economic Development on the occasion of the meeting with donors" (London, April 25).

—, 1995a: *Summary of the recommendations of the Mwanakatwe constitutional review commission and government reactions to the report.* Government Paper No. 1. Lusaka: Government Printers.

—, 1995b: *Draft Constitution of the Republic of Zambia* (June 16).

—, 1995c: *Policy Framework Paper 1995–1998.* Prepared by the Zambian Government in collaboration with the International Monetary Fund and World Bank. Lusaka (November 29).

—, 1995d: "Opening statement by the Minister of Finance to the Consultative Group Meeting for Zambia". (Bournemouth, December 14–15)

—, 1995e: "Closing Statement to the Consultative Group Meeting for Zambia by the Honorary Ronald Penza, Minister of Finance". Bournemouth, December 15.

—, 1994: "Report of the Zambian Government to the Consultative Group meeting" (March 22–23).

—, 1993: *Policy Framework Paper 1990–1993.* Prepared in collaboration with the Word Bank and the International Monetary Fund.

—, 1993a: "Closing statement by the Minister of Finance to the Consultative Group Meeting" (December 10).

—, 1992: *Policy Framework Paper 1992–1995.* Prepared by the Zambian Government in collaboration with the International Monetary Fund and World Bank. Lusaka (November).

—, 1991a: *Economic and Financial Policy Framework Paper* 1991–1993. Prepared by the Zambian Authorities in collaboration with the IMF and World Bank (February 1).

—, 1991b: *Opening of Parliament.* Speech by F.J.T. Chiluba 29 November 1991. Lusaka: Government Printer.

—, 1989: *Economic and Financial Policy Framework Paper* 1989–1991. Prepared by the Zambian Authorities in collaboration with the IMF and World Bank.

—, 1971: *Industrial Relations Act.* No. 36 of 1971. Lusaka: Government Printers.

—, 1966: *First National Development Plan, 1960–70.* Lusaka: Office of National Development and Planning.

Government of the Republic of Zambia (GRZ); Ministry of Agriculture Food and Fisheries (MAFF) 1996: "Zambia: From transition to consolidation. A critical policy review of the liberalization of maize and agricultural input markets 1993–1996", *Market Liberalization Impact Studies* No. 18. Lusaka (December).

—, 1995: Ministry of Agriculture Food and Fisheries (MAFF): "The adjustment by the cooperative sector to the liberalised marketing environment", *Market Liberalization Impact Studies* No. 6. Lusaka (May).

—, 1995a: Ministry of Agriculture Food and Fisheries (MAFF): "Maize marketing costs and margins", *Market Liberalization Impact Studies* No. 4. Lusaka (February).

Government of the Republic of Zambia/Planning and Development Division (GRZ); NORAD, Mellomfolkeligt Samvirke and Finnish Volunteer Service, 1993: *A Directory of Non-Governmental Organisations in Zambia*, Lusaka.

Graham, C., 1995: "The political economy of adjustment and sectoral reforms in Zambia: A stakeholders approach?" Unpublished draft. Washington DC: The Brookings Institution.

—, 1994: *Safety Nets, Politics and the Poor. Transitions to Market Economies.* Washington DC: The Brookings Institution.

Grindle, M. and J. Thomas, 1991: *Public Choices and Policy Change: The Political Economy of Reform in Developing Countries.* Baltimore: Johns Hopkins University Press.

Grosh, B. and R. Mukandala (eds), 1994: *State-Owned Enterprises in Africa.* Boulder and London: Lynne Rienner Publishers.

Gulhati, R., 1989: *Impasse in Zambia. The Economics and Politics of Reform.* Development Political Case Series, No. 2. Economic Development Institute, Washington DC: World Bank.

Gwin, C. and J. M. Nelson (eds), 1997: *Perspectives on Aid and Development.* Policy Essay No. 22. Washington DC: Overseas Development Council.

Haggard, S., 1994: "Introduction", in Haggard, S. and S.B. Webb (eds), *Voting for Reform: Democracy, Political Liberalization, and Economic Adjustment.* New York: Oxford University Press for the World Bank, pp. 1–36.

Haggard, S. and R.R. Kaufman, 1992: "The political economy of inflation and stabilization in middle-income countries", in Haggard, S. and R. Kaufman (eds), *The Politics of Economic Adjustment.* Princeton: Princeton University Press, pp. 270–313.

—, 1989: "Economic adjustment in new democracies", in Nelson, J.M. et al., *Fragile Coalitions: The Politics of Economic Adjustment.* New Brunswick and Oxford: Transaction Books, pp. 57–77.

Haggard, S. and R. R. Kaufman, (eds) 1995: *The Political Economy of Democratic Transitions.* Princeton: Princeton University Press.

—, (eds) 1992: *The Politics of Economic Adjustment.* Princeton: Princeton University Press.

Haggard S. and S.B. Webb (eds), 1994: *Voting for Reform: Democracy, Political Liberalization, and Economic Adjustment.* New York: Oxford University Press.

—, (eds) 1993: "What do we know about the political economy of economic policy reform?", *The World Bank Research Observer* 8, 2 (July):143–68.

Haggard, S. and J. Williamson, 1994: "The Political Conditions for Economic Reform", in J. Williamson (ed.), *The Political Economy of Policy Reform.* Washington DC: Institute of International Economics.

Harvey, C., 1978: "The structure of Zambian development", in Damachi, U. and G. Routh (eds), *Development Paths in Africa and China.* London: Macmillan, pp. 136–51.

Havnevik, K. (ed.), 1987: *The IMF and the World Bank in Africa. Conditionality, Impact and Alternatives*. Uppsala: The Scandinavian Institute of African Studies.

Havnevik, K. and B. van Arkadie (eds), 1996: *Domination or Dialogue? Experiences and Prospects for African Development Cooperation.* Uppsala: The Scandinavian Institute of African Studies.

Hawkins, J., 1991: "Understanding the failure of IMF reform: The Zambian case", *World Development,* Vol. 19, No. 7:839–49.

Healey, J. and M. Robinson, 1992: *Democracy, Governance and Economic Policy. Sub-Saharan Africa in Comparative Perspective.* London: Overseas Development Institute (ODI): Russell Press.

Heijden, H., van der, 2000: *The Effectiveness of Economic Policy Reform, Foreign Aid and External Debt Relief in Zambia.* (Unpublished) report commissioned by the Norwegian and Swedish Ministries of Foreign Affairs.

Heilman B. and J. Lucas, 1997: "A social movement for African capitalism? A comparison of business associations in two African cities", *African Studies Review,* Vol. 40, No. 3:141–71.

Helleiner, G.K. (ed.), 1986: *Africa and the International Monetary Fund.* Washington: International Monetary Fund.

Hellman, J.S., 1998: "Winners take all: The politics of partial reform in postcommunist transitions", *World Politics*, Vol. 50, No. 2:203–35.

Henley, A. and E. Tsakalotos, 1993: *Corporatism and Economic Performance.* Aldershot: Edward Elgar.

Herbst, J., 1993: *The Politics of Reform in Ghana, 1982–1991.* Berkeley and Los Angeles: University of California Press.

—, 1990: "The structural adjustment of politics in sub-Saharan Africa", *World Development,* Vol. 18, No. 7:949–58.

Hewitt, A.P. and T. Killick, 1996: "Bilateral aid conditionality and policy leverage", in Stokke, O. (ed.), *Foreign Aid Towards the Year 2000: Experiences and Challenges.* London: Frank Cass.

Hibbs, D., 1977: "Political parties and macroeconomic policy", *The American Political Science Review,* Vol. 7:1467–87.

Holm, J.D., N. Simutanyi and D. Pfeiffer, 1997: "Zambia democratic governance project: Final evaluation". Washington DC (USAID) June.

Hopkins, R., A. Powell, A. Roy and C. Gilbert, 1997: "The World Bank and conditionality", *Journal of International Development,* Vol. 9, No. 4, (June):507–16.

Hulme, D. and M. Edwards (eds), 1997: *NGOs, States and Donors. Too Close for Comfort?* London: Macmillan Press.

Human Rights Watch/Africa Report, 1996: *Zambia: Elections and human rights in the Third Republic,* Vol. 8, No. 4, December.

Huntington, S., 1991: "Democracy's Third Wave", *Journal of Democracy,* No. 2, Vol. 2, (Spring).

—, 1968: *Political Order in Changing Societies.* New Haven: Yale University Press.

Ihonvbere, J., 1996: *Economic Crisis, Civil Society and Democratization: The Case of Zambia.* Trenton and Asmara: Africa World Press, Inc.

International Institute for Democracy and Electoral Assistance (IDEA), 1997: *The Stromsborg Statement* (Stockholm, June 10).

International Monetary Fund (IMF), 2000: *Zambia: Improving public expenditure management.* Washington DC, IMF Fiscal Department (June).

—, 1995: *Zambia: Staff report for accumulation of rights and economic program for 1995–1998.* Washington DC: November 2.

—, 1995b: *Zambia: Request for extension of the period of the first annual arrangement under the Enhanced Structural Adjustment Facility.* Washington DC: November 26.

—, 1980: *World Economic Outlook 1980.* Washington DC: International Monetary Fund, International Financial Statistics 1992–1997.

Jackson R. and C. Rosberg, 1982: *Personal Rule in Black Africa: Prince, Autocrat, Prophet and Tyrant.* Berkeley: Berkeley University Press.

Jeffries, R., 1993: "The state, structural adjustment, and good governance in Africa", *Journal of Commonwealth and Comparative Politics,* No. 31.

Johns, S., 1980: "The Parastatal Sector", in W. Tordoff (ed.), *Administration in Zambia.* Manchester: Manchester University Press.

Johnson, J. and S. Wasty, 1993: "Borrower ownership of adjustment programs and the political economy of reform", *World Bank Discussion Paper,* No. 199. Washington DC: World Bank.

Jones, S. 1994: "Structural adjustment in Zambia", in Geest, W. van der (ed.), *Negotiating Structural Adjustment in Africa.* London and Portsmouth: James Currey and Heinemann.

Joseph, R. (ed.), 1999: *State, Conflict and Democracy in Africa.* Boulder: Lynne Rienner Publishers.

—, 1998: "Africa, 1990–1997: From *abertura* to closure", *Journal of Democracy,* Vol. 9:3–17.

—, 1992: "Zambia: A model for democratic change", *Current History* (May):199–201.

Kahler, M., 1992: "External influence, conditionality, and the politics of adjustment", in Haggard, S. and R. Kaufman (eds), *The Politics of Economic Adjustment* Princeton: Princeton University Press.

—, 1990: "Orthodoxy and its alternatives: Explaining approaches to stabilisation and adjustment", in Nelson, J.M. (ed.), *Economic Crisis and Policy Choice. The Politics of Adjustment in the Third World.* Princeton: Princeton University Press.

Kalyalya, D. and J. Lushinga (Bank of Zambia) 1996: "Economic liberalisation and the development of the domestic money market in Zambia". Paper prepared for the Bank of Zambia international conference on "Economic Liberalisation: Experiences and the Way Forward". Lusaka (August 21–23).

Kani, F. (Bank of Zambia), 1996: "Central banking and macro-economic stability in a liberalised environment. The case of Zambia". Paper prepared for the Bank of Zambia international conference on "Economic Liberalisation: Experiences and the Way Forward". Lusaka (August 21–23).

Kanyinga, K., 1993: "The social-political context of the growth of non-governmental organisations in Kenya", in Gibbon, P. (ed.), *Social Change and Economic Reform in Africa.* Uppsala: The Nordic Africa Institute.

Kaplan, I., 1979: *Zambia: A Country Study.* Washington DC: The American University.

Kapur, D., 1997: "The weakness of strength: The challenge of Sub-Saharan Africa", in *The World Bank. Its First Half Century* (Volume I). Washington DC: The Brookings Institution, pp. 683–805.

Kapur, D., J.P. Lewis and R. Webb, 1997: *The World Bank. Its First Half Century* (Volume I and Volume II). Washington DC: The Brookings Institution.

Kaufman, R., 1985, "Democratic and authoritarian responses to the debt issue: Argentina, Brazil and Mexico", *International Organization,* Vol. 39, No. 3 (Summer):473–503.

Kaufman, R. and B. Stallings, 1989: "Debt and democracy in the 1980s: The Latin American experience", in Stallings, B. and R. Kaufman (eds), *Debt and Development in Latin America.* Boulder: Westview Press, pp. 201–23.

Kaunda, K., 1974: *Humanism Part II.* Lusaka: Government Printers.

—, 1967: *Humanism Part I,* Lusaka: Government Printers.

Kifle, H., A.O. Olukoshi and L. Wohlgemuth, 1997: *A New Partnership for African Development. Issues and Parameters.* Uppsala: The Nordic Africa Institute.

Killick, T., 1998: *Aid and the Political Economy of Policy Change.* London: ODI.

—, 1997: "Principals, agents and the failings of conditionality", *Journal of International Development,* Vol. 9, No. 4, (June):483–97.

—, 1996: "Principals, agents and the limitations of BWI conditionality", *World Economy,* Vol. 19, No. 2 (March):211–30.

—, 1995: *IMF Programmes in Developing Countries. Design and Impact.* London and New York: Routledge.

Kinley, L., 1995: "Privatization in Africa: The case of Zambia". Mimeo. Lusaka: USAID, (June).

Kochanowicz, J., 1994: "The transition to market and democratisation in Poland", in Nelson, J.M. (ed.), *A Precarious Balance Volume I: Democracy and Economic Reforms in Eastern Europe.* Washington DC: Overseas Development Council (ODC).

Krennerich, M., 1999: "Zambia", in Nohlen, D., M. Krennerich and B. Thibant (eds), *Elections in Africa.* Oxford: Oxford University Press, pp. 939–62.

Lal, D., 1983: *The Poverty of 'Development Economics'.* London: Institute of Economic Affairs, Hobart Paperback 16.

Lancaster, C., 1997: "The World Bank in Africa since 1980: The politics of structural adjustment lending", in Kapur, D., J.P. Lewis and R. Webb (eds), *The World Bank. Its First Half Century (*Volume II) Washington DC: The Brookings Institution, pp. 161–95.

—, 1993: "Governance and development: The views from Washington", *IDS Bulletin* Vol. 24, No. 1.

Landell-Mills, P., 1992: "Governance, cultural change, and empowerment", *Journal of Modern African Studies,* Vol. 30, No. 4.

Lehman, H. and J. McCoy, 1992: "The dynamics of the two-level bargaining game. The 1988 Brazilian debt negotiations", *World Politics* (July):600–44.

Leith, C. and M. Lofchie, 1993: "The political economy of structural adjustment in Ghana", in Bates, R. and A. Krueger (eds), *Political and Economic Interactions in Economic Policy Reform.* Oxford and Cambridge: Blackwell.

Lemarchand, R., 1992: "Africa's troubled transitions", *Journal of Democracy,* Vol. 3, No. 4.

Lewanika, A. and D. Chitala, 1990: *The Hour Has Come! Proceedings From the National Conference on the Multi-Party Option.* Lusaka: Zambia Research Foundation.

Lewis, P., 1996: "Economic reform and political transition in Africa: The quest for a policy of development", *World Politics,* Vol. 49, No. 1 (October):92–129.

Liberal Progressive Front (LPF), 1996: *Party Manifesto 1996.* Lusaka, October.

Lijphart, A., 1971: "Comparative politics and comparative method", *American Political Science Review,* Vol. 65, No. 3.

Limongi, F. and A. Przeworski, 1997: "Modernization: Theories and facts", *World Politics,* Vol. 49, No. 2 (January):155–83.

—, 1993: "Political regimes and economic growth", *Journal of Economic Perspectives,* Vol. 7, No. 3 (Summer):51–69.

Lindenberg, M. and S. Devarajan, 1993: "Prescribing strong economic medicine: Revisiting the myths about structural adjustment, democracy and economic performance in developing countries", *Comparative Politics,* 26, (January):169–82.

Linz, J. and A. Stepan, 1996: "Towards consolidated democracies", *Journal of Democracy,* Vol. 7, No. 2, (April):14–33.

Lipset, S.M. (ed.), 1995: *The Encyclopaedia of Democracy.* London: Routledge.

—, 1959: "Some social requisites of democracy, economic development and political legitimacy", *American Political Science Review,* 53.

Loxley, J., 1986: "Alternative approaches to stabilization in Africa", in Helleiner, G.K. (ed.), *Africa and the International Monetary Fund.* Washington DC: International Monetary Fund.

Loxley, J. and R. Young, 1990: *Zambia: An Assessment of Zambia's Structural Adjustment Experience.* Ottawa: The North South Institute.

Lucas, J., 1997: "The politics of business associations in the developing world", *Journal of Developing Areas,* Vol. 32, No. 1:71–96.

Luckham, R. and G. White (eds), 1996: *Democratization in the South. The Jagged Wave.* Manchester: Manchester University Press.

Mahmud, S., 1996: "Africa's democratic transitions, change, and development", *Africa Today,* Vol. 43, No. 4:405–15.

Mailafia, O., 1997: *Europe and Economic Reform in Africa. Structural Adjustment and Economic Diplomacy.* London and New York: Routledge.

Makgetla, N.S, 1994: "Control in the parastatal sector in Zambia:1976–1986", in Grosh, B. and R. Mukandala (eds), *State-Owned Enterprises in Africa.* Boulder and London: Lynne Rienner Publishers, pp. 107–25.

Marks, G. and L. Diamond (eds), 1992: *Re-examining Democracy: Essays in Honor of Seymour Martin Lipset.* Newbury Park: Sage Publications.

Maxfield, S. and B.R. Schneider, 1997: *Business and the State in Developing Countries.* Ithaca: Cornell University Press.

McPherson, M.F., 1995: "The sequencing of economic reforms: Lessons from Zambia", *Development Discussion Paper,* No. 516, Harvard Institute for International Development (HIID), (November).

Meadowcroft, M., 2002: "The elections that might have been", *Southern African Human Rights Review,* 9 (special issue):1–3.

Meebelo, H.S., 1986: *African Proletarians and Colonial Capitalism. The Origins of Growth and Struggles of the Zambian Labour Movement to 1964*. Lusaka: Kenneth Kaunda Foundation.

Migdal J.S., A. Kohli and V. Shue (eds), 1994: *State Power and Social Forces: Domination and Transformation in the Third World*. Cambridge: Cambridge University Press.

Milner, H.V., 1997: *Interests, Institutions, and Information: Domestic Politics and International Relations*. Princeton: Princeton University Press.

Mine Workers Union of Zambia (MUZ), 1996a: "1996 16th Bi-ennial Conference". Mimeo.

—, 1996b: "Union's view on the management of privatisation". Brief No. 1. Kitwe, December 5.

—, 1994: "Zambia's agenda for development and the option of privatisation—the union's view" (Kitwe).

Ministry of Finance (MOF), *Economic Reports 1991–2001*. Lusaka.

Mkandawire, T. 1999: "Crisis management and the making of 'choiceless democracies' in Africa", in Joseph, R. (ed.), *State, Conflict and Democracy in Africa*. Boulder: Lynne Rienner Publishers.

—, 1996: "Economic policy-making and the consolidation of democratic institutions in Africa", in Havnevik, K. and B. van Arkadie (eds), *Domination or Dialogue? Experiences and Prospects for African Development Cooperation*. Uppsala: The Scandinavian Institute of African Studies, pp. 24–48.

Mkandawire, T. and A. Olukoshi, 1995: *Between Liberalisation and Repression: The Politics of Adjustment in Africa*. Dakar: CODESRIA.

Moore, M. (ed.), 1993: "Declining to Learn from the East? The World Bank on Governance and Development?", *IDS Bulletin*, Vol. 24, No. 1, (January).

Moore, M. and L. Hamalai, 1993: "Economic liberalization, political pluralism and business associations in developing countries", *World Development*, Vol. 21, No 12:1895–1912.

Mosley, P., J. Harrigan and John Toye 1991: *Aid and Power: The World Bank and Policy-Based Lending*, Volume 1 and 2. London: Routledge.

Movement for Multiparty Democracy (MMD), 2001: *Party Manifesto* 2001–2006. Lusaka.

—, 1996: *Party Manifesto* 1996–2001. Lusaka.

—, 1991: *Party Manifesto* 1991–1996, Lusaka.

Mulwanda, R.S., 2002: "Corruption and the abuse of office in Zambia's 2001 General Elections", *The Corruption Eye*, Vol. 1, No. 2 (February).

Mulenga, C.L., 2001: "Elections 2001: Advance or Retreat from High Moral Ground?" Paper presented at the seminar "The 2001 local government, parliamentary and presidential elections in Zambia", held at the Chr. Michelsen Institute, Bergen, Norway, January 14–15.

Munck, G.L., 1994: "Democratic transitions in comparative perspective", *Comparative Politics*, Vol. 27, (April):355–75.

Mwanawina, I., E. Kaunga, A. Mwanza, N. Mwikisa and V. Seshamani, 1996: "The 1996 Budget analysis". Mimeo. Department of Economics, University of Zambia, March.

Mwanza A.M. (ed.), 1992: *The Structural Adjustment Programme in Zambia. Lessons From Experience*. Harare: SAPES Books.

Mwenda, A., 1996: "Foreign exchange liberalisation in Zambia: Nature, performance and prospects". Paper prepared for the Bank of Zambia international conference on "Economic Liberalisation: Experiences and the Way Forward". Lusaka: (August 21–23).

National Assembly, 1993: Official Verbatim Report of the Parliamentary Debates of the Third Session of the 7th National Assembly, 1993, No. 93 (15 January to 18 March).

—, 1992: Official Verbatim Report of the Parliamentary Debates of the First Session of the 7th National Assembly, 1992 No. 91 (16 June to 9 July)

—, 1992b: Official Verbatim Report of the Parliamentary Debates of the Second Session of the 7th National Assembly, 1992, No. 92 (27 October to 4 November).

National Lima Party (NLP), 1996: *Party Manifesto 1996.*

National Party (NP), 1996: *Manifesto of the National Party 1996* (February 24).

Ncube, P.D., M. Ndulu and M. Sakala, 1987: "The International Monetary Fund and the Zambian economy—a case", in Havnevik, K. (ed.), *The IMF and the World Bank in Africa. Conditionality, Impact and Alternatives*. Uppsala: The Scandinavian Institute of African Studies.

Ndegwa, P., 1997: "Appendix: A view from Africa", in Kapur, D., J.P. Lewis and R. Webb, *The World Bank. Its First Half Century (*Volume II). Washington DC: The Brookings Institution, pp. 189–94.

Nelson, Joan M., 1996: "Promoting policy reforms: The twilight of conditionality?", *World Development*, Vol. 24, No. 9:1551–59.

—, 1994: "Labor and business roles in dual transitions: Building blocks or stumbling blocks?", in Nelson, J.M. (ed.), *Intricate Links: Democratization and Market Reforms in Latin America and Eastern Europe.* New Brunswick: Transaction, pp. 147–94.

—, 1994a: "The political economy of stabilization: Commitment, capacity and public response", *World Development*, Vol. 12, No. 10 (October).

—, (ed.), 1994b: *A Precarious Balance Volume I: Democracy and Economic Reforms in Eastern Europe.* Washington DC: Overseas Development Council.

—, 1993: "The politics of economic transformation: Is third world experience relevant in Eastern Europe?", *World Politics*, Vol. 45, No. 3 (April):433–63.

—, 1991: "Organized labor, politics, and labor market flexibility in developing countries", *The World Bank Research Observer,* 6, 1 (January):37–56.

—, (ed.), 1990: *Economic Crisis and Policy Choice. The Politics of Adjustment in the Third World.* Princeton: Princeton University Press.

—, 1989: *Fragile Coalitions: The Politics of Economic Adjustment.* New Brunswick: Transaction Books.

Nelson, J. and S. Eglington, 1993: *Global Goals, Contentious Means: Issues of Multiple Aid and Conditionality.* Policy Essay No. 10. Washington DC: Overseas Development Council (ODC).

—, 1992: *Encouraging democracy: What role for conditioned aid?* Policy Essay No 4. Washington DC: Overseas Development Council (ODC).

Njobvu, E., 1996: "The conduct of fiscal policy in a liberalised economy. The case of Zambia". Paper prepared for the Bank of Zambia international conference on "Economic Liberalisation Experiences and the Way Forward". Lusaka (August 21–23).

Nordhaus W., 1975: "The political business cycle", *Review of Economic Studies*, Vol. 42:169–90.

Nordhaus, W.D., P.A. Samuelsen and M.J. Mandel (eds), 1995: *Macroeconomics.* New York: McGraw-Hill.

Nordlund, P., 1996: *Organising the Political Agora. Domination and Democratisation in Zambia and Zimbabwe.* Unpublished PhD Dissertation thesis, University of Uppsala.

Norwegian Ministry of Foreign Affairs, 1997: "Norwegian statement to the Zambia Consultative Group Meeting" (Paris July 10–11).

—, 1995: "Statement by the Norwegian delegation to the Consultative Group Meeting for Zambia" (December 9–10).

—, 1994: "Review of Consultative Group Meeting for Zambia. Paris March 21–23, 1994" (April 13, 1994. Confidential).

—, 1993: "Statement by the Norwegian delegation to the Consultative Group meeting for Zambia" (April 6–7).

—, 1993a: "Statement of the Norwegian delegation to the Consultative Group Meeting for Zambia" (December 9–10).

—, 1992: "Norwegian statement to the CG-meeting for Zambia" 22.3 1992.

O'Donnell, G., 1996: "Illusions about consolidation", *Journal of Democracy*, Vol. 7. No. 2 (April):34–51.

—, 1994: "Delegative democracy", *Journal of Democracy*, Vol. 5, No. 1 (January):55–67.

Ollawa, P., 1979: *Participatory Democracy in Zambia: The Political Economy of National Development.* Elms Court, Ilfracombe, Devon, UK: Arthur H. Stockwell Ltd.

Olson, M., 1982: *The Rise and Decline of Nations.* New Haven: Yale University Press.

—,1965: *The Logic of Collective Action.* Cambridge: Harvard University Press.

Olukoshi, A., 1996: "The impact of recent reform efforts on the African state", in Havnevik, K. and B. van Arkadie (eds), *Domination or Dialogue? Experiences and prospects for African Development Cooperation.* Uppsala: The Scandinavian Institute of African Studies, pp. 48–70.

Ostrom, E., 1986: "An agenda for the study of institutions", *Public Choice*, No. 48:3–25.

Ostrom, E., C. Gibson, S. Shivakumar and K. Andersson, 2001: *Aid, Incentives and Sustainability. An Institutional Analysis of Development Cooperation.* Stockholm: Sida Studies in Evaluation.

Panter-Brick, K., 1994: "Prospects for democracy in Zambia", *Government and Opposition,* Vol. 29, No. 2, (Spring):230–47.

Parliamentary Debates, No. 112, January 22–March 18, 1999.

Pausewang, S. and H. Hedlund, 1986: *Zambia. Country Study and Norwegian Aid Review.* Bergen: Chr.Michelsen Institute.

Please, S., 1984: *The Hobbled Giant: Essays on the World Bank.* Boulder: Lynne Rienner Publishers.

Polhemus, J.H., 1997: "Zambia's 1996 elections: Lessons for the future?" Paper prepared for the Southern African Regional Institute for Policy Studies seminar. Harare: 31 January.

Powell, W. and P. DiMaggio (eds), 1991: *The New Institutionalism in Organizational Analysis.* Chicago and London: The University of Chicago Press.

Pritchett, L., 1998: "Patterns of economic growth: Hills, plateaus, mountains and plains", *Policy Research Working Paper*, 1947. Washington DC: The World Bank.

Przeworski, A., 1991: *Democracy and the Market.* Cambridge: Cambridge University Press.

Putnam, R., 1988: "Diplomacy and domestic politics. The logic of two-level games", *International Organization,* Vol. 42, (Summer):427–60.

Rakner, L., 2001: "The pluralist paradox: The decline of economic interest groups in Zambia", *Development and Change*, Vol. 32, No. 3: 521–43.

—, 1992: *Trade Unions in Processes of Democratisation. A Study of Party Labour Relations in Zambia.* Bergen: Chr. Michelsen Institute Report series R:6.

Rakner, L. and S. Gloppen, 2003: "Taxation and Accountability in sub-Saharan Africa", in van de Walle, N., N. Ball and V. Ramachandram (eds), 2003: *Beyond Structural Adjustment: The Institutional Context of African Development.* New York: Palgrave Macmillan.

Rakner, L. and L. Svåsand, 2003: "From Dominant to Competitive Party System: The Zambian Experiences 1991–2001", *Party Politics,* Vol. 9, No. 6 (December) (forthcoming).

Rakner, L., N.van de Walle and D. Mulaisho, 2001: "Zambia", in Devajaran et al., *Aid and Reform in Africa: Lessons from Ten Country Cases.* Washington DC: The World Bank, pp. 533–89.

Ravenhill, J. (eds), 1986: *Africa in Economic Crisis.* Hampshire: Macmillan Press Ltd.

Remmer, K., 1995: "New theoretical perspectives on democratization", *Comparative Politics* (October):103–22.

Roberts, A.D., 1976: *A History of Zambia.* London: Heinemann.

Roberts, K.M., 1995: "Neoliberalism and the transformation of populism in Latin America. The Peruvian case", *World Politics* 48 (October):82–116.

Robinson, M. (ed.), 1995: "Strengthening Civil Society in Africa: The Role of Foreign Political Aid", *IDS Bulletin*, Vol. 26, No. 2 (April).

—, 1993: "Aid, democracy and political conditionality in Sub-Saharan Africa", in Sørensen, G., *Political Conditionality, The European Journal of Development Research*, Vol. 5, No. 1:85–99.

Saasa, O., 1997: "Reducing Africa's aid dependence. Lessons from Zambia on capacity building and external support", in Kifle, H., A.O. Olukoshi and L. Wohlgemuth: *A New Partnership for African Development. Issues and Parameters.* Uppsala: The Nordic Africa Institute, pp. 189–203.

—, 1996: *Policy reforms and structural adjustment in Zambia. The case of agriculture and trade.* Washington DC: USAID, Technical Paper No. 35 (October).

—, 1994: "Structural adjustment and governance capacity in Zambia 1983–1994". Paper presented at the conference on "Governance and Successful Adjustment Conference" sponsored by the World Bank. Lusaka, November 9–11.

Saasa, O. with J. Carlsson, 2002: *Aid and Poverty Reduction in Zambia. Mission Unaccomplished.* Uppsala: The Nordic Africa Institute.

Sachs, J. (ed.), 1989: *Developing Country Debt and Economic Performance.* Chicago: University of Chicago Press.

Sandberg, E. (ed.), 1994: *The Changing Politics of Non-Governmental Organizations and African States.* Westport and London: Praeger Publishing.

—, 1990: *International Foreign Aid, Donor Cohesion, and Donor Bounded Decision making in Zambia's Agricultural Sector.* PhD Dissertation thesis, Yale University.

Sandbrook, R., 1985: *The Politics of Africa's Economic Stagnation.* Cambridge: Cambridge University Press.

SAPRIN (The Structural Adjustment Participatory Review International Network), 2002: "The policy roots of economic crisis and poverty. A multi-country participatory assessment of structural adjustment" (http//:www.saprin.org).

Schafer, M.D., 1994: *Winners and Losers: How Sectors Shape the Development Prospects of States.* Ithaca: Cornell University Press.

Schamis, H., 1999: "Distributional Coalitions and the Politics of Economic Reform in Latin America", *World Politics*, No. 51:236–68.

Schuknecht, L., 1996: "Political business cycles and fiscal policies in developing countries", *Kyklos*, Vol. 49, No. 2:155–70.

Scott, G., E. Sjaastad and D. Aarnes, 1998: *The potential for market-based agricultural development in Zambia. An appraisal for further NORAD support to agricultural development in the Northern Province in Zambia.* Report commissioned by the Norwegian Agency for Development Cooperation. Oslo/Lusaka, September 19.

Scott, I., 1980: "Party administration under the one-party state", in Tordoff, W. (ed.), *Administration in Zambia.* Manchester: Manchester University Press, pp. 185–213.

Selbervik, H., 1997: *Aid as a Tool for the Promotion of Human Rights: What Can Norway Do?* Oslo: Norwegian Ministry of Foreign Affairs, Report No. 7.

Seshamani, V., 1996: "The macro development context of macroeconomic policy in Zambia". Mimeo. Lusaka: Department of Economics, University of Zambia.

Sichone, O. and B.C. Chikulo (eds), 1996: *Democracy in Zambia. Challenges for the Third Republic.* Harare: SAPES Books.

Simutanyi, N., 1997: "Democracy on trial. Political opposition and the 1996 Zambian elections". Paper presented at the conference on "African Renewal", Massachusetts Institute of Technology (MIT), March 6–9.

—, 1996: "Organised Labour, Economic Crisis and Structural Adjustment in Africa", in Sichone, O. and B. Chikulo (eds), *Democracy in Zambia. Challenges for the Third Republic*, Harare: SAPES Books, pp. 151–72.

—, 1996a: "The politics of structural adjustment in Zambia", *Third World Quarterly*, Vol. 17, No. 4:825–39.

—, 1995: *The Politics of Economic Reform: Trade Unions and Structural Adjustment in Zambia.* Unpublished PhD dissertation, University of Cambridge (UK).

—, 1990: "Unions and democratisation processes: The case of Zambia". Mimeo.

Skålnes, T., 1995: *The Politics of Economic Reform in Zimbabwe: Continuity and Change in Economic Development.* Basingstoke and London: Macmillan.

Skidmore, T.E., 1977, "The politics of economic stabilization in postwar Latin America", in Malloy, J.M. (ed.), *Authoritarianism and Corporatism in Latin America.* Pittsburgh: University of Pittsburgh Press.

Sklar, R.L., 1975: *Corporate Power in an African State: The Political Impact of Multinational Mining Companies in Zambia.* Berkeley: University of California Press.

Snyder, R., 1999: "After Neoliberalism: The Politics of Reregulation in Mexico", *World Politics*, No. 51:173–204.

Sørensen, G., 1993: "Democracy, Authoritarianism and State Strength", *The European Journal of Development Research*, Vol. 5, No. 1.

—, 1991: *Democracy, Dictatorship and Development.* London: Macmillan Press Ltd.

Stepanek, J., 1999: *Wringing Success From Failure in Late-Developing Countries: Lessons From the Field.* Westport: Praeger Publishers.

Stokke, O. (ed.), 1996: *Foreign Aid Towards the Year 2000: Experiences and Challenges.* London and Portland: Frank Cass.

—, (ed.), 1995: *Aid and Political Conditionality.* London and Portland: Frank Cass.

Swedish International Development Corporation (SIDA), 1995: "General Statement by the Swedish delegation by Jan Cedergren to the Consultative Group Meeting for Zambia" (December 9–10).

Taylor, M. and D. Aarnes, 2002: "Confidence, investment and growth: Economic Developments and the 2001 elections in Zambia". Report presented at the workshop "Analysing political processes in the context of multiparty elections", held at Institute for Social and Economic Research, University of Zambia (Lusaka), October 6–7.

Taylor, S., 2003: "Resource Networks, Political Movements and the MDC in Zimbabwe: Opposition Prospects and a Framework for Analysis". Chr. Michelsen Institute: CMI Working Paper (forthcoming).

—, 1999: "Race, class and neopatrimonial politics in Zimbabwe", in Joseph, R. (ed.), *State, Conflict and Democracy in Africa.* Boulder: Lynne Rienner Publishers.

— 1997: "Open for Business? Business Associations and the State in Zambia". Mimeo. Paper prepared for the Business Associations and the State in Africa Project, February 6. Washington DC: American University.

Tordoff, W. (ed.), 1980: *Administration in Zambia.* Manchester: Manchester University Press.

—, 1974: *Government and Politics in Zambia.* London: Macmillan.

Tripp, A.M., 2000: "Political reform in Tanzania. The struggle for associational autonomy", *Comparative Politics*, Vol. 32, No. 2:191–215.

—, 1997: *Changing the Rules. The Politics of Liberalisation and the Urban Informal Economy in Tanzania.* Berkeley and Los Angeles: University of California Press.

Turok, B., 1989: *Mixed Economy in Focus: Zambia.* London: Institute for African Alternatives.

United Nations Development Program (UNDP), 2001: *Human Development Report: Zambia.* (Lusaka.)

United National Independence Party (UNIP), 2001: *Manifesto 2001.*

—,1996: *Manifesto 1996.*

United Party for National Development (UPND) 2001: *Manifesto for the Presidential, Parliamentary and Local Government Elections for 2001.* Lusaka.

USAID, 1997: *Zambia Democratic Governance Project: Final Evaluation.* Washington DC (June).

—, 1995: "Closing statement by the US delegation to the Consultative Group Meeting" (December 14–15).

—, 1994: *Zambia: Consultative Group Meeting. Interagency Review Paper* (December).

—, 1993: "Opening Statement by United States Government Delegation to the Zambia Consultative Group Meeting, December 9–19".

van de Walle, N., 2001: *African Economies and the Politics of Permanent Crisis 1979–1999.* Cambridge University Press.

—, 1994: "Political liberalization and economic policy reform in Africa", *World Development*, Vol. 22, No. 4:483–500.

van de Walle, N., N. Ball and V. Ramachandram (eds), 2003: *Beyond Structural Adjustment: The Institutional Context of African Development.* New York: Palgrave Macmillan (forthcoming).

van de Walle, N. and D. Chiwele, 1994: *Democratization and economic reform in Zambia.* MSU Working Papers on Political Reform in Africa, No. 9. Michigan: Michigan State University.

van de Walle, N. and T. A. Johnston, 1996: *Improving Aid to Africa.* Policy Essay No. 21. Washington DC: Overseas Development Council (ODC).

van de Walle, N. and K. Smiddy Butler, 1999: "Political parties and party systems in Africa's illiberal democracies", *Cambridge Review of International Affairs,* Vol. XIII, No. 1:14–28.

West, T., 1992: "Politics of implementation of structural adjustment in Zambia, 1985–1987", in *Politics of Economic Reform in Sub-Saharan Africa.* Washington DC: USAID.

—, 1989: *The Politics of Hope: Zambia's Structural Adjustment Programme, 1985–1987.* Unpublished PhD dissertation, Yale University.

White, G., 1996: "Civil society, democratization and development", in Luckham, R. and G. White, *Democratization in the South. The Jagged Wave.* Manchester: Manchester University Press, pp. 178–220.

White, H., 1998: *Aid and Macroeconomic Performance: Theory, Empirical Evidence, and Four Country Cases.* London: Macmillan.

White, H. and T. Edstrand, 1994: "Aid impact in a debt stressed economy: The case of Zambia", in *The Macroeconomics of Aid: Case Studies of Four Countries.* Stockholm: SASDA.

Widner, J. (ed.), 1994: *Economic Change and Political Liberalization in Sub-Saharan Africa.* Baltimore: The Johns Hopkins Press.

Williamson, J., (ed.), 1993: *The Political Economy of Policy Reform* Washington DC: Institute for International Economics.

Williamson, J. and S. Haggard, 1993: "The political conditions for economic reform", in Williamson, J. (ed.), *The Political Economy of Policy Reform.* Washington DC: Institute of International Economics.

Wilson, B., 1999: "Leftist Parties, Neoliberal Policies, and Reelection Strategies", *Comparative Political Studies*, 32:752–79.

Wiseman, J. (ed.), 1995: *Democracy and Political Change in Sub-Saharan Africa.* London: Routledge.

Woods, D., 1992: "Civil society in Europe and Africa. Limiting state power through a public sphere", *African Studies Review,* No. 2, Vol. 35:77–100.

World Bank, 2000a: *World Development Report 2000/2001: Attacking Poverty.* New York: Oxford University Press for the World Bank.

—, 2000b: *The President Report on the Fiscal Sustainability Credit.* Report P-7379-ZA, Washington DC.

—, 1998a: *Assessing Aid: What Works, What Doesn't and Why.* New York: Oxford University Press for the World Bank.

—, 1998b: *Zambia: Fiscal Management Report.* Report 18552-ZA, Washington DC.

—, 1996a: *Zambia: Prospects for Sustainable Growth 1995–2005.* Report 15477-ZA. Washington DC (August).

—, 1996b: *Implementation completion report, Zambia: Economic and social adjustment credit* (credit 2577-ZA). Washington DC (July).

—, 1996c: *Zambia: Country assistance strategy* (15761-ZA). Washington DC (June).

—, 1996d: "Report and recommendation of the President of the International Development Association to the Executive Directors on a proposed credit in the amount equivalent to SDR 62.4 million to the Republic of Zambia for a second Economic and Social Adjustment Credit". Washington DC (June 25, congress).

—, 1995a: *Zambia: Agricultural sector investment programme.* Staff appraisal report, No. 13518-ZA. Washington DC (March).

—, 1994: *Governance: The World Bank's Experience.* Washington DC: The World Bank.

—, 1994a: *Zambia. Poverty Assessment* (Vol. I–V). Report 12985-ZA (November).

—, 1993: *Zambia: Prospects for Sustainable and Equitable Growth.* Report 11570-ZA. Washington DC: The World Bank (August 23).

—, 1992: *Governance and Development.* Washington DC: The World Bank.

—, 1992a: "Consultative Group meeting for Zambia" March 23–24. Press release.

—, 1991: *World Bank Debt Tables 1990–91.* Washington DC: The World Bank.

—, 1990: *The Long-Term Perspective Study for Sub-Saharan Africa* (Vol. 1–4). Washington DC: The World Bank.

—, 1989: *From Crisis to Sustainable Growth.* Washington DC.

—, 1988: *Adjustment Lending*: Washington, DC: The World Bank.

—, 1984: *Towards Sustained Development in Sub-Saharan Africa.* Washington DC: The World Bank.

—, 1981: *Accelerated Development in Sub-Saharan Africa. An Agenda for Action.* Washington DC.

World Bank/IBRD, 1997a: "Chair's Closing Statement at Zambia's Consultative Group Meeting" (Paris, July 10).

—, 1997b: "The Consultative Group meeting for Zambia pledges renewed partnership". Press release July 11.

—, 1995b: "Consultative Group Meeting for Zambia". Press release; "Closing Statement by the Chairman (December 8–9)".

—, 1994b: "Note on Consultative Group Meeting for Zambia. March 22–23." (Report from the Deputy Secretary, April 4, 1993. Confidential.)

—, 1994c: "Consultative Group meeting for Zambia (December 8–9)"; Report from the vice-President and Secretary (December 23)". Press release; "Closing Statement by the Chairman".

—, 1993a: "Consultative Group Meeting for Zambia", Paris April 6–7, 1993. Press release.

—, 1993b: "Closing remarks" by the Chairman of the World Bank (April).

—, 1993c: "Consultative Group Meeting for Zambia (December 9–10)"; Press release; "Closing statement by the Chairman".

—, 1992b: *Summary of Discussions on Zambia: Economic and Financial Policy Framework Paper 1992–94*", March 23.

Young, A., 1973: *Industrial Diversification in Zambia.* New York: Praeger Publishers.

Zambia Congress of Trade Unions (ZCTU), 1996: "The case of Zambia". Paper presented to the SATUCC/FES Regional Labour Symposium, Gaborone, Botswana, 26–29 November 1996.

—, 1995: "Prevailing situation in the Zambian labour movement from the period leading to the 9th Quadrennial Congress". Kitwe: ZCTU Secretariat, April.

—, 1994a: "Summary of items on the agenda of meeting with the President" (December 30).

—, 1994b: "Managing the human resources in a liberalised economy" (September 5–9).

—, 1994c: "ZCTU position on privatisation in Zambia", Kitwe.

—, 1994d: "Report of the Secretary General to the 9th Quadrennial Congress (Livingstone October 27–28 1994).

—, 1994e: "On the current social and economic situation in the country". Meeting with Head of State, State House, December 22. Kitwe: ZCTU Secretariat.

—, 1987: "ZCTU's Response to the Recent Developments vis-à-vis Press Statement on the Economic Recovery Programme in which Zambia Ditched the IMF". Kitwe: ZCTU Secretariat Archives, (undated).

—, 1986: "Report of the General Secretary to the 7th Quadrennial Congress". Kitwe: ZCTU Secretariat.

Zambia Democratic Congress (ZDC): *Manifesto 1996.*

Zambia Independent Monitoring Team (ZIMT), 1991: *Parliamentary and Presidential Election Results.* Lusaka.

Zambia National Farmers Union (ZNFU): *Annual Reports 1991–2002.*

Zambia Republican Party (ZRP), 2001: *Party Manifesto.* Lusaka.

Zambia Privatisation Agency (ZPA): *Progress Reports* 1993–2001.

—, *Status Reports* 1992–2000.

Periodicals

Africa Confidential
Africa Report
ANC Network News
EIU Country Risk Service
Economist Intelligence Unit: Country Profile: Zambia (1991–2002)
Economist Intelligence Unit: Country Report: Zambia (1991–2002)
*The Farmer (*Lusaka: Monthly magazine December 1995–)
Financial Mail (Lusaka: Weekly financial newspaper)
Financial Times (London)
New African
Inter-Press Services
Mail and Guardian
The Post (Lusaka: Daily newspaper 1995–)
Profit Magazine (Lusaka: Monthly magazine))
SAPEM (Harare: Southern Africa Political and Economic Monthly)
Southern African Economist,
Times of Zambia (Lusaka: Daily newspaper)
The Weekly Post (Lusaka: Weekly newspaper 1991–1994)
World Bank Findings (Washington DC)
ZACCI Business Line (Lusaka)
Zambia Daily Mail (Lusaka: Daily newspaper)

Index